A PRIMER ON
PARTIAL LEAST SQUARES
STRUCTURAL EQUATION
MODELING (PLS-SEM)

To the Academy of Marketing Science (AMS) and its members

A PRIMER ON PARTIAL LEAST SQUARES STRUCTURAL EQUATION MODELING (PLS-SEM)

Joseph F. Hair, Jr.
Kennesaw State University

G. Tomas M. Hult
Michigan State University, East Lansing

Christian M. Ringle
Technical University of Hamburg-Harburg, Germany

Marko Sarstedt
Otto-von-Guericke University, Magdeburg

Los Angeles | London | New Delhi
Singapore | Washington DC

Los Angeles | London | New Delhi
Singapore | Washington DC

FOR INFORMATION:

SAGE Publications, Inc.

2455 Teller Road

Thousand Oaks, California 91320

E-mail: order@sagepub.com

SAGE Publications Ltd.

1 Oliver's Yard

55 City Road

London EC1Y 1SP

United Kingdom

SAGE Publications India Pvt. Ltd.

B 1/I 1 Mohan Cooperative Industrial Area

Mathura Road, New Delhi 110 044

India

SAGE Publications Asia-Pacific Pte. Ltd.

3 Church Street

#10-04 Samsung Hub

Singapore 049483

Acquisitions Editor: Vicki Knight

Editorial Assistant: Kalie Koscielak

Production Editor: Laura Barrett

Copy Editor: Gillian Dickens

Typesetter: C&M Digitals (P) Ltd.

Proofreader: Scott Oney

Indexer: Will Ragsdale

Cover Designer: Rose Storey

Marketing Manager: Nicole Elliott

Permissions Editor: Adele Hutchinson

Printed in the United States of America

Library of Congress Cataloging-in-Publication Data

A primer on partial least squares structural equation modeling (PLS-SEM) / Joseph F. Hair, Jr. . . . [et al.].

p. cm.
Includes bibliographical references and index.

ISBN 978-1-4522-1744-4 (pbk.)

1. Least squares. 2. Structural equation modeling.
I. Hair, Joseph F.

QA275.P88 2014
511'.42—dc23   2012041594

This book is printed on acid-free paper.

MIX
Paper from
responsible sources
FSC
www.fsc.org
FSC® C014174

13 14 15 16 17 10 9 8 7 6 5 4 3 2

Table of Contents

Detailed Table
of Contents

Preface

Academics, industry, government, and individuals are confronted with an explosion of data. The data increasingly are emerging from sources such as web traffic, social networking interactions, search behavior, sensors that track suppliers, customers, and shipments, and GPS systems that monitor traffic, to name only some of the more visible sources. This trend, often referred to as the age of big data, is pushing the world toward data-driven discovery and decision making.

This abundance of data presents both opportunities and challenges for scholars, practitioners, and government. While more data are available, there are not enough individuals with the analytical skills to probe and understand the data. Analysis requires a rigorous scientific approach dependent on knowledge of statistics, mathematics, measurement, logic, theory, experience, intuition, and many other variables affecting the situational context. Statistical analysis is perhaps the most important skill because, while the other areas facilitate better understanding of data patterns, statistics supported by user-friendly software makes the process efficient and cost-effective, in both time and money.

Descriptive statistics and the application of multivariate data analysis techniques such as regression analysis and factor analysis belong to the core set of statistical instruments, and their use has generated findings that have significantly shaped the way we see the world today. The increasing reliance on and acceptance of statistical analysis, as well as the advent of powerful computer systems that allow for handling large amounts of data, paved the way for the development of more advanced next-generation analysis techniques. Structural equation modeling (SEM) is among the most useful advanced statistical analysis techniques that have emerged in the social sciences in recent decades. SEM is a class of multivariate techniques that combine aspects of factor analysis and regression, enabling the researcher to simultaneously examine relationships among measured variables and latent variables as well as between latent variables.

Considering the ever-increasing importance of understanding latent phenomena such as consumer perceptions, attitudes, or intentions and their influence on organizational performance measures (e.g., stock prices), it is not surprising that SEM has become one of the most prominent statistical analysis techniques today. While there are many approaches to conducting SEM, the most widely applied method is certainly covariance-based SEM (CB-SEM). Since its introduction by Karl Jöreskog in 1973, CB-SEM has received considerable interest among empirical researchers across virtually all social sciences disciplines. However, the predominance of LISREL and AMOS, certainly the most well-known software tools to perform this kind of analysis, has led to the fact that not all researchers are aware of the variance-based partial least squares SEM (PLS-SEM) approach, an alternative technique for SEM, which lately has become a key research method.

Figure 1.1 summarizes the studies on PLS-SEM use in the top journals in the marketing and strategic management disciplines as well as *MIS Quarterly,* the flagship journal in management information systems research.[1] PLS-SEM use has increased exponentially in a variety of disciplines with the recognition that PLS-SEM's distinctive methodological features make it a viable alternative to the more popular CB-SEM approach. Specifically, PLS-SEM has several advantages over CB-SEM in many situations commonly encountered in social sciences research—for example, when sample sizes are small, the data are nonnormally distributed, or when complex models with many indicators and model relationships are estimated. However, PLS-SEM should not simply be viewed as a less stringent alternative to CB-SEM but rather as a complementary modeling approach to SEM. If correctly applied, PLS-SEM indeed can be a silver bullet in many research situations. (Hair, Sarstedt, and Ringle, 2011)

PLS-SEM is evolving as a statistical modeling technique, and while there are several published articles on the method, there is no comprehensive book that explains the fundamental aspects of the method, particularly in a way that can be comprehended by individuals with limited statistical and mathematical training. This book clarifies the nature and role of PLS-SEM in social sciences research and hopefully makes researchers aware of a tool that will enable them to pursue research opportunities in new and different ways.

The approach of this book is based on the authors' many years of conducting and teaching research, as well as the desire to communicate the fundamentals of the PLS-SEM method to a broad audience. To

---

[1]For the selection of journals and details on the use of PLS-SEM in the three disciplines, see Hair, Sarstedt, Ringle, and Mena (2012); Hair, Sarstedt, Pieper, and Ringle (2012a); and Ringle, Sarstedt, and Straub (2012).

Figure I.1   Number of PLS-SEM Studies in Marketing, Strategic Management, and MIS Quarterly

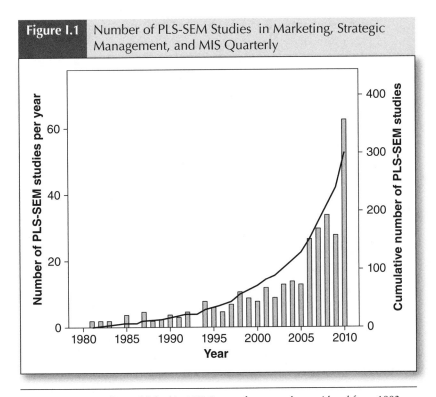

Note: PLS-SEM studies published in *MIS Quarterly* were only considered from 1992 on.

accomplish this goal, we have limited the emphasis on equations, formulas, Greek symbols, and so forth that are typical of most books and articles. Instead, we explain in detail the basic fundamentals of PLS-SEM and provide rules of thumb that can be used as general guidelines for understanding and evaluating the results of applying the method. We also rely on a single software package (SmartPLS; http://www.smartpls .de) that is available for download at no charge and can be used not only with exercises in this book but also in the reader's own research.

As a further effort to facilitate learning, we use a single case study throughout the book. The case is drawn from a published study on corporate reputation, and we believe it is general enough to be understood by many different areas of social science research, thus further facilitating comprehension of the method. Review and critical thinking questions are posed at the end of the chapters, and key terms are defined to better understand the concepts. Finally, suggested readings and extensive references are provided to enhance more advanced coverage of the topic.

The book chapters and learning support supplements are organized around the learning outcomes shown at the beginning of each chapter. Moreover, instead of a single summary at the end of each chapter, we present a separate topical summary for each learning outcome. This approach makes the book more understandable and usable for both students and teachers. The www.pls-sem.com website for the book also includes other support materials to facilitate learning and applying the PLS-SEM method.

We would like to acknowledge the many insights and suggestions provided by the reviewers: Eleanor Witta (University of Central Florida), Richard S. Mohn (University of Southern Mississippi) and Edward Markowski (Old Dominion University), as well as a number of our colleagues and students. Most notably, we would like to thank Adamantios Diamantopoulos (University of Vienna), Markus Eberl (TNS Infratest), /Jeannette A. Mena (University of South Florida), Verena Gruber (University of Vienna), Karl-Werner Hansmann (University of Hamburg), Jörg Henseler (Radboud University Nijmegen), Geoffrey Hubona (Virginia Commonwealth University), Arthur Money (Henley Business School), Christian Nitzl (Universität der Bundeswehr München), Sascha Raithel (Ludwig-Maximilians-University Munich), Edward E. Rigdon (Georgia State University), Rainer Schlittgen (University of Hamburg), Phillip Samouel (University of Kingston), Manfred Schwaiger (Ludwig-Maximilians-University Munich), Donna Smith (Ryerson University), and Anita Whiting (Clayton State University) for their helpful remarks and support throughout the project. In addition, at SAGE we thank our publisher Vicki Knight, as well as Gillian Dickens, Nicole Elliott, Kalie Koscielak, Lyndsi Stephens, and Laura Barrett. We hope this book will expand knowledge of the capabilities and benefits of PLS-SEM to a much broader group of researchers and practitioners. Last, if you have any remarks, suggestions, or ideas to improve this book, please get in touch with us. We appreciate any feedback on the book's concept and contents!

Joe F. Hair, Jr., Kennesaw State University, USA

G. Tomas M. Hult, Michigan State University, USA

Christian M. Ringle, Hamburg University of Technology (TUHH), Germany

Marko Sarstedt, Otto-von-Guericke University Magdeburg, Germany

About the Authors

Joseph F. Hair, Jr., is Founder and Senior Scholar of the Doctoral Degree in Business Administration, Coles College, Kennesaw State University, Kennesaw, Georgia. He previously held the Copeland Endowed Chair of Entrepreneurship and was Director, Entrepreneurship Institute, Ourso College of Business Administration, Louisiana State University. He has authored more than 40 books, including *Multivariate Data Analysis* (7th edition, 2010 [cited 22,000+ times]), *Marketing* (12th edition, 2012), *Essentials of Business Research Methods* (2011), *Research Methods for Business* (2007), and *Essentials of Marketing Research* (3rd edition, 2013). He also has published numerous articles in scholarly journals and was recognized as the 2011 Academy of Marketing Science Marketing Educator of the year. He often presents seminars on research techniques, multivariate data analysis, and marketing issues for organizations in Europe, Australia, and other locations outside the United States.

G. Tomas M. Hult is the Eli Broad Professor of Marketing and International Business and Director of the International Business Center at Michigan State University. He has been Executive Director of the Academy of International Business and President of the AIB Foundation since 2004, Editor-in-Chief of the *Journal of the Academy of Marketing Science* since 2009, and on the U.S. Department of Commerce's District Export Council since 2012. He is one of the world's leading authorities in global strategy, with a particular focus on the intersection of global marketing and supply chain management. Ranked the 75th "most-cited scientist in economics and business" in the world by Thomson Reuters, his research has been cited more than 10,000 times, per Google Scholar. Hult teaches doctoral seminars on multivariate statistics, structural equation modeling, and hierarchical linear modeling worldwide and is a dual citizen of Sweden and the United States.

Christian M. Ringle is a Full Professor and Managing Director of the Institute for Human Resource Management and Organizations at the Hamburg University of Technology and Visiting Professor at the Faculty of Business Law at the University of Newcastle, Australia. He holds a master's degree in business administration from the University of Kansas and received his doctor of philosophy from the University of Hamburg. His widely published research addresses the management of organizations, strategic and human resource management, marketing, and quantitative methods for business and market research. He is cofounder and the Managing Director of SmartPLS (www.smaprtpls.com), a software tool with a graphical user interface for the application of the partial least squares structural equation modeling (PLS-SEM) method. Besides supporting consultancies and international corporations, he regularly teaches doctoral seminars on multivariate statistics, the PLS-SEM method, and the use of SmartPLS worldwide.

Marko Sarstedt is a Full Professor of Marketing at the Otto-von-Guericke-University Magdeburg (Germany) and Visiting Professor to the Faculty of Business and Law at the University of Newcastle (Australia). He previously was an Assistant Professor of Quantitative Methods in Marketing and Management at the Ludwig-Maximilians-University Munich (Germany). His main research is in the application and advancement of structural equation modeling methods to further the understanding of consumer behavior and to improve marketing decision making. His research has been published in journals such as *Journal of the Academy of Marketing Science, MIS Quarterly, Long Range Planning, Journal of World Business*, and *Journal of Business Research*. According to the 2012 Handelsblatt ranking, Dr. Sarstedt is among the top five marketing researchers younger than age 40 in Germany. He regularly teaches doctoral seminars on multivariate statistics, structural equation modeling, and measurement worldwide.

CHAPTER 1

An Introduction to Structural Equation Modeling

CHAPTER PREVIEW

Social science researchers have been using statistical analysis tools for many years to extend their ability to develop and confirm research findings. Application of first-generation statistical methods dominated the research landscape through the 1980s. But since the early 1990s, second-generation methods have expanded rapidly and, in some disciplines, represent almost 50% of the statistical tools applied in empirical research. In this chapter, we explain the fundamentals of second-generation statistical methods and establish a foundation that will enable you to understand and apply one of the emerging second-generation tools, referred to as partial least squares structural equation modeling (PLS-SEM).

WHAT IS STRUCTURAL EQUATION MODELING?

Statistical analysis has been an essential tool for social science researchers for more than a century. Applications of statistical methods have expanded dramatically with the advent of computer hardware and software, particularly in recent years with widespread access to many more methods due to user-friendly interfaces with technology-delivered knowledge. Researchers initially relied on univariate and bivariate analysis to understand data and relationships. To comprehend more complex relationships associated with current research directions in the social sciences, it is increasingly necessary to apply more sophisticated multivariate data analysis methods.

Multivariate analysis involves the application of statistical methods that simultaneously analyze multiple variables. The variables typically represent measurements associated with individuals, companies, events, activities, situations, and so forth. The measurements are often obtained from surveys or observations that are used to collect primary data, but they may also be obtained from databases consisting of secondary data. Exhibit 1.1 displays some of the major types of statistical methods associated with multivariate data analysis.

Exhibit 1.1	Organization of Multivariate Methods	
	Primarily Exploratory	*Primarily Confirmatory*
First-generation techniques	• Cluster analysis • Exploratory factor analysis • Multidimensional scaling	• Analysis of variance • Logistic regression • Multiple regression
Second-generation techniques	• PLS-SEM	• CB-SEM, *including* • Confirmatory factor analysis

The statistical methods often used by social scientists are typically called **first-generation techniques** (Fornell, 1982, 1987). These techniques, shown in the upper part of Exhibit 1.1, include regression-based approaches such as multiple regression, logistic regression, and analysis of variance but also techniques such as exploratory factor analysis, cluster analysis, and multidimensional scaling. When applied to a research problem, these methods can be used to either confirm a priori established theories or identify data patterns and relationships. Specifically, they are **confirmatory** when testing the hypotheses of existing theories and concepts and **exploratory** when they search for latent patterns in the data in case there is no or only little prior knowledge on how the variables are related.

It is important to note that the distinction between confirmatory and exploratory is not always as clear-cut as it seems. For example, when running a regression analysis, researchers usually select the dependent and independent variables based on a priori established theories and concepts. The goal of the regression analysis is then to test these theories and concepts. However, the technique can also be used to explore whether additional independent variables prove valuable for extending the concept being tested. The findings typically focus first on which independent variables are statistically significant predictors of the single dependent variable (more confirmatory) and then which independent variables are, relatively speaking, better predictors of the dependent variable (more exploratory). In a similar fashion, when exploratory factor analysis is applied to a data set, the method searches for relationships between the variables in an effort to reduce a large number of variables to a smaller set of composite factors (i.e., combinations of variables). The final set of composite factors is a result of exploring relationships in the data and reporting the relationships that are found (if any). Nevertheless, while the technique is exploratory in nature (as the name already suggests), researchers often have a priori knowledge that may, for example, guide their decision on how many composite factors to extract from the data (Mooi & Sarstedt, 2011).

First-generation techniques have been widely applied by social science researchers. However, for the past 20 years, many researchers have increasingly been turning to **second-generation techniques** to overcome the weaknesses of first-generation methods (Exhibit 1.1). These methods, referred to as **structural equation modeling** (SEM), enable researchers to incorporate unobservable variables measured indirectly by indicator variables. They also facilitate accounting for measurement error in observed variables (Chin, 1998).

There are two types of SEM. **Covariance-based SEM (CB-SEM)** is primarily used to confirm (or reject) theories (i.e., a set of systematic relationships between multiple variables that can be tested empirically). It does this by determining how well a proposed theoretical model can estimate the covariance matrix for a sample data set. In contrast, **PLS-SEM** (also called **PLS path modeling**) is primarily used to develop theories in exploratory research. It does this by focusing on explaining the variance in the dependent variables when examining the model. We explain this difference in more detail later in the chapter.

PLS-SEM is evolving as a statistical modeling technique, and while there are several published articles on the method (Chin, 2010; Haenlein & Kaplan, 2004; Hair, Ringle, & Sarstedt, 2011; Hair et al., 2012a; Henseler, Ringle, & Sarstedt, 2012; Henseler, Ringle, & Sinkovics, 2009; Ringle, Götz, Wetzels, & Wilson, 2009), there is no comprehensive text that explains the fundamental aspects of the method, particularly in a way that can be comprehended by the non-statistician. This book clarifies the nature and role of PLS-SEM in social sciences research and hopefully makes researchers aware of a tool that will enable them to pursue research opportunities in new and different ways.

CONSIDERATIONS IN USING STRUCTURAL EQUATION MODELING

Regardless whether a researcher is using first- or second-generation multivariate analysis methods, several considerations are necessary in deciding to use multivariate analysis, particularly SEM. Among the most important are the following five elements: (1) the variate, (2) measurement, (3) measurement scales, (4) coding, and (5) data distributions.

The Variate

The **variate** is the fundamental building block of multivariate analysis (Hair, Black, Babin, & Anderson, 2010). The variate is a linear combination of several variables that are chosen based on the research problem at hand. The process for combining the variables involves calculating a set of weights, multiplying the weights (e.g., w_1 and w_2) times the associated data observations for the variables (e.g., x_1 and x_2), and summing them. The mathematical formula for this linear combination with five variables is shown as follows (note that the variate value can be calculated for any number of variables):

$$\text{Variate value} = x_1 w_1 + x_2 w_2 + \ldots + x_5 w_5,$$

where x stands for the individual variables and w represents the weights. All x variables (e.g., questions in a questionnaire) have responses from many respondents that can be arranged in a data matrix. Exhibit 1.2 shows such a data matrix, where i is an index that stands for the number of responses (i.e., cases). A variate value is calculated for each of the i respondents in the sample.

Measurement

Measurement is a fundamental concept in conducting social science research. When we think of measurement, the first thing that comes to mind is often a ruler, which could be used to measure someone's height or the length of a piece of furniture. But there are many other examples of measurement in life. When you drive, you use a speedometer to measure the speed of your vehicle, a heat gauge to measure the temperature of the engine, and a gauge to determine how much fuel remains in your tank. If you are sick, you use a thermometer to measure your temperature, and when you go on a diet, you measure your weight on a bathroom scale.

Measurement is the process of assigning numbers to a variable based on a set of rules (Hair, Wolfinbarger Celsi, Money, Samouel, & Page, 2011). The rules are used to assign the numbers to the variable

Exhibit 1.2 Data Matrix					
Case	x_1	x_2	. . .	x_5	Variate Value
1	x_{11}	x_{21}	. . .	x_5	v_1
. . .	. . .	. . .	. . .	. . .	. . .
i	x_{1i}	x_{2i}	. . .	x_{5i}	v_i

in a way that accurately represents the variable. With some variables, the rules are easy to follow, while with other variables, the rules are much more difficult to apply. For example, if the variable is gender, then it is easy to assign a 1 for females and a 0 for males. Similarly, if the variable is age or height, it is again easy to assign a number. But what if the variable is satisfaction or trust? Measurement in these situations is much more difficult because the phenomenon that is supposed to be measured is abstract, complex, and not directly observable. We therefore talk about the measurement of **latent** (i.e., unobservable) **variables** or **constructs.**

We cannot directly measure abstract concepts such as satisfaction or trust. However, we can measure indicators or manifestations of what we have agreed to call satisfaction or trust, for example, in a brand, product, or company. Specifically, when concepts are difficult to measure, one approach is to measure them indirectly with a set of indicators that serve as proxy variables. Each item represents a single separate aspect of a larger abstract concept. For example, if the concept is restaurant satisfaction, then the several proxy variables that could be used to measure this might be the following:

1. The taste of the food was excellent.

2. The speed of service met my expectations.

3. The waitstaff was very knowledgeable about the menu items.

4. The background music in the restaurant was pleasant.

5. The meal was a good value compared with the price.

By combining several items to form a scale (or index), we can indirectly measure the overall concept of restaurant satisfaction. Usually, researchers use several items to form a multi-item scale, which indirectly measures a concept, as in the restaurant satisfaction example above. The several measures are combined to form a single composite score (i.e., the score of the variate). In some instances, the composite score is a simple summation of the several measures. In other instances, the scores of the individual measures are combined to form a composite score using a linear weighting process for the several individual measures. The logic of using several individual variables to measure an abstract concept such as restaurant satisfaction is that the measure will be more accurate. The anticipated improved accuracy is based on the assumption that using several items to measure a single concept is more likely to represent all the different aspects of the concept. This involves reducing **measurement error,** which is the difference between the true value of a variable and the value obtained by a measurement. There are many sources of measurement error, including poorly worded questions on a survey, misunderstanding of the scaling approach, and incorrect application of a statistical method. Indeed, all measurements used in multivariate analysis are likely to contain some measurement error. The objective, therefore, is to reduce the measurement error as much as possible.

Rather than using multiple items, researchers sometimes opt for the use of **single items** to measure concepts such as satisfaction or purchase intention. For example, we may use only "Overall, I'm satisfied with this restaurant" to measure restaurant satisfaction instead of all five items described above. While this is a good way to make the questionnaire shorter, it also reduces the quality of your measurement. We are going to discuss the fundamentals of measurement and measurement evaluation in the following chapters.

Measurement Scales

A **measurement scale** is a tool with a predetermined number of closed-ended responses that can be used to obtain an answer to a question. There are four types of measurement scales, each representing a different level of measurement—nominal, ordinal, interval, and ratio. Nominal scales are the lowest level of scales because they are the most restrictive in terms of the type of analysis that can be carried out. A **nominal scale** assigns numbers that can be used to identify and classify objects (e.g., people, companies, products, etc.) and is also referred to as a categorical scale. For example, if a survey asked a respondent to identify his or her profession and the categories are doctor, lawyer, teacher, engineer, and so forth, the question has a nominal scale. Nominal scales can have two or more categories, but each category must be mutually exclusive, and all possible categories must be included. A number could be assigned to identify each category, and the numbers could be used to count the number of responses in each category, or the modal response or percentage in each category.

The next higher level of scale is called **ordinal.** If we have a variable measured on an ordinal scale, we know that if the value of that variable increases or decreases, this gives meaningful information. For example, if we code customers' use of a product as nonuser = 0, light user = 1, and heavy user = 2, we know that if the value of the use variable increases, the level of use also increases. Therefore, something measured on an ordinal scale provides information about the order of our observations. However, we cannot assume that the differences in the order are equally spaced. That is, we do not know if the difference between "nonuser" and "light user" is the same as between "light user" and "heavy user," even though the differences in the values (i.e., 0 – 1 and 1 – 2) are equal. Therefore, it is not appropriate to calculate arithmetic means or variances for ordinal data.

If something is measured with an **interval scale,** we have precise information on the rank order at which something is measured and, in addition, we can interpret the magnitude of the differences in values directly. For example, if the temperature is 80°F, we know that if it drops to 75°F, the difference is exactly 5°F. This difference of 5°F is the same as the increase from 80°F to 85°F. This exact "spacing" is called **equidistance,** and equidistant scales are necessary for certain analysis techniques, such as SEM. What the interval scale does not give us is an absolute zero point. If the temperature is 0°F, it may feel cold, but the temperature can drop further. The value of 0 therefore does not mean that there is no temperature at all (Mooi & Sarstedt, 2011). The value of interval scales is that almost any type of mathematical computations can be carried out, including the mean and standard deviation.

The **ratio scale** provides the most information. If something is measured on a ratio scale, we know that a value of 0 means that a particular characteristic for a variable is not present. For example, if a customer buys no products (value = 0), then he or she really buys no products. Or, if we spend no money on advertising a new product (value = 0), we really spend no money. Therefore, the zero point or origin of the variable is equal to 0. With ratio scales, all types of mathematical computations are possible.

Coding

The assignment of numbers to categories in a manner that facilitates measurement is referred to as **coding.** In survey research, data are often precoded. Precoding is assigning numbers ahead of time to answers (e.g., scale points) that are specified on a questionnaire. For example, a 10-point agree-disagree scale typically would assign the number 10 to the highest endpoint "agree" and a 1 to the lowest endpoint "disagree," and the points between would be coded 2 to 9. Postcoding is assigning numbers to categories of responses after data are collected. The responses might be to an open-ended question on a quantitative survey or to an interview response in a qualitative study.

Coding is very important in the application of multivariate analysis because it determines when and how various types of scales can be used. For example, variables measured with interval and ratio scales can always be used with multivariate analysis. However, when using ordinal scales such as Likert scales (which is common within an SEM context), researchers have to pay special attention to the coding to fulfill the requirement of equidistance. For example, when using a typical 5-point Likert scale with the categories (1) *strongly disagree*, (2) *disagree*, (3) *neither agree nor disagree*, (4) *agree*, and (5) *strongly agree*, the inference is that the "distance" between categories 1 and 2 is the same as between categories 3 and 4. In contrast, the same type of Likert scale but using the categories (1) *disagree*, (2) *neither agree nor disagree*, (3) *somewhat agree*, (4) *agree*, and (5) *strongly agree* is unlikely to be equidistant as only one item can receive a rating below the neutral category "neither agree nor disagree." This would clearly bias any result in favor of a better outcome. A good Likert scale, as above, will present symmetry of Likert items about a middle category that have clearly defined linguistic qualifiers for each category. In such symmetric scaling, equidistant attributes will typically be more clearly observed or, at least, inferred. When a Likert scale is perceived as symmetric and equidistant, then it will behave more like an interval scale. So while a Likert scale is ordinal, if it is well presented, then it is likely the Likert scale can approximate an interval-level measurement, and the corresponding variables can be used in SEM.

Data Distributions

When researchers collect quantitative data, the answers to the questions asked are reported as a distribution across the available (predefined) response categories. For example, if responses are requested using a 10-point agree-disagree scale, then a distribution of the answers in each of the possible response categories $(1, 2, 3, \ldots, 10)$ can be calculated and displayed in a table or chart. Exhibit 1.3

shows an example of the frequencies of a corresponding variable *x*. As can be seen, most respondents indicated a 5 on the 9-point scale, followed by 4 and 6, as well as 3 and 7, and so on. Overall, the frequency count approximately follows a bell-shaped, symmetric curve around the mean value of 5. This bell-shaped curve is the normal distribution, which many analysis techniques require to render correct results.

While many different types of distributions exist (e.g., normal, binomial, Poisson), researchers working with SEM generally only need to distinguish normal from nonnormal distributions. Normal distributions are usually desirable, especially when working with CB-SEM. In contrast, PLS-SEM generally makes no assumptions about the data distributions. However, for reasons discussed in later chapters, it is nevertheless worthwhile to consider the distribution when working with PLS-SEM. To assess whether the data are normal, researchers can revert to statistical tests such as the Kolmogorov-Smirnov test and

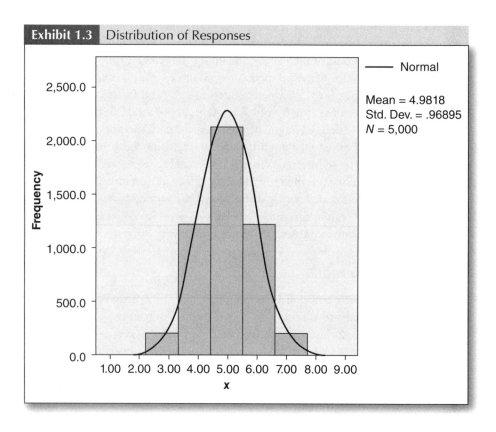

Exhibit 1.3   Distribution of Responses

Normal

Mean = 4.9818
Std. Dev. = .96895
N = 5,000

Shapiro-Wilk test (Mooi & Sarstedt, 2011). In addition, researchers can examine two measures of distributions—skewness and kurtosis (Chapter 2)—which allow assessing to what extent the data deviate from normality (Hair et al., 2010).

STRUCTURAL EQUATION MODELING WITH PARTIAL LEAST SQUARES PATH MODELING

Path Models With Latent Variables

Path models are diagrams used to visually display the hypotheses and variable relationships that are examined when SEM is applied (Hair, Ringle, & Sarstedt, 2011; Hair, Wolfinbarger Celsi, et al., 2011). An example of a path model is shown in Exhibit 1.4.

Constructs (i.e., variables that are not directly measured) are represented in path models as circles or ovals (Y_1 to Y_4). The **indicators**, also called **items** or **manifest variables**, are the directly measured proxy variables that contain the raw data. They are represented in path models as rectangles (x_1 to x_{10}). Relationships between constructs

| Exhibit 1.4 | A Simple Path Model |

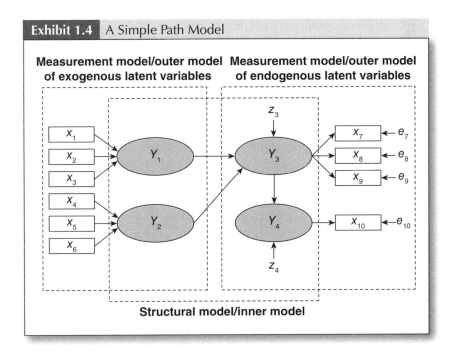

as well as between constructs and their assigned indicators are shown as arrows. In PLS-SEM, the arrows are always single-headed, thus representing directional relationships. Single-headed arrows are considered a predictive relationship and, with strong theoretical support, can be interpreted as causal relationships.

A PLS path model consists of two elements. First, there is a **structural model** (also called the **inner model** in the context of PLS-SEM) that represents the constructs (circles or ovals). The structural model also displays the relationships (paths) between the constructs. Second, there are the **measurement models** (also referred to as the **outer models** in PLS-SEM) of the constructs that display the relationships between the constructs and the indicator variables (rectangles). In Exhibit 1.4, there are two types of measurement models: one for the **exogenous latent variables** (i.e., those constructs that explain other constructs in the model) and one for the **endogenous latent variables** (i.e., those constructs that are being explained in the model). Rather than referring to measurement models of exogenous and endogenous latent variables, researchers often refer to the measurement model of one specific latent variable. For example, x_1 to x_3 are the indicators used in the measurement model of Y_1 while Y_4 has only the x_{10} indicator in the measurement model.

The **error terms** (e.g., e_7 or e_8; Exhibit 1.4) are connected to the (endogenous) constructs and (reflectively) measured variables by single-headed arrows. Error terms represent the unexplained variance when path models are estimated. In Exhibit 1.4, error terms e_7 to e_{10} are on those indicators whose relationships go from the construct to the indicator (i.e., reflectively measured indicators). In contrast, the formatively measured indicators x_1 to x_6, where the relationship goes from the indicator to the construct, do not have error terms. The structural model also contains error terms. In Exhibit 1.4, z_3 and z_4 are associated with the endogenous latent variables Y_3 and Y_4 (note that error terms on constructs and measured variables are labeled differently). In contrast, the exogenous latent variables that only explain other latent variables in the structural model do not have an error term.

Path models are developed based on theory. **Theory** is a set of systematically related hypotheses developed following the scientific method that can be used to explain and predict outcomes. Thus, hypotheses are individual conjectures, whereas theories are multiple hypotheses that are logically linked together and can be tested empirically. Two types of theory are required to develop path models:

measurement theory and structural theory. The latter specifies how the constructs are related to each other in the structural model, while measurement theory specifies how each construct is measured.

Measurement Theory

Measurement theory specifies how the latent variables (constructs) are measured. Generally, there are two different ways to measure unobservable variables. One approach is referred to as reflective measurement, and the other is a formative measurement. Constructs Y_1 and Y_2 in Exhibit 1.4 are modeled based on a **formative measurement model.** Note that the directional arrows are pointing from the indicator variables (x_1 to x_3 for Y_1 and x_4 to x_6 for Y_2) to the construct, indicating a causal (predictive) relationship in that direction.

In contrast, Y_3 and Y_4 in the exhibit are modeled based on a **reflective measurement model.** With multiple reflective indicators, the direction of the arrows is from the construct to the indicator variables, indicating the assumption that the construct causes the measurement (more precisely, the covariation) of the indicator variables. As indicated in Exhibit 1.4, reflective measures have an error term associated with each indicator, which is not the case with formative measures. The latter are assumed to be error free (Diamantopoulos, 2011). Last, note that Y_4 is measured using a single item rather than multi-item measures.

The approach to modeling constructs (i.e., formative vs. reflective and multi-items vs. single items) is an important consideration in developing path models. These approaches to modeling constructs are explained in more detail in Chapter 2.

Structural Theory

Structural theory shows how the latent variables are related to each other (i.e., it shows the constructs and the path relationships between them in the structural model). The location and sequence of the constructs are based on theory or the researcher's experience and accumulated knowledge. When path models are developed, the sequence is from left to right. The variables on the left side of the path model are independent variables, and any variable on the right side is the dependent variable. Moreover, variables on the left are shown as sequentially preceding and predicting the variables on the right. However, variables may also serve as both the independent and dependent variable.

When latent variables serve only as independent variables, they are called *exogenous latent variables* (Y_1 and Y_2). When latent variables serve only as dependent variables (Y_4) or as both independent and dependent variables (Y_3), they are called *endogenous latent variables*. Any latent variable that has only single-headed arrows going out of it is an exogenous latent variable. In contrast, endogenous latent variables can have either single-headed arrows going both into and out of them (Y_3) or only going into them (Y_4). Note that the exogenous latent variables Y_1 and Y_2 do not have error terms since these constructs are the entities (independent variables) that are explaining the dependent variables in the path model.

PLS-SEM AND CB-SEM

There are two approaches to estimate the relationships in a structural equation model (Hair et al., 2010; Hair, Ringle, & Sarstedt, 2011; Hair et al., 2012a). One is the more widely applied CB-SEM approach. The other is PLS-SEM, which is the focus of this book. Each is appropriate for a different research context, and researchers need to understand the differences in order to apply the correct method.

To answer the question of when to use PLS-SEM versus CB-SEM, researchers should focus on the characteristics and objectives that distinguish the two methods (Hair et al., 2012b). In situations where theory is less developed, researchers should consider the use of PLS-SEM as an alternative approach to CB-SEM. This is particularly true if the primary objective of applying structural modeling is prediction and explanation of target constructs.

The estimation procedure for PLS-SEM is an ordinary least squares (OLS) regression-based method rather than the maximum likelihood (ML) estimation procedure for CB-SEM. PLS-SEM uses available data to estimate the path relationships in the model with the objective of minimizing the error terms (i.e., the residual variance) of the endogenous constructs. In other words, PLS-SEM estimates coefficients (i.e., path model relationships) that maximize the R^2 values of the (target) endogenous constructs. This feature achieves the prediction objective of PLS-SEM. PLS-SEM is therefore the preferred method when the research objective is theory development and explanation of variance (prediction of the constructs). For this reason, PLS-SEM is regarded as a **variance-based** approach to SEM.

Note that PLS-SEM is similar but not equivalent to **PLS regression,** another popular multivariate data analysis technique. PLS regression is a regression-based approach that explores the linear relationships between multiple independent variables and a single or multiple dependent variable(s). PLS regression differs from regular regression, however, because in developing the regression model, it constructs composite factors from both the multiple independent variables and the dependent variable(s) by means of principal component analysis. PLS-SEM, on the other hand, relies on prespecified networks of relationships between constructs as well as between constructs and their measures (see Mateos-Aparicio [2011] for a more detailed comparison between PLS-SEM and PLS regression).

Several considerations are important when deciding whether or not to apply PLS-SEM. These considerations also have their roots in the method's characteristics. The statistical properties of the PLS-SEM algorithm have important features associated with the characteristics of the data and model used. Moreover, the properties of the PLS-SEM method also affect the evaluation of the results. There are four critical issues relevant to the application of PLS-SEM (Hair, Ringle, & Sarstedt, 2011; Hair et al., 2012a; Hair et al., 2012b; Ringle, Sarstedt, & Straub, 2012): (1) the data, (2) model properties, (3) the PLS-SEM algorithm, and (4) model evaluation issues. Exhibit 1.5 summarizes the key characteristics of PLS-SEM. An initial overview of these issues is provided in this chapter, and a more detailed explanation is provided in later sections of the book, particularly as they relate to the PLS-SEM algorithm and evaluation of results.

PLS-SEM works efficiently with small sample sizes and complex models and makes practically no assumptions about the underlying data (for example, in terms of data distributions, see Cassel, Hackyl, and Westlund, 1999). In addition, PLS-SEM can easily handle reflective and formative measurement models, as well as single-item constructs, with no identification problems. It can therefore be applied in a wide variety of research situations. When applying PLS-SEM, researchers also benefit from high efficiency in parameter estimation, which is manifested in the method's greater **statistical power** than that of CB-SEM. Greater statistical power means that PLS-SEM is more likely to render a specific relationship significant when it is in fact significant in the population.

There are, however, several limitations of PLS-SEM. The technique cannot be applied when structural models contain causal loops or

Exhibit 1.5	Key Characteristics of PLS-SEM
Data Characteristics	
Sample sizes	• No identification issues with small sample sizes • Generally achieves high levels of statistical power with small sample sizes • Larger sample sizes increase the precision (i.e., consistency) of PLS-SEM estimations
Distribution	• No distributional assumptions; PLS-SEM is a nonparametric method
Missing values	• Highly robust as long as missing values are below a reasonable level
Scale of measurement	• Works with metric data, quasi-metric (ordinal) scaled data, and binary coded variables (with certain restrictions) • Some limitations when using categorical data to measure endogenous latent variables
Model Characteristics	
Number of items in each construct measurement model	• Handles constructs measured with single and multi-item measures
Relationships between constructs and their indicators	• Easily incorporates reflective and formative measurement models
Model complexity	• Handles complex models with many structural model relations • Larger numbers of indicators are helpful in reducing the PLS-SEM bias
Model setup	• No causal loops allowed in the structural model (only recursive models)
PLS-SEM Algorithm Properties	
Objective	• Minimizes the amount of unexplained variance (i.e., maximizes the R^2 values)
Efficiency	• Converges after a few iterations (even in situations with complex models and/or large sets of data) to the optimum solution; efficient algorithm

Construct scores	• Estimated as linear combinations of their indicators • Used for predictive purposes • Can be used as input for subsequent analyses • Not affected by data inadequacies
Parameter estimates	• Structural model relationships are generally underestimated (PLS-SEM bias) • Measurement model relationships are generally overestimated (PLS-SEM bias) • Consistency at large • High levels of statistical power
Model Evaluation Issues	
Evaluation of the overall model	• No global goodness-of-fit criterion
Evaluation of the measurement models	• Reflective measurement models: reliability and validity assessments by multiple criteria • Formative measurement models: validity assessment, significance and relevance of indicator weights, indicator collinearity
Evaluation of the structural model	• Collinearity among sets of constructs, significance of path coefficients, coefficient of determination (R^2), effect size (f^2), predictive relevance (Q^2 and q^2 effect size)
Additional analyses	• Impact-performance matrix analysis • Mediating effects • Hierarchical component models • Multigroup analysis • Uncovering and treating unobserved heterogeneity • Measurement model invariance • Moderating effects

Source: Adapted from *The Journal of Marketing Theory and Practice* 19(2) (Spring 2011), 139–151. Copyright © 2011 by M. E. Sharpe, Inc. Used by permission. All Rights Reserved. Not for reproduction.

circular relationships between the latent variables (i.e., when the model is nonrecursive). Since PLS-SEM does not have an adequate global goodness-of-model fit measure, its use for theory testing and confirmation is limited. In addition, in general, PLS-SEM parameter estimates are not optimal regarding bias and consistency—a property frequently referred to as PLS-SEM bias (Chapter 3). Although CB-SEM advocates strongly emphasize this limitation, simulation studies show that the differences between CB-SEM and PLS-SEM estimates are very small (e.g., Reinartz, Haenlein, & Henseler, 2009). Thus, the extensively discussed PLS-SEM bias is not relevant for most applications.

The results for CB-SEM and PLS-SEM typically do not differ much, and PLS-SEM estimates can therefore be good proxies of CB-SEM results. In certain cases, particularly when there is little a priori knowledge on structural model relationships or the measurement of the constructs or when the emphasis is more on exploration than confirmation, PLS-SEM is an attractive alternative to CB-SEM. Furthermore, when CB-SEM assumptions are violated with regard to normality of distributions, minimum sample size, and maximum model complexity, or related methodological anomalies occur in the process of model estimation, PLS-SEM is a good methodological alternative for theory testing. Thus, researchers should consider both CB-SEM and PLS-SEM when deciding on the appropriate analysis approach for structural model assessment.

Exhibit 1.6 displays the rules of thumb (RoT) that can be applied when deciding whether to use CB-SEM or PLS-SEM. As can be seen, PLS-SEM is not recommended as a universal alternative to CB-SEM. Both methods differ from a statistical point of view, so neither of the techniques is generally superior to the other and neither of them is appropriate for all situations. In general, the strengths of PLS-SEM are CB-SEM's weaknesses, and vice versa. It is important that researchers understand the different applications each approach was developed for and use them accordingly. Researchers need to apply the SEM technique that best suits their research objective, data characteristics, and model setup (see Roldán and Sánchez-Franco [2012] for a more detailed discussion).

Data Characteristics

Minimum Sample Size Requirements

Data characteristics such as minimum sample size, non-normal data, and scale of measurement (i.e., the use of different scale types) are among the most often stated reasons for applying PLS-SEM (Hair et al., 2012b; Henseler et al., 2009). While some of the arguments are consistent with the method's capabilities, others are not. For example, small sample size is probably the most often abused argument

Exhibit 1.6	Rules of Thumb for Choosing Between PLS-SEM and CB-SEM

Use PLS-SEM when

- The goal is predicting key target constructs or identifying key "driver" constructs.
- Formatively measured constructs are part of the structural model. Note that formative measures can also be used with CB-SEM, but doing so requires construct specification modifications (e.g., the construct must include both formative and reflective indicators to meet identification requirements).
- The structural model is complex (many constructs and many indicators).
- The sample size is small and/or the data are non-normally distributed.
- The plan is to use latent variable scores in subsequent analyses.

Use CB-SEM when

- The goal is theory testing, theory confirmation, or the comparison of alternative theories.
- Error terms require additional specification, such as the covariation.
- The structural model has non-recursive relationships.
- The research requires a global goodness-of-fit criterion.

Source: Adapted from *The Journal of Marketing Theory and Practice* 19(2) (Spring 2011), 139–151. Copyright © 2011 by M. E. Sharpe, Inc. Used by permission. All Rights Reserved. Not for reproduction.

associated with the use of PLS-SEM (Goodhue, Lewis, & Thompson, 2012; Marcoulides & Saunders, 2006). The result of these misrepresentations has been skepticism in general about the use of PLS-SEM.

The overall complexity of a structural model has little influence on the sample size requirements for PLS-SEM. The reason is the algorithm does not compute all relationships in the structural model at the same time. Instead, it uses OLS regressions to estimate the model's partial regression relationships. Two early studies systematically evaluated the performance of PLS-SEM with small sample sizes and concluded it performed well (e.g., Chin & Newsted, 1999; Hui & Wold, 1982). More recently, a simulation study by Reinartz et al. (2009) indicated that PLS-SEM is a good choice when the sample size is small. Moreover, compared with its covariance-based counterpart,

PLS-SEM has higher levels of statistical power in situations with complex model structures or smaller sample sizes.

Unfortunately, some researchers believe that sample size considerations do not play a role in the application of PLS-SEM. This idea is fostered by the often-cited 10 times rule (Barclay, Higgins, & Thompson, 1995), which indicates the sample size should be equal to the larger of

1. 10 times the largest number of formative indicators used to measure a single construct, or

2. 10 times the largest number of structural paths directed at a particular construct in the structural model.

This rule of thumb is equivalent to saying that the minimum sample size should be 10 times the maximum number of arrowheads pointing at a latent variable anywhere in the PLS path model. While the 10 times rule offers a rough guideline for minimum sample size requirements, PLS-SEM—like any statistical technique—requires researchers to consider the sample size against the background of the model and data characteristics (Hair, Ringle, & Sarstedt, 2011). Specifically, the required sample size should be determined by means of power analyses based on the part of the model with the largest number of predictors.

Since sample size recommendations in PLS-SEM essentially build on the properties of OLS regression, researchers can revert to more differentiated rules of thumb such as those provided by Cohen (1992) in his statistical power analyses for multiple regression models, provided that the measurement models have an acceptable quality in terms of outer loadings (i.e., loadings should be above the common threshold of 0.70). Alternatively, researchers can use programs such as G*Power (which is available free of charge at http://www.psycho .uni-duesseldorf.de/aap/projects/gpower/) to carry out power analyses specific to model setups.

Exhibit 1.7 shows the minimum sample size requirements necessary to detect minimum R^2 values of 0.10, 0.25, 0.50 and 0.75 in any of the endogenous constructs in the structural model for significance levels of 1%, 5%, and 10%, assuming the commonly used level of statistical power of 80% and a specific level of complexity of the PLS path model (i.e., the maximum number of arrows pointing at a construct in the PLS path model). For instance, when the maximum number of independent variables in the measurement and structural models is five,

Exhibit 1.7 Sample Size Recommendation a in PLS-SEM for a Statistical Power of 80%

	Significance Level											
	1%				5%				10%			
Maximum Number of Arrows Pointing at a Construct	Minimum R²				Minimum R²				Minimum R²			
	0.10	0.25	0.50	0.75	0.10	0.25	0.50	0.75	0.10	0.25	0.50	0.75
2	158	75	47	38	110	52	33	26	88	41	26	21
3	176	84	53	42	124	59	38	30	100	48	30	25
4	191	91	58	46	137	65	42	33	111	53	34	27
5	205	98	62	50	147	70	45	36	120	58	37	30
6	217	103	66	53	157	75	48	39	128	62	40	32
7	228	109	69	56	166	80	51	41	136	66	42	35
8	238	114	73	59	174	84	54	44	143	69	45	37
9	247	119	76	62	181	88	57	46	150	73	47	39
10	256	123	79	64	189	91	59	48	156	76	49	41

Source: Cohen, J. A power primer. Psychological Bulletin, 112, 155–519.

one would need 70 observations to achieve a statistical power of 80% for detecting R^2 values of at least 0.25 (with a 5% probability of error).

Data Distribution and Measurement Scales

As with other statistical analyses, missing values should be dealt with when using PLS-SEM. For reasonable limits (i.e., less than 5% values missing per indicator), missing value treatment options such as mean replacement, EM (expectation-maximization algorithm), and nearest neighbor (e.g., Hair et al., 2010) generally result in only slightly different PLS-SEM estimations. Alternatively, researchers can opt for deleting all observations with missing values, which, however, decreases variation in the data and may introduce biases when certain groups of observations have been deleted systematically.

The use of PLS-SEM has not been challenged on the two other key reasons related to data characteristics (i.e., distribution and scales). Thus, in situations where it is difficult or impossible to meet the stricter requirements of more traditional multivariate techniques (e.g., normal data distribution), PLS-SEM is the preferred method. PLS-SEM's greater flexibility is described by the label "soft modeling," coined by Wold (1982), who developed the method. It should be noted, however, that "soft" is attributed only to the distributional assumptions and not to the concepts, models, or estimation techniques (Lohmöller, 1989). PLS-SEM's statistical properties provide very robust model estimations with data that have normal as well as extremely non-normal (i.e., skewness and/or kurtosis) distributional properties (Reinartz et al., 2009; Ringle et al., 2009). It must be remembered, however, that influential outliers, and collinearity do influence the OLS regressions in PLS-SEM, and researchers should evaluate the data and results for these issues (Hair et al., 2010).

The PLS-SEM algorithm generally requires metric data for the measurement model indicators. But the method also works well with ordinal scales with equidistant data points (i.e., quasi-metric scales; Mooi & Sarstedt, 2011) and with binary coded data. The use of binary coded data is often a means of including categorical control variables or moderators in PLS-SEM models. In short, dummy-coded indicators can be included in PLS-SEM models but require special attention (see some note of caution by Hair et al., 2012b). When using both metric and dummy variables, researchers must consider the role of the dummy-coded variables in the model (Hair, Wolfinbarger Celsi, et al., 2011). Exhibit 1.8 summarizes key considerations related to data characteristics.

Model Characteristics

PLS-SEM is very flexible in its modeling properties. The PLS-SEM algorithm requires all models to be **recursive**. That is, circular relationships or loops of relationships between the latent variables are not allowed in the structural model. While non-recursive models are seldom specified in business research, this characteristic does limit the applicability of PLS-SEM if nonrecursive models are required. Other model specification requirements that constrain the use of CB-SEM, such as distribution assumptions, are not relevant with PLS-SEM.

Measurement model difficulties are one of the major obstacles to obtaining a solution with CB-SEM. For instance, estimation of complex models with many latent variables and/or indicators is often impossible with CB-SEM. In contrast, PLS-SEM can be used in such situations since it is not constrained by identification and other technical issues. Consideration of reflective and formative measurement models is a key issue in the application of SEM. PLS-SEM can easily handle both

Exhibit 1.8	Data Considerations When Applying PLS-SEM

- As a rough guideline, the minimum sample size in a PLS-SEM analysis should be equal to the larger of the following (10 times rule): (1) 10 times the largest number of formative indicators used to measure one construct or (2) 10 times the largest number of structural paths directed at a particular construct in the structural model. Researchers should, however, follow more elaborate recommendations such as those provided by Cohen (1992) that also take statistical power and effect sizes into account. Alternatively, researchers should run individual power analyses, using programs such as G*Power.
- With larger data sets (N = 250+), CB-SEM and PLS-SEM results are very similar when an appropriate number of indicator variables (4+) are used to measure each of the constructs (consistency at large).
- PLS-SEM can handle extremely non-normal data (e.g., high levels of skewness).
- Most missing value treatment procedures (e.g., mean replacement, pairwise deletion, EM, and nearest neighbor) can be used for reasonable levels of missing data (less than 5% missing per indicator) with limited effect on the analysis results.
- PLS-SEM works with metric, quasi-metric, and categorical (i.e., dummy-coded) scaled data, albeit with certain limitations.

formative and reflective measurement models and is considered the primary approach when the hypothesized model incorporates formative measures. CB-SEM can accommodate formative indicators, but to ensure model identification, they must follow distinct specification rules (Diamantopoulos & Riefler, 2011). In fact, the requirements often prevent running the analysis as originally planned. In contrast, PLS-SEM does not have such requirements, and both formative and reflective measurement models are handled equally well. The only problematic issue is when a high level of collinearity exists between the indicator variables of a formative measurement model.

Finally, PLS-SEM is capable of estimating very complex models. For example, if theoretical or conceptual assumptions support large models and sufficient data are available (i.e., meeting minimum sample size requirements), PLS-SEM can handle models of almost any size, including those with dozens of constructs and hundreds of indicator variables. As noted by Wold (1985), PLS-SEM is virtually without competition when path models with latent variables are complex in their structural relationships (Chapter 3). Exhibit 1.9 summarizes rules of thumb for PLS-SEM model characteristics.

Exhibit 1.9	Model Considerations When Choosing PLS-SEM

- Measurement model requirements are quite flexible. PLS-SEM can handle reflective and formative measurement models as well as single-item measures without additional requirements or constraints.
- Model complexity is generally not an issue for PLS-SEM. As long as appropriate data meet minimum sample size requirements, the complexity of the structural model is virtually unrestricted.

ORGANIZATION OF REMAINING CHAPTERS

The remaining chapters provide more detailed information on PLS-SEM, including specific examples of how to use software to estimate simple and complex PLS path models. In doing so, the chapters follow a multistage procedure that should be used as a blueprint when conducting PLS-SEM analyses (Exhibit 1.10).

Specifically, the process starts with the specification of structural and measurement models, followed by the collection and examination of data (Chapter 2). Next, we discuss the PLS-SEM algorithm and provide an overview of important considerations when running the

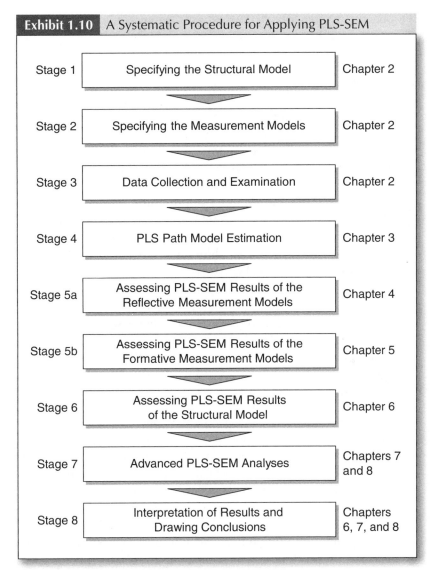

Exhibit 1.10 A Systematic Procedure for Applying PLS-SEM

Stage 1	Specifying the Structural Model	Chapter 2
Stage 2	Specifying the Measurement Models	Chapter 2
Stage 3	Data Collection and Examination	Chapter 2
Stage 4	PLS Path Model Estimation	Chapter 3
Stage 5a	Assessing PLS-SEM Results of the Reflective Measurement Models	Chapter 4
Stage 5b	Assessing PLS-SEM Results of the Formative Measurement Models	Chapter 5
Stage 6	Assessing PLS-SEM Results of the Structural Model	Chapter 6
Stage 7	Advanced PLS-SEM Analyses	Chapters 7 and 8
Stage 8	Interpretation of Results and Drawing Conclusions	Chapters 6, 7, and 8

analyses (Chapter 3). On the basis of the results of the computation, the researcher then has to evaluate the results. To do so, researchers must know how to assess both reflective and formative measurement models (Chapters 4 and 5). When the data for the measures are considered reliable and valid (based on established criteria), researchers can then evaluate the structural model (Chapter 6). Finally, Chapters 7 and 8 cover advanced topics in PLS-SEM, such as mediating and moderating variables, hierarchical component models, testing for unobserved heterogeneity in sample data, invariance, and multigroup modeling. On the basis of the results of Chapters 6, 7, and 8, researchers interpret their findings and draw their final conclusions.

SUMMARY

SEM is a powerful statistical method that can identify relationships in social science research that likely would not otherwise be found. This chapter introduced you to the topic, explained why researchers are increasingly using the method, and helped you do the following:

• **Understand the meaning of structural equation modeling (SEM) and its relationship to multivariate data analysis.** SEM is a second-generation multivariate data analysis method. Multivariate data analysis involves the application of statistical methods that simultaneously analyze multiple variables representing measurements associated with individuals, companies, events, activities, situations, and so forth. SEM is used to either explore or confirm theory. Exploratory modeling involves developing theory while confirmatory modeling tests theory. There are two types of SEM—one is covariance based, and the other is variance based. CB-SEM is used to confirm (or reject) theories. Variance-based structural equation modeling (i.e., PLS-SEM) is primarily used to develop theories.

• **Describe the basic considerations in applying multivariate data analysis.** Several considerations are necessary when applying multivariate analysis, including the following five elements: (1) the variate, (2) measurement, (3) measurement scales, (4) coding, and (5) data distributions. It is the fundamental building block of multivariate analysis. The variate is a linear combination of several variables that are chosen based on the research problem at hand. Measurement is the process of assigning numbers to a variable based on a set of rules. **Multivariate measurement** involves using several variables to indirectly measure a concept to improve measurement accuracy. The anticipated improved accuracy is based on the assumption that using several variables (indicators) to measure a single concept is more likely to represent all the different aspects of the concept and thereby result in a more valid measurement of the concept. The ability to identify measurement error using multivariate measurement also helps researchers obtain more accurate measurements. Measurement error is the difference between the true value of a variable and the value obtained by a measurement. A measurement scale is a tool with a predetermined number of closed-ended responses that can be used to obtain an answer to a question. There are four types of measurement scales: nominal, ordinal, interval, and ratio. When researchers collect quantitative data using scales, the answers to the questions can be shown as a distribution across the available (predefined) response categories. The type of distribution must always be considered when working with SEM.

- **Comprehend the basic concepts of partial least squares SEM (PLS-SEM).** Path models are diagrams used to visually display the hypotheses and variable relationships that are examined when structural equation modeling is applied. Four basic elements must be understood when developing path models: (1) constructs, (2) measured variables, (3) relationships, and (4) error terms. Constructs are latent variables that are not directly measured and are sometimes called unobserved variables. They are represented in path models as circles or ovals. Measured variables are directly measured observations (raw data), generally referred to as either indicators or manifest variables, and are represented in path models as rectangles. Relationships represent hypotheses in path models and are shown as arrows that are single-headed, indicating a predictive/causal relationship. Error terms represent the unexplained variance when path models are estimated and are shown as circles connected to the (endogenous) constructs and (reflectively) measured variables by single-headed arrows. Path models also distinguish between the structural (inner) model and the measurement (outer) models. The role of theory is important when developing structural models. Theory is a set of systematically related hypotheses developed following the scientific method that can be used to explain and predict outcomes. Measurement theory specifies how the latent unobservable variables (constructs) are modeled. Latent variables can be modeled as either reflective or formative. Structural theory shows how the latent unobservable variables are related to each other. Latent variables are classified as either endogenous or exogenous.

- **Explain the differences between covariance-based SEM (CB-SEM) and PLS-SEM and when to use each.** As an alternative to CB-SEM, PLS-SEM emphasizes the prediction objective while simultaneously relaxing the demands regarding the data and specification of relationships. PLS-SEM maximizes the endogenous latent variables' explained variance by estimating partial model relationships in an iterative sequence of OLS regressions. In contrast, CB-SEM estimates model parameters so that the discrepancy between the estimated and sample covariance matrices is minimized. PLS-SEM is not constrained by identification issues, even if the model becomes complex—a situation that typically restricts CB-SEM use—and does not require accounting for most distributional assumptions. Moreover, PLS-SEM can better handle formative measurement models and has advantages when sample sizes are relatively small. Researchers should consider the two SEM approaches as complementary and apply the SEM technique that best suits their research objective, data characteristics, and model setup.

REVIEW QUESTIONS

1. What is multivariate analysis?

2. Describe the difference between first- and second-generation multivariate methods.

3. What is structural equation modeling?

4. What is the value of structural equation modeling in understanding relationships between variables?

CRITICAL THINKING QUESTIONS

1. When would SEM methods be more advantageous in understanding relationships between variables?

2. What are the most important considerations in deciding whether to use CB-SEM or PLS-SEM?

3. Under what circumstances is PLS-SEM the preferred method over CB-SEM?

4. Why is an understanding of theory important when deciding whether to use PLS-SEM or CB-SEM?

5. Why should social science researchers consider using SEM instead of multiple regression?

KEY TERMS

CB-SEM: see *Covariance-based structural equation modeling.*
Coding: is the assignment of numbers to scales in a manner that facilitates measurement.
Confirmatory: see *Confirmatory applications.*

Confirmatory applications: aim at empirically testing theoretically developed models.

Constructs (also called latent variables): measure concepts that are abstract, complex, and cannot be directly observed by means of (multiple) items. Constructs are represented in path models as circles or ovals.

Covariance-based structural equation modeling: is used to confirm (or reject) theories. It does this by determining how well a proposed theoretical model can estimate the covariance matrix for a sample data set.

Endogenous latent variables: serve only as dependent variables, or as both independent and dependent variables in a structural model.

Equidistance: is given when the distance between data points of a scale is identical.

Error terms: capture the unexplained variance in constructs and indicators when path models are estimated.

Exogenous latent variables: are latent variables that serve only as independent variables in a structural model.

Exploratory: see *Exploratory applications.*

Exploratory applications: focus on exploring data patterns and identifying relationships.

First-generation techniques: are statistical methods traditionally used by researchers, such as regression and analysis of variance.

Formative measurement model: is a type of measurement model setup in which the direction of the arrows is from the indicator variables to the construct, indicating the assumption that the indicator variables cause the measurement of the construct.

Indicators: are directly measured observations (raw data), generally referred to as either *items* or *manifest variables,* represented in path models as rectangles.

Inner model: see *Structural model.*

Interval scale: can be used to provide a rating of objects and has a constant unit of measurement so the distance between the scale points is equal.

Items: see *Indicators.*

Latent variable: see *Constructs.*

Manifest variables: see *Indicators.*

Measurement: is the process of assigning numbers to a variable based on a set of rules.

Measurement error: is the difference between the true value of a variable and the value obtained by a measurement.

Measurement model: is an element of a path model that contains the indicators and their relationships with the constructs and is also called the *outer model* in PLS-SEM.

Measurement scale: is a tool with a predetermined number of closed-ended responses that can be used to obtain an answer to a question.

Measurement theory: specifies how the latent variables are measured.

Multivariate analyses: are statistical methods that simultaneously analyze multiple variables.

Multivariate measurement: involves using several variables to indirectly measure a concept.

Nominal scale: is a measurement scale where numbers are assigned that can be used to identify and classify objects (e.g., people, companies, products, etc.).

Ordinal scale: is a measurement scale where numbers are assigned that indicate relative positions of objects in an ordered series.

Outer models: see *Measurement model.*

Partial least squares path modeling: see *Partial least squares structural equation modeling.*

Partial least squares structural equation modeling: is a variance-based method to estimate structural equation models. The goal is to maximize the explained variance of the endogenous latent variables.

Path models: are diagrams that visually display the hypotheses and variable relationships that are examined when structural equation modeling is applied.

PLS regression: is an analysis technique that explores the linear relationships between multiple independent variables and a single or multiple dependent variable(s). In developing the regression model, it constructs composites from both the multiple independent variables and the dependent variable(s) by means of principal component analysis.

PLS-SEM: see *Partial least squares structural equation modeling.*

Ratio scales: are the highest level of measurement because they have a constant unit of measurement and an absolute zero point; a ratio can be calculated using the scale points.

Recursive model: is a PLS path model that does not have a causal loop of relationships between latent variables in the structural model (i.e., no circular relationships).

Reflective measurement model: is a type of measurement model setup in which the direction of the arrows is from the construct to the indicator variables, indicating the assumption that the construct causes the measurement (more precisely, the covariation) of the indicator variables.

Second-generation techniques: overcome the limitations of first-generation techniques, for example, in terms of accounting for measurement error. SEM is the most prominent second-generation data analysis technique.

SEM: see *Structural equation modeling.*

Single-item constructs: have only a single item to measure the construct.

Statistical power: the probability to detect a significant relationship significant when it is in fact significant in the population.

Structural equation modeling: is used to measure relationships between latent variables.

Structural model: is an element of a PLS path model that contains the constructs as well as the relationships between them. It is also called the *inner model* in PLS-SEM.

Structural theory: specifies how the latent variables are related to each other. That is, it shows the constructs and the paths between them.

Theory: is a set of systematically related hypotheses developed following the scientific method that can be used to explain and predict outcomes and can be tested empirically.

Variance-based SEM: see *Partial least squares structural equation modeling*.

Variate: is a linear combination of several variables.

SUGGESTED READINGS

Esposito Vinzi, V., Trinchera, L., & Amato, S. (2010). PLS path modeling: From foundations to recent developments and open issues for model assessment and improvement. In V. Esposito Vinzi, W. W. Chin, J. Henseler & H. Wang (Eds.), *Handbook of partial least squares: Concepts, methods and applications* (Springer Handbooks of Computational Statistics Series, vol. II) (pp. 47–82). New York: Springer.

Gefen, D., Straub, D. W., & Boudreau, M. C. (2000). Structural equation modeling techniques and regression: Guidelines for research practice. *Communications of the AIS, 1*(7), 1–78.

Hair, J. F., Black, W. C., Babin, B. J., & Anderson, R. E. (2010). *Multivariate data analysis.* Englewood Cliffs, NJ: Prentice Hall.

Hair, J. F., Ringle, C. M., & Sarstedt, M. (2011). PLS-SEM: Indeed a silver bullet. *Journal of Marketing Theory and Practice, 19,* 139–151.

Hair, J. F., Wolfinbarger Celsi, M., Money, A. H., Samouel, P., & Page, M. J. (2011). *Essentials of business research methods.* Armonk, NY: Sharpe.

Henseler, J., Ringle, C. M., & Sarstedt, M. (2012). Using partial least squares path modeling in international advertising research: Basic concepts and recent issues. In S. Okazaki (Ed.), *Handbook of research in international advertising* (pp. 252–276). Cheltenham, UK: Edward Elgar.

Jöreskog, K. G., & Wold, H. (1982). The ML and PLS techniques for modeling with latent variables: Historical and comparative aspects. In H. Wold & K. G. Jöreskog (Eds.), *Systems under indirect observation*, Part I (pp. 263–270). Amsterdam: North-Holland.

Lohmöller, J. B. (1989). *Latent variable path modeling with partial least squares.* Heidelberg: Physica.

Mateos-Aparicio, G. (2011). Partial Least Squares (PLS) methods: Origins, evolution, and application to social sciences. *Communications in Statistics: Theory and Methods, 40*(13), 2305–2317.

Rigdon, E. E. (2012). Rethinking partial least squares path modeling: In praise of simple methods. *Long Range Planning, 45*(5/6), 341–358.

CHAPTER 2

Specifying the Path Model and Collecting Data

LEARNING OUTCOMES

1. Understand the basic concepts of structural model specification, including mediation, moderation, and higher-order models.

2. Explain the differences between reflective and formative measures and be able to specify the appropriate measurement model.

3. Explain the difference between multi-item and single-item measures and be able to assess when to use each measurement type.

4. Describe the data collection and examination considerations necessary to apply PLS-SEM.

5. Learn how to develop a PLS path model using the SmartPLS software.

CHAPTER PREVIEW

Chapter 2 introduces the basic concepts of structural and measurement model specification when PLS-SEM is used. The concepts are associated with completing the first three stages in the application of PLS-SEM, as described in Chapter 1. Stage 1 is specifying the structural model. Stage 2 is selecting and specifying the measurement models. Stage 3 summarizes the major guidelines for data collection when application of PLS-SEM is anticipated, as well as the need to examine your data after they have been collected to ensure the results from applying PLS-SEM are valid and reliable. An understanding of these three topics will prepare you for Stage 4, estimating the model, which is the focus of Chapter 3.

STAGE 1: SPECIFYING THE STRUCTURAL MODEL

In the initial stages of a research project that involves the application of SEM, an important first step is to prepare a diagram that illustrates the research hypotheses and displays the variable relationships that will be examined. This diagram is often referred to as a *path model*. Recall that a **path model** is a diagram that connects variables/constructs based on theory and logic to visually display the hypotheses that will be tested (Chapter 1). Preparing a path model early in the research process enables researchers to organize their thoughts and visually consider the relationships between the variables of interest. Path models also are an efficient means of sharing ideas between researchers working on or reviewing a research project.

Path models are made up of two elements, the **structural model** (also called the **inner model** in PLS-SEM), which describes the relationships between the latent variables, and the measurement models, which describe the relationships between the latent variables and their measures (i.e., their indicators). We discuss structural models first, which are developed in Stage 1. The next section covers Stage 2, measurement models.

When a structural model is being developed, two primary issues need to be considered: the sequence of the constructs and the relationships between them. Both issues are critical to the concept of modeling because they represent the hypotheses and their relationship to the theory being tested.

The sequence of the constructs in a structural model is based on theory, logic, or practical experiences observed by the researcher. The sequence is displayed from left to right, with independent (predictor) constructs on the left and dependent (outcome) variables to the right. That is, constructs to the left side are assumed to precede and predict constructs to the right. Constructs that only act as independent variables are generally referred to as **exogenous latent**

variables and are on the extreme left side of the structural model. Exogenous latent variables only have arrows that point out of them and never have arrows pointing into them. Constructs considered as dependent in a structural model (i.e., those that have an arrow pointing into it) often are called **endogenous latent variables** and are on the right side of the structural model. Constructs that operate as both independent and dependent variables in a model also are considered endogenous and, if they are part of a model, appear in the middle of the diagram.

The structural model in Exhibit 2.1 illustrates the three types of constructs and the relationships. The reputation construct on the far left is an independent (exogenous) variable. It is modeled as predicting the satisfaction construct. The satisfaction construct is an endogenous variable that has a dual relationship as both independent and dependent. It is a dependent construct because it is predicted by reputation. But it is also an independent construct because it predicts loyalty. The loyalty construct on the far right is a dependent (endogenous) latent variable predicted by satisfaction.

Determining the sequence of the constructs is seldom an easy task because contradictory theoretical perspectives can lead to different sequencing of latent variables. For example, some researchers assume that customer satisfaction precedes and predicts corporate reputation (e.g., Walsh, Mitchell, Jackson, & Beatty, 2009), while others argue that corporate reputation predicts customer satisfaction (Eberl, 2010; Sarstedt, Wilczynski, & Melewar, in press). Theory and logic should always determine the sequence of constructs in a conceptual model, but when the literature is inconsistent or unclear, researchers must use their best judgment to determine the sequence. In large, complex models, researchers may adjust the sequence of constructs several times while trying to accurately portray the

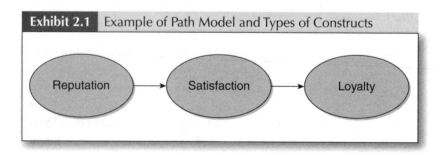

Exhibit 2.1   Example of Path Model and Types of Constructs

theoretical concepts. Likewise, it is possible to have alternative competing models that test a different sequence (Sattler, Völckner, Riediger, & Ringle, 2010; Wilson, Callaghan, Ringle, & Henseler, 2007). However, selecting the best sequence among several competing alternatives can be challenging.

When the sequence of the constructs has been decided, then the relationships between them must be established by drawing arrows. The arrows are inserted with the arrow pointed to the right. This approach indicates the sequence and that the constructs on the left predict the constructs to the right. The predictive relationships are sometimes referred to as **causal links,** if the **structural theory** supports a causal relationship. In drawing arrows between the constructs, researchers face a trade-off between theoretical soundness (i.e., including those relationships that are strongly supported by theory) and model parsimony (i.e., using fewer relationships). The latter should be of crucial concern as the most non-restrictive statement "everything is predictive of everything else" is also the most uninformative. As pointed out by Falk and Miller (1992), "A parsimonious approach to theoretical specification is far more powerful than the broad application of a shotgun" (p. 24).

In most instances, researchers examine linear independent-dependent relationships between two or more constructs in the path model. Theory may suggest, however, that model relationships are more complex and involve mediation or moderation relationships. In the following section, we briefly introduce these different relationship types. In Chapters 7 and 8, we explain how they can be estimated and interpreted using PLS-SEM.

Mediation

A **mediating effect** is created when a third variable or construct intervenes between two other related constructs, as shown in Exhibit 2.2. To understand how mediating effects work, let's consider a path model in terms of direct and indirect effects. **Direct effects** are the relationship linking two constructs with a single arrow; **indirect effects** are those relationships that involve a sequence of relationships with at least one intervening construct involved. Thus, an indirect effect is a sequence of two or more direct effects (compound path) that are represented visually by multiple arrows. This indirect effect is characterized as the *mediating effect*. In Exhibit 2.2, satisfaction is modeled as a possible mediator between reputation and loyalty.

From a theoretical perspective, the most common application of mediation is to "explain" why a relationship between an exogenous and endogenous construct exists. For example, a researcher may observe a relationship between two constructs but not be sure "why" the relationship exists or if the observed relationship is the only relationship between the two constructs. In such a situation, a researcher might posit an explanation of the relationship in terms of an intervening variable that operates by receiving the "inputs" from an exogenous construct and translating them into an "output," which is an endogenous construct. The role of the mediator variable then is to clarify or explain the relationship between the two original constructs.

Consider the example in Exhibit 2.2, in which we want to examine the effect of corporate reputation on customer loyalty. On the basis of theory and logic, we know that a relationship exists between reputation and loyalty, but we are unsure how the relationship actually works. As researchers, we might want to explain how companies translate their reputation into higher loyalty among their customers. We may observe that sometimes a customer perceives a company as being highly reputable, but this perception does not translate into high levels of loyalty. In other situations, we observe that some customers with lower reputation assessments are highly loyal. These observations are confusing and lead to the question as to whether there is some other process going on that translates corporate reputation into customer loyalty.

| **Exhibit 2.2** | Example of a Mediating Effect |

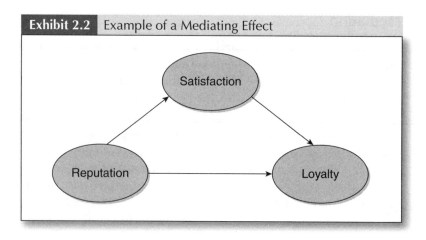

In the diagram, the intervening process (mediating effect) is modeled as satisfaction. If a respondent perceives a company to be highly reputable, this assessment may lead to higher satisfaction levels and ultimately to increased loyalty. In such a case, the relationship between reputation and loyalty may be explained by the reputation → loyalty sequence, or the reputation → satisfaction → loyalty sequence, or perhaps even by both sets of relationships (Exhibit 2.2). The reputation → loyalty sequence is an example of a direct relationship. In contrast, the reputation → satisfaction → loyalty sequence is an example of an indirect relationship. After empirically testing these relationships, the researcher would be able to explain how reputation is related to loyalty, as well as the role that satisfaction might play in mediating that relationship. Chapter 7 offers additional details on mediation and explains how to test mediating effects in PLS-SEM.

Moderation

Related to the concept of mediation is moderation. With **moderation,** the construct could also directly affect the relationship between the exogenous and endogenous latent variables but in a different way. Referred to as a **moderator effect,** this situation occurs when the moderator (an independent variable or construct) changes the strength or even the direction of a relationship between two constructs in the model.

For example, income has been shown to significantly affect the strength of the relationship between customer satisfaction and customer loyalty (Homburg & Giering, 2001). In that context, income serves as a moderator variable on the satisfaction → loyalty relationship, as shown in Exhibit 2.3. Specifically, the relationship between satisfaction and loyalty has been shown to be weaker for people with high income than for people with low income. That is, for higher-income individuals, there may be little or no relationship between satisfaction and loyalty. But for lower-income individuals, there often is a strong relationship between the two variables. As can be seen, both the mediator and the moderator concept affect the strength of a relationship between two latent variables. The crucial distinction between both concepts is that the moderator variable (income in our moderator example) does not depend on the predictor variable (satisfaction in our moderator example).

There are two types of moderating relationships. One is referred to as *continuous* and the other as *categorical.* The difference in the two types of relationships is that a continuous moderating effect

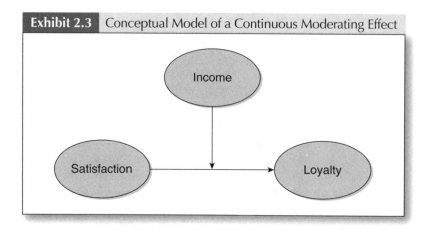

Exhibit 2.3 Conceptual Model of a Continuous Moderating Effect

exists when the moderating variable is metrically measured (e.g., income in Exhibit 2.3), whereas a categorical moderating effect is when the moderating variable is categorical, such as gender.

When a moderator effect is categorical, the variable serves as a grouping variable that divides the data into subsamples. The same theoretical model is then estimated for each of the distinct subsamples. Since researchers are usually interested in comparing the models and learning about significant differences between the subsamples, the model estimates for the subsamples are usually compared by means of **multigroup analysis** (Chapter 8). Specifically, multigroup analysis enables the researcher to test for differences between identical models estimated for different groups of respondents. The general objective is to see if there are statistically significant differences between individual group models. This procedure is different from testing different theoretical models for the same sample of respondents. With multigroup analysis, we are comparing the same model across different samples of respondents. For example, we might be interested in evaluating whether the effect of satisfaction on loyalty is significantly different for males compared with females (Exhibit 2.4). Specifically, a researcher might want to determine whether the relationship is statistically significant for both males and females and if the strength of the relationship is similar or quite different.

Another situation researchers often encounter is where they have a continuous moderator variable, but instead of modeling its original effect on the relationship as continuous, they transform

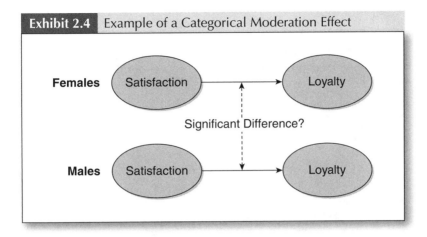

Exhibit 2.4   Example of a Categorical Moderation Effect

the continuous variable into a categorical variable and then conduct a multigroup analysis. Different approaches transform the continuous variable into a categorical one, such as mean and median splits. We will discuss these approaches in greater detail in Chapter 8, which deals with the modeling of categorical and continuous moderator effects.

Higher-Order and Hierarchical Component Models

In some instances, the constructs that researchers wish to examine are quite complex. Thus far, we have dealt with first-order components in which we consider a single layer of constructs. However, constructs can also be operationalized at higher levels of abstraction. **Higher-order models** or **hierarchical component models (HCM)** most often involve testing second-order structures that contain two layers of components (e.g., Ringle et al., 2012; Wetzels, Odekerken-Schroder, & van Oppen, 2009). For example, satisfaction can be defined at different levels of abstraction. Specifically, satisfaction can be represented by numerous first-order components that capture separate attributes of satisfaction. In the context of services, these might include satisfaction with the quality of the service, the service personnel, the price, or the servicescape. These first-order components might form the more abstract second-order component satisfaction, as shown in Exhibit 2.5.

Instead of modeling the attributes of satisfaction as drivers of the respondent's overall satisfaction on a single construct layer,

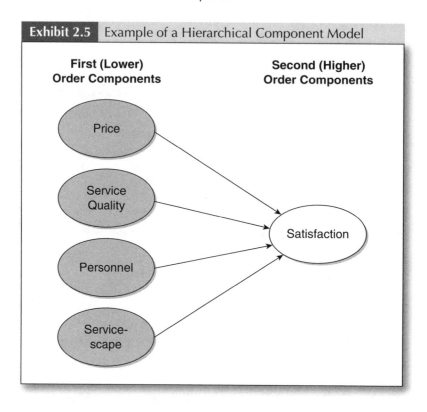

Exhibit 2.5 Example of a Hierarchical Component Model

higher-order modeling involves summarizing the lower-order components (LOCs) into a single multidimensional higher-order construct (HOC). This modeling approach leads to more theoretical parsimony and reduces model complexity. Theoretically, this process can be extended to any number of multiple layers, but researchers usually restrict their modeling approach to two layers. We discuss the application of hierarchical component models using PLS-SEM in Chapter 7.

STAGE 2: SPECIFYING THE MEASUREMENT MODELS

The structural model describes the relationships between latent variables (constructs). In contrast, the **measurement models** represent the relationships between constructs and their corresponding indicator variables (generally called the **outer models** in PLS-SEM). The basis for determining these relationships is **measurement theory**. A sound measurement theory is a necessary condition to obtain useful results from PLS-SEM. Hypothesis tests involving the structural relationships among constructs will only be as reliable or valid as are the measurement models explaining how these constructs are measured.

Researchers typically have several established measurement approaches to choose from, each a slight variant from the others. In fact, almost all social science research today uses measurement approaches published in prior research studies or scale handbooks (e.g., Bearden, Netemeyer, & Haws, 2011; Bruner, James, & Hensel, 2001) that performed well (Ramirez, David, & Brusco, in press). In some situations, however, the researcher is faced with the lack of an established measurement approach and must develop a new set of measures (or substantially modify an existing approach). A description of the general process for developing **indicators** to measure a construct can be long and detailed. Hair et al. (2010) describe the essentials of this process. Likewise, Diamantopoulos and Winklhofer (2001), DeVellis (2011), and MacKenzie, Podsakoff, and Podsakoff (2011) offer thorough discussions of different approaches to measurement development. In each case, decisions regarding how the researcher selects the indicators to measure a particular construct provide a foundation for the remaining analysis.

The path model shown in Exhibit 2.6 shows an excerpt of the path model we use as an example throughout the book. The model has two exogenous constructs—*corporate social responsibility* (*CSOR*) and *attractiveness* (*ATTR*)—and one endogenous construct, which is *competence* (*COMP*). Each of these constructs is measured by means of multiple indicators. For instance, the endogenous construct *COMP* has three measured indicator variables, *comp_1* to *comp_3*. Using a scale from 1 to 7 (*totally disagree* to *fully agree*), respondents had to evaluate the following statements: "[The company] is a top competitor in its market," "As far as I know, [the company] is recognized worldwide," and "I believe that [the company] performs at a premium level." The answers to these three questions represent the measures for this construct. The construct itself is measured indirectly by these three indicator variables and for that reason is referred to as a latent variable.

The other two constructs in the model, *CSOR* and *ATTR*, can be described in a similar manner. That is, the two exogenous constructs are measured by indicators that are each directly measured

Exhibit 2.6 Example of a Path Model With Three Constructs

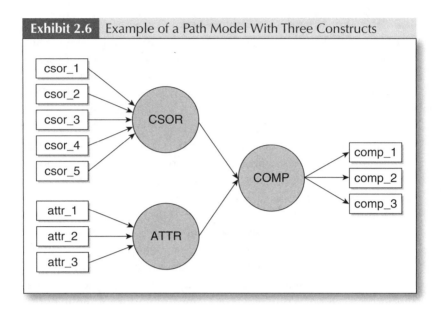

by responses to specific questions. Note that the relationship between the indicators and the corresponding construct is different for *COMP* compared with *CSOR* and *ATTR*. When you examine the *COMP* construct, the direction of the arrows goes from the construct to the indicators. This type of measurement model is referred to as *reflective*. When you examine the *CSOR* and *ATTR* constructs, the direction of the arrows is from the measured indicator variables to the constructs. This type of measurement model is called *formative*. As discussed in Chapter 1, an important characteristic of PLS-SEM is that the technique readily incorporates both reflective and formative measures. Likewise, PLS-SEM can easily be used when constructs are measured with only a single item (rather than multiple items). Both of these measurement issues are discussed in the following sections.

Reflective and Formative Measurement Models

When developing constructs, researchers must consider two broad types of measurement specification: reflective and formative measurement models. The **reflective measurement** model (also referred to as **Mode A** measurement in PLS-SEM) has a long tradition in the social sciences and is directly based on classical test theory. According to this theory, measures represent the effects (or manifestations) of an underlying construct. Therefore, causality is from the construct to its measures (*COMP* in Exhibit 2.6). Reflective indicators can be viewed as a representative sample of all the possible items available within the conceptual domain of the construct. Therefore, since a reflective measure dictates that all indicator items are caused by the same construct (i.e., they stem from the same domain), indicators associated with a particular construct should be highly correlated with each other. In addition, individual items should be interchangeable, and any single item can generally be left out without changing the meaning of the construct, as long as the construct has sufficient reliability. The fact that the relationship goes from the construct to its measures implies that if the evaluation of the latent trait changes (e.g., because of a change in the standard of comparison), all indicators will change simultaneously. A set of reflective measures is commonly called a **scale.**

In contrast, **formative measurement** models (also referred to as **Mode B** measurement in PLS-SEM) are based on the assumption that the indicators cause the construct. Therefore, researchers typically refer to this type of measurement model as being a formative **index.** An important characteristic of formative indicators is that they are not interchangeable, as is true with reflective indicators. Thus, each indicator for a formative construct captures a specific aspect of the construct's domain. Taken jointly, the items ultimately determine the meaning of the construct, which implies that omitting an indicator potentially alters the nature of the construct. As a consequence, breadth of coverage of the construct domain is extremely important to ensure that the domain of content of the focal construct is adequately captured (Diamantopoulos & Winklhofer, 2001).

Exhibit 2.7 illustrates the key difference between the reflective and formative measurement perspective. The black circle illustrates the construct domain, which is the domain of content the construct is intended to measure. The gray circles represent the scope each indicator captures. Whereas the reflective measurement approach aims at maximizing the overlap between interchangeable indicators, the formative measurement approach tries to fully cover the construct domain (black circle) by the different formative indicators (gray circles), which should have small overlap.

Many authors note that a census of indicators rather than a sample is needed when measuring constructs formatively (e.g., Bollen &

Exhibit 2.7	Difference Between Reflective and Formative Measures

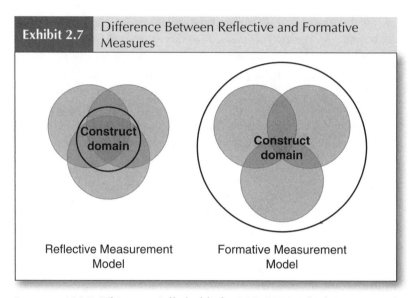

Reflective Measurement Model   Formative Measurement Model

Lennox, 1991). This especially holds for PLS-SEM, which is restricted to estimating formative constructs without error terms (Diamantopoulos, 2011). In practice, this circumstance is difficult to achieve because scholars cannot be certain that all possible causes related to the formatively measured latent variable are accounted for by the indicators (Diamantopoulos, 2006). That is why establishing an acceptable level of measurement validity before analysis of the structural relationships is essential in PLS-SEM studies that include formative measures. Specifically, researchers need to pay special attention to the content validity of the measures by determining how well the indicators represent the entire domain of the content (or at least its major aspects) of the content domain.

Unlike the reflective measurement approach that tries to maximize the overlap between interchangeable indicators, there are no specific expectations about patterns or magnitude of intercorrelations between formative indicators (Diamantopoulos, Riefler, & Roth, 2008). Since there is no "common cause" for the items in the construct, there is not any requirement for the items to be correlated, and they may be completely independent. In fact, collinearity among formative indicators can present significant problems because the weights linking the formative indicators with the construct can become unstable and nonsignificant. Furthermore, formative indicators have no individual measurement error terms. That is, they are assumed to be error free in a conventional sense.

These characteristics have broad implications for the evaluation of constructs based on a formative measurement model. For example, a reliability analysis based on item correlations (internal consistency) could remove important items and decrease the validity of the index (Diamantopoulos & Siguaw, 2006). Therefore, researchers must consider different measures when evaluating formative constructs, which we discuss in Chapter 5.

But when do we measure a construct reflectively or formatively? There is not a definite answer to this question since constructs are not inherently reflective or formative. Instead, the specification depends on the construct conceptualization and the objective of the study. Consider Exhibit 2.8, which shows how the construct "satisfaction with hotels" can be operationalized in both ways (Albers, 2010).

The left side of Exhibit 2.8 shows a reflective measurement model setup. This type of model setup is likely to be more appropriate when a researcher wants to test theories with respect to satisfaction. In many managerially oriented business studies, however, the aim is to identify the most important drivers of satisfaction that

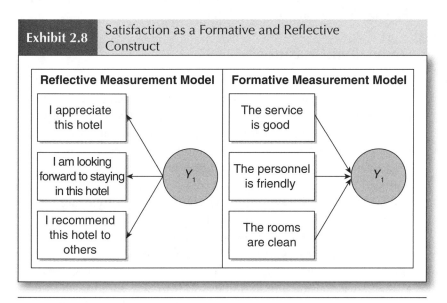

| Exhibit 2.8 | Satisfaction as a Formative and Reflective Construct |

Source: Albers, S. (2010). PLS and Success Factor Studies in Marketing. In: Esposito Vinzi V, Chin WW, Henseler J, et al. (eds) *Handbook of Partial Least Squares: Concepts, Methods and Applications in Marketing and Related Fields.* Berlin et al.: Springer, 409–425. With kind permission of Springer Science+Business Media.

ultimately lead to customer loyalty. In this case, researchers should consider the different facets of satisfaction, such as satisfaction with the service or the personnel, as shown on the right side of Exhibit 2.8. Obviously, the specification of the content of the construct (i.e., the domain content the construct is intended to capture) guides the measurement perspective.

The decision of whether to measure a construct reflectively or formatively is not clear-cut. In fact, the decision as to which measurement model is appropriate has been the subject of considerable debate in a variety of disciplines and is not fully resolved. In Exhibit 2.9, we present a set of guidelines that researchers can use to guide their decision of whether to measure a construct reflectively or formatively. Note that there are also empirical means to determine the measurement perspective. Gudergan, Ringle, Wende, and Will (2008) propose the so-called **confirmatory tetrad analysis for PLS-SEM** (CTA-PLS), which allows testing the null hypothesis that the construct measures are reflective in nature. Rejecting the null hypothesis in a tetrad test implies, therefore, that formative measures should be used for construct operationalization. Clearly, a purely data-driven perspective needs to be supplemented with theoretical considerations based on the guidelines summarized in Exhibit 2.9.

Single-Item Measures

Rather than using multiple items to measure a construct, researchers sometimes choose to use a single item. Single items have practical advantages such as ease of application, brevity, and lower costs associated with their use. Unlike long and complicated scales, which often result in a lack of understanding and mental fatigue for respondents, single items promote higher response rates as the questions can be easily and quickly answered (Fuchs & Diamantopoulos, 2009; Sarstedt & Wilczynski, 2009). However, single-item measures do not offer more for less. For instance, single items leave researchers with fewer degrees of freedom when partitioning the data into subgroups since scores from only a single variable are available to assign observations into groups. Similarly, there is less information available when using imputation methods to deal with missing values. Finally, from a psychometric perspective, single-item measures do not allow for adjustment of measurement error (as is the case with multiple items), and this generally decreases their reliability. Note

Exhibit 2.9	Guidelines for Choosing the Measurement Model Mode	
Criterion	*Decision*	*Reference*
Causal priority between the indicator and the construct	• From the construct to the indicators: reflective • From the indicators to the construct: formative	Diamantopoulos and Winklhofer (2001)
Is the construct a trait explaining the indicators or rather a combination of the indicators?	• If trait: reflective • If combination: formative	Fornell and Bookstein (1982)
Do the indicators represent consequences or causes of the construct?	• If consequences: reflective • If causes: formative	Rossiter (2002)
Is it necessarily true that if the assessment of the trait changes, all items will change in a similar manner (assuming they are equally coded)?	• If yes: reflective • If no: formative	Chin (1998)
Are the items mutually interchangeable?	• If yes: reflective • If no: formative	Jarvis, MacKenzie, and Podsakoff (2003)

that, contrary to commonly held beliefs, single-item reliability can be estimated (e.g., Loo, 2002; Wanous, Reichers, & Hudy, 1997).

Most important, from a validity perspective, opting for single-item measures in most empirical settings is a risky decision when it comes to predictive validity considerations. Specifically, the set of circumstances that would favor the use of single-item measures rather than multiple items is very unlikely to be encountered in practice. This conclusion is even more relevant for PLS-SEM since the utilization of a small number of items for construct measurement (in the extreme, the use of a single item) is inconsistent with the desire of reducing PLS-SEM's tendency to develop biased estimates (i.e., overestimation of the measurement model relationships and underestimation of the structural model relationships; PLS-SEM bias). Recall that with PLS-SEM, this bias is reduced when the number of indicators and/or the number of observations increases (i.e., consistency at large). According to guidelines by Diamantopoulos, Sarstedt, Fuchs, Kaiser, and Wilczynski (2012), single-item measures should only be considered in situations when (1) small sample sizes are present (i.e., $N < 50$), (2) path coefficients (i.e., the coefficients linking constructs in the structural model) of 0.30 and lower are expected, (3) items of the originating multi-item scale are highly homogeneous (i.e., Cronbach's alpha > 0.90), and (4) the items are semantically redundant (Exhibit 2.10).

Nevertheless, when setting up measurement models, this purely empirical perspective should be complemented with practical considerations. Some research situations call for or even necessitate the use of single items. Respondents frequently feel they are oversurveyed, which contributes to low response rates. The difficulty of obtaining large sample sizes in surveys, often due to a lack of willingness to take the time to complete questionnaires, leads to the necessity of considering reducing the length of construct measures where possible. Therefore, if the population being surveyed is small or only a limited sample size is available (e.g., due to budget constraints, difficulties in recruiting respondents, or dyadic data), the use of single-item measures is a pragmatic solution. Thus, if single-item measures are used, researchers typically must accept the consequences of lower predictive validity. Last, it is important to note that the above issues must be considered for the measurement of unobservable phenomena, such as perceptions or attitudes. But single-item measures are clearly appropriate when used to measure observable characteristics such as sales, quotas, profits, and so on.

At this point, you should be prepared to create a path model. Exhibit 2.11 summarizes some key guidelines you should consider when preparing your path model. The next section continues with collecting the data needed to empirically test your PLS path model.

STAGE 3: DATA COLLECTION AND EXAMINATION

The data collection and examination stage is very important in the application of SEM. This stage is important in all types of research but is particularly important when a researcher anticipates using SEM.

Exhibit 2.10	Guidelines for Single-Item Use (Diamantopoulos et al., 2012)

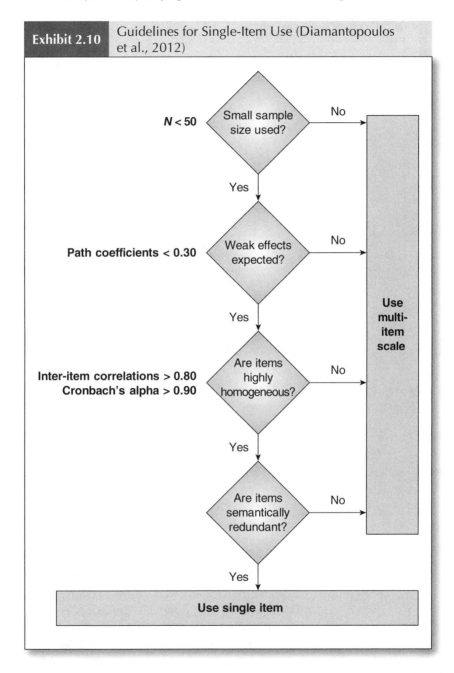

With first-generation statistical methods, the general assumption is that the data are error free. With second-generation statistical methods, the measurement model stage attempts to identify the error

Exhibit 2.11	Guidelines for Preparing Your PLS Path Model

- The variables/constructs considered relevant to the study must be clearly identified and defined.
- The measurement discussion states how the constructs are related to each other, that is, which constructs are dependent (endogenous) or independent (exogenous). If applicable, this also includes more complex relationships such as mediators or moderators.
- If possible, the nature (positive or negative) of the relationships as well as the direction is hypothesized on the basis of theory, logic, previous research, or researcher judgment.
- There is a clear explanation of why you expect these relationships to exist. The explanation cites theory, qualitative research, business practice, or some other credible source.
- A conceptual model or framework is prepared to clearly illustrate the hypothesized relationships.
- The measurement discussion states whether constructs are conceptualized as first- or second-order constructs.
- The measurement perspective (i.e., reflective vs. formative) has to be clearly stated and motivated. A construct's conceptualization and the aim of the study guide this decision.
- Single-item measures should only be used if indicated by Diamantopoulos et al.'s (2012) guidelines or for pragmatic reasons.

component of the data and remove it from that analysis. As a result, the research design phase of any project must be carefully planned and executed so the answers to questions are as valid and reliable as possible for social science research.

Application of SEM methods requires that quantitative data be available. Many research applications in scholarly research involve primary data, but it is possible to use secondary data. Social science researchers in general have relied on primary data obtained from structured questionnaires for their SEM analyses. This is true for both CB-SEM and PLS-SEM and particularly for academic research.

When empirical data are collected using questionnaires, typically data collection issues must be addressed after the data are collected. The primary issues that need to be examined include missing data, suspicious response patterns (straight lining or inconsistent answers), outliers, and data distribution. We briefly address each of these on the following pages. The reader is referred to more comprehensive discussions of these issues in Hair et al. (2010).

Missing Data

Missing data are often a problem in social science research because many projects obtain data using survey research. Missing data occur when a respondent either purposely or inadvertently fails to answer one or more question(s). When the amount of missing data on a questionnaire exceeds 15%, the observation is typically removed from the data file. Indeed, an observation may be removed from the data file even if the overall missing data on the questionnaire does not exceed 15%. For example, if a high proportion of responses are missing for a single construct, then the entire observation may have to be removed. A high proportion of missing data on a single construct is more likely to occur if the construct is measuring a sensitive topic, such as racism, sexual orientation, or even firm performance.

The proportion of survey data collected in the United States using online data collection methods now exceeds 60% and is above 50% in many developed countries. The increased use of online data collection approaches has reduced missing data because it is possible to prevent respondents from going to the next question if they do not answer a particular question. This forced-answer approach does motivate some individuals to stop answering the survey. But more often than not, it means respondents answer the question and move on because the reason for skipping questions was inadvertence.

The software used in the book, *SmartPLS 2.0* (Ringle, Wende, & Will, 2005), offers two ways of handling missing values. In **mean value replacement,** the missing values of an indicator variable are replaced with the mean of valid values of that indicator. While easy to implement, mean value replacement decreases the variability in the data and likely reduces the possibility of finding meaningful relationships. It should therefore be used only when the data exhibit extremely low levels of missing data. As a rule of thumb, we recommend using mean value replacement when there are less than 5% values missing per indicator.

Alternatively, SmartPLS offers an option to remove all cases from the analysis that include missing values in any of the indicators used in the model (**casewise deletion**). When casewise deletion is being used, two issues warrant further attention. First, we need to ensure that we do not systematically delete a certain group of respondents. For example, market researchers frequently observe that wealthy respondents are more likely to refuse answering questions related to their income. Running casewise deletion would systematically omit this group of respondents and therefore likely yield biased results. Second, using casewise deletion can dramatically diminish the number of observations in our data set. It is therefore crucial to carefully check the number of observations used in the final model estimation when this type of missing value treatment is used.

In addition, more complex procedures for handling missing values can be conducted before analyzing the data with SmartPLS. Among the best approaches to overcoming missing data is to first determine the demographic profile of the respondent with missing data and then calculate the mean for the sample subgroup representing the identified demographic profile. For example, if the respondent with missing data is male, aged 25 to 34, with 14 years of education, then calculate the mean for that group on the questions with missing data. Next determine if the question with missing data is associated with a construct with multiple items. If yes, then calculate an average of the responses to all the items associated with the construct. The final step is to use the subgroup mean and the average of the construct indicator responses to decide what value to insert for the missing response. This approach minimizes the decrease in variability of responses and also enables the researcher to know specifically what is being done to overcome missing data problems. Last, numerous complex statistical procedures rely on regression approaches or the expectation maximization algorithm to impute missing data (Little & Rubin, 2002; Schafer & Graham, 2002). However, as knowledge on their suitability in a PLS-SEM context is scarce, we recommend drawing on the methods described above when treating missing values in PLS-SEM analyses.

Suspicious Response Patterns

Before analyzing their data, researchers should also examine response patterns. In doing so, they are looking for a pattern often described as straight lining. **Straight lining** is when a respondent marks the same response for a high proportion of the questions. For example, if a 7-point scale is used to obtain answers and the response pattern is all 4s (the middle response), then that respondent in most cases should be removed from the data set. Similarly, if a respondent selects only 1s or only 7s, then that respondent should in most cases be removed.

Inconsistency in answers may also need to be addressed before analyzing your data. Many surveys start with one or more screening questions. The purpose of a screening question is to ensure that only individuals who meet the prescribed criteria complete the survey. For example, a survey of mobile phone users may screen for individuals who own an Apple iPhone. But a question later in the survey is posed and the individual indicates he or she is an Android user. This respondent would therefore need to be removed from the data set. Surveys often ask the same question with slight variations, especially when reflective measures are used. If a respondent gives a very different answer to the same question asked in a slightly different way, this too raises a red flag and suggests the respondent was not reading the questions closely or simply was marking answers to complete and exit the survey as quickly as possible.

Outliers

An **outlier** is an extreme response to a particular question, or extreme responses to all questions. The first step in dealing with outliers is to identify them. Many statistical software packages have options to help identify outliers. For example, IBM SPSS Statistics has an option called Explore that develops box plots and stem-and-leaf plots that facilitate the identification of outliers by respondent number (Mooi & Sarstedt, 2011).

Once the respondents are identified, the researcher must decide what to do. For example, if there are only a few identified outliers, the approach most often followed is to simply remove them from the data set. On the other hand, as the number of outliers increases, at some point the researcher must decide if the outlier group represents a distinct and unique subgroup of the sample.

There are two approaches to use in deciding if a unique subgroup exists. First, a subgroup can be identified based on prior knowledge. For example, if the research involves examining binge drinking among college students, the researcher should have knowledge (based on previous studies) of the proportion of students who are binge drinkers as well as how binge drinkers should be defined. If several respondents indicate their alcohol consumption is much higher than known patterns, these individuals likely should be removed from the data set. However, if the corresponding information is not available, researchers can revert to data-driven approaches to identify distinct subgroups. In the context of PLS-SEM, the finite mixture PLS (FIMIX-PLS) approach has gained prominence, which can be used to identify (latent) subgroups of respondents. We will discuss the FIMIX-PLS approach (Ringle, Wende, & Will, 2010; Sarstedt & Ringle, 2010) in the context of unobserved heterogeneity in greater detail in Chapter 8.

Data Distribution

PLS-SEM is a nonparametric statistical method. Different from maximum likelihood (ML)-based CB-SEM, it does not require the data to be normally distributed. Nevertheless, it is important to verify that the data are not too far from normal as extremely non-normal data prove problematic in the assessment of the parameters' significances. Specifically, extremely non-normal data inflate standard errors obtained from bootstrapping (see Chapter 5 for more details) and thus decrease the likelihood some relationships will be assessed as significant (Hair, Ringle, & Sarstedt, 2011; Henseler et al., 2009).

The Kolmogorov-Smirnov test and Shapiro-Wilks test are designed to test normality by comparing the data to a normal distribution with the same mean and standard deviation as in the sample (Mooi & Sarstedt, 2011). However, both tests only indicate whether the null hypothesis of normally distributed data should be rejected or not. As the bootstrapping procedure performs fairly robustly when data are non-normal, these tests provide only limited guidance when deciding whether the data are too far from being normally distributed. Instead, researchers should examine two measures of distributions—skewness and kurtosis.

Skewness assesses the extent to which a variable's distribution is symmetrical. If the distribution of responses for a variable stretches toward the right or left tail of the distribution, then the distribution is characterized as skewed. **Kurtosis** is a measure of whether the distribution is too peaked (a very narrow distribution with most of the responses in the center). When both skewness and kurtosis are close to zero (a situation that researchers are very unlikely to ever encounter), the pattern of responses is considered a normal distribution. A general guideline for skewness is that if the number is greater than +1 or lower than −1, this is an indication of a substantially skewed distribution. For kurtosis, the general guideline is that if the number is greater than +1, the distribution is too peaked. Likewise, a kurtosis of less than −1 indicates a distribution that is too flat. Distributions exhibiting skewness and/or kurtosis that exceed these guidelines are considered non-normal.

Serious effort, considerable amounts of time, and a high level of caution are required when collecting and analyzing the data that you need for carrying out multivariate techniques. Always remember the garbage in, garbage out rule. All your analyses are meaningless if your data are inappropriate. Exhibit 2.12 summarizes some key guidelines you should consider when examining your data and preparing them for PLS-SEM. For more detail on examining your data, see Chapter 2 of Hair et al. (2010).

CASE STUDY ILLUSTRATION: SPECIFYING THE PLS-SEM MODEL

The most effective way to learn how to use a statistical method is to actually apply the method to a set of data. Throughout this book, we use a single example that enables you to do that. We start the example with a simple model, and in Chapter 5, we expand that same model to a much broader, more complex model. For our initial model, we hypothesize a path model to estimate the relationships between corporate reputation, customer satisfaction, and customer loyalty. The example will provide insights on (1) how to develop the structural model representing the underlying concepts/theory, (2) the setup of measurement models for the latent variables, and (3) the structure of the empirical data used. Then, our focus shifts to setting up the SmartPLS software (Ringle et al., 2005) for PLS-SEM.

Exhibit 2.12	Guidelines for Examining Data Used With PLS-SEM

- Missing data must be identified. When missing data for an observation exceed 15%, it should be removed from the data set. Other missing data should be dealt with before running a PLS-SEM analysis. When less than 5% of values *per indicator* are missing, use mean replacement. Otherwise, use casewise replacement, but make sure that the deletion of observations did not occur systematically and that enough observations remain for the analysis. Also consider using more complex imputation procedures.

- Straight lining and inconsistent response patterns typically justify removing a response from the data set.

- Outliers should be identified before running a PLS-SEM, and in most instances, the offending responses should be removed from the data set. Subgroups that are substantial in size should be identified based on prior knowledge or by statistical means (e.g., FIMIX-PLS).

- Lack of normality in variable distributions can distort the results of multivariate analysis. This problem is much less severe with PLS-SEM, but researchers should still examine PLS-SEM results carefully when distributions deviate substantially from normal. *Absolute* skewness and/or kurtosis values of greater than 1 are indicative of highly non-normal data.

Application of Stage 1: Structural Model Specification

To specify the structural model, we must begin with some fundamental explications about conceptual/theoretical models. The corporate reputation model by Eberl (2010) is the basis of our theory. The goal of the model is to explain the effects of corporate reputation on customer satisfaction (*CUSA*) and, ultimately, customer loyalty (*CUSL*). Corporate reputation represents a company's overall evaluation by its stakeholder (Helm, Eggert, and Garnefeld, 2010). It is measured using two dimensions. One dimension represents cognitive evaluations of the company, and the construct is the company's competence (*COMP*). The second dimension captures affective judgments, which determine the company's likeability (*LIKE*). This two-dimensional approach to measure reputation was developed by Schwaiger (2004). It has been validated in different countries (e.g., Eberl, 2010; Zhang & Schwaiger, 2009) and applied in various research studies (e.g., Eberl & Schwaiger, 2005; Raithel, Wilczynski, Schloderer, & Schwaiger, 2010; Sarstedt & Schloderer, 2010; Sarstedt & Ringle, 2010; Schwaiger, Raithel, & Schloderer, 2009). Recent research shows that the approach performs favorably (in terms of convergent validity and predictive validity) compared with alternative reputation measures (Sarstedt et al., 2013).

Building on a definition of corporate reputation as an attitude-related construct, Schwaiger (2004) further identified four antecedent dimensions of reputation—quality, performance, attractiveness, and corporate social responsibility—measured by a total of 21 formative indicators. These driver constructs of corporate reputation are components of the more complex example we will use in the book and will be added in Chapter 5. Likewise, we do not consider more complex model setups such as higher-order models, mediation, or moderation effects yet. These aspects will be covered in the case studies in Chapters 7 and 8.

In summary, the simple corporate reputation model has two main conceptual/theoretical components: (1) the target constructs of interest—namely, *CUSA* and *CUSL* (dependent variables)—and (2) the two corporate reputation dimensions *COMP* and *LIKE* (independent variables), which represent key determinants of the target constructs. Exhibit 2.13 shows the constructs and their relationships, which represent the structural model for the PLS-SEM case study.

To propose a theory/concept, researchers usually build on existing research knowledge. When PLS-SEM is applied, the structural

Exhibit 2.13 Example of a Conceptual/Theoretical Model

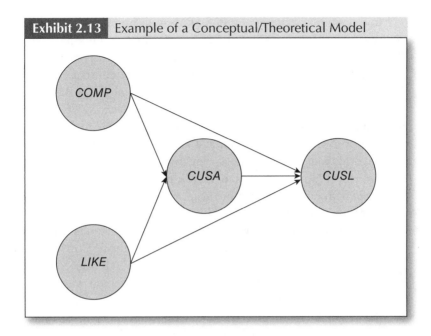

model displays the concept/theory with its key elements (i.e., constructs) and cause-effect relationships (i.e., paths). Researchers typically develop hypotheses for the constructs and their path relationships in the structural model. For example, consider Hypothesis 1 (H_1): Customer satisfaction has a positive effect on customer loyalty. PLS-SEM enables statistically testing the significance of the hypothesized relationship (Chapter 6). When conceptualizing the theoretical constructs and their hypothesized structural relationships for PLS-SEM, it is important to make sure the model has no circular relationships (i.e., causal loops) and thus is recursive. A circular relationship would occur if, for example, we reversed the relationship between *COMP* and *CUSL* as this would yield the causal loop *COMP → CUSA → CUSL → COMP*.

Application of Stage 2: Measurement Model Specification

Since the constructs are not directly observed, we need to specify a measurement model for each construct. The specification of the measurement models (i.e., multi-item vs. single-item measures and reflective vs. formative measures) draws on prior research studies by Schwaiger (2004) and Eberl (2010).

In our simple example of a PLS-SEM application, we have three constructs (*COMP, CUSL,* and *LIKE*) measured by multiple items (Exhibit 2.14). All three constructs have reflective measurement models as indicated by the arrows pointing from the construct to the indicators. For example, *COMP* is measured by means of the three reflective items *comp_1, comp_2,* and *comp_3,* which relate to the following survey questions (Exhibit 2.15): "[The company] is a top competitor in its market," "As far as I know, [the company] is recognized worldwide," and "I believe that [the company] performs at a premium level." Respondents had to indicate the degree to which they (dis)agree with each of the statements on a 7-point scale from 1 = *fully disagree* to 7 = *fully agree.*

Different from *COMP, CUSL,* and *LIKE,* the customer satisfaction construct (*CUSA*) is operationalized by a single item (*cusa*) that is related to the following question in the survey: "If you consider your experiences with [company], how satisfied are you with [company]?" The single indicator is measured with a 7-point scale indicating the respondent's degree of satisfaction (1 = *very dissatisfied;* 7 = *very satisfied*). The single item has been used due to practical considerations in an effort to decrease the overall number of items in the questionnaire. As customer satisfaction items are usually highly homogeneous, the loss in predictive validity compared with a multi-item measure is not considered severe. As *cusa* is the only item measuring customer satisfaction, construct and item are equivalent (as indicated by the fact that the relationship between construct and single-item measure is always one in PLS-SEM). Therefore, the choice of the measurement perspective (i.e., reflective vs. formative) is of no concern. By convention, single-item measures are included as reflective in a PLS path model (Exhibit 2.15).

Application of Stage 3: Data Collection and Examination

To estimate the PLS-SEM, data were collected using computer-assisted telephone interviews (Mooi & Sarstedt, 2011) that asked about the respondents' perception of and their satisfaction with four major mobile network providers in Germany's mobile communications market. Respondents rated the questions on 7-point Likert scales, with higher scores denoting higher levels of agreement with a particular statement. In the case of *cusa,* higher scores

Exhibit 2.14 Types of Measurement Models in the PLS-SEM Example

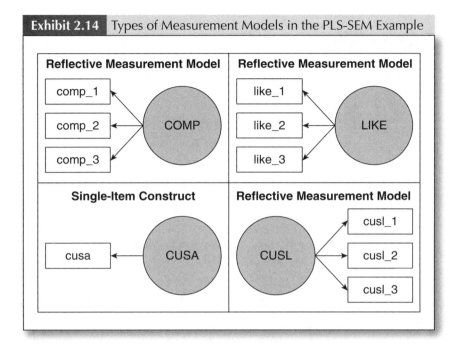

denote higher levels of satisfaction. Satisfaction and loyalty were asked with respect to the respondents' own service providers. The data set has 344 responses (sample size).

Exhibit 2.16 shows the data matrix for the model. The 10 columns represent the variables (i.e., specific questions in the survey as described in the previous section) and the 344 rows (i.e., cases) contain the answers of every respondent to these questions. For example, the first row contains the answers of Respondent 1 while the last row contains the answers of Respondent 344. The columns show the answers to the 10 survey questions. Data in the first nine columns are for the indicators associated with the three constructs, and the tenth column includes the data for the single indicator for *CUSA*.

If you are using a data set in which a respondent did not answer a specific question, you need to insert a number that does not appear otherwise in the responses to indicate the missing values. Researchers commonly use −99 to indicate missing values, but you can use any other value that does not normally occur in the data set. In the following, we will also use −99 to indicate missing values. If, for example, the first data point of *comp_1* were a missing value, the −99 value would be inserted into the space as a missing value space holder instead of the

Exhibit 2.15	Indicators for Reflective Measurement Model Constructs

Competence (COMP)	
comp_1	[The company] is a top competitor in its market.
comp_2	As far as I know, [the company] is recognized worldwide.
comp_3	I believe that [the company] performs at a premium level.

Likeability (LIKE)	
like_1	[The company] is a company that I can better identify with than other companies.
like_2	[The company] is a company that I would regret more not having if it no longer existed than I would other companies.
like_3	I regard [the company] as a likeable company.

Customer Loyalty (CUSL)	
cusl_1	I would recommend [company] to friends and relatives.
cusl_2	If I had to choose again, I would choose [company] as my mobile phone services provider.
cusl_3	I will remain a customer of [company] in the future.

Note: For data collection, the actual name of the company was inserted in the bracketed space that indicates company.

Exhibit 2.16	Data Matrix for the Indicator Variables									
	Variable Name									
Case Number	1 comp_1	2 comp_2	3 comp_3	4 like_1	5 like_2	6 like_3	7 cusl_1	8 cusl_2	9 cusl_3	10 cusa
1	4	5	5	3	1	2	5	3	3	5
2	6	7	6	6	6	6	7	7	7	7
...	...	...	...	...	...	...	...	...	...	...
344	6	5	6	6	7	5	7	7	7	7

value of 4 that you see in Exhibit 2.16. Missing value treatment procedures (e.g., mean replacement) could then be applied to these data (e.g., Hair et al., 2010). Again, if the number of missing values in your data set per indicator is relatively small (i.e., less than 5% missing per indicator), we recommend mean value replacement instead of casewise deletion to treat the missing values when running PLS-SEM. Furthermore, we need to ascertain that the number of missing values per observation does not exceed 15%. If this was the case, the corresponding observation should be eliminated from the data set.

The data example shown in Exhibit 2.16 (and in the book's example) has only very few missing values. More precisely, *cusa* has one missing value (0.29%), *cusl_1* and *cusl_3* have three missing values (0.87%), and *cusl_2* has four missing values (1.16%). Thus, mean value replacement can be used. Furthermore, none of the observations has more than 15% missing values, so we can proceed analyzing all 344 respondents.

Outlier diagnostics by means of boxplots using IBM SPSS Statistics indicate some influential observations but no outliers. Moreover, nonnormality of data regarding skewness and kurtosis is not an issue. The kurtosis and skewness values of the indicators are within the −1 and +1 acceptable range. The only exception is the *cusl_2* indicator, which has a skewness of −1.3 and thus exhibits a slight degree of nonnormality. However, as the degree of skewness is not severe and because *cusl_2* is one of three indicators measuring the (reflective) *CUSL* construct, this deviation from normality is not considered an issue and the indicator is retained.

Finally, the data set contains two types of customers. The variable *plan* (not shown in Exhibit 2.16) distinguishes customers with a contract plan ($plan = 1$; $n^{(1)} = 219$) from those with a prepaid plan ($plan = 2$; $n^{(2)} = 125$). These groups will be examined in later PLS-SEM analyses by means of multigroup comparisons (Chapter 8).

PATH MODEL CREATION USING THE SMARTPLS SOFTWARE

The SmartPLS software (Ringle et al., 2005) is used to execute all the PLS-SEM analyses in this book. It is available free of charge at http://www.smartpls.de. SmartPLS has a graphical user interface that enables the user to estimate the PLS path model. Our discussion includes an overview of the software's functionalities. The SmartPLS download area on the website includes tutorial videos for getting started using the software, and the SmartPLS discussion forum answers the most frequently asked questions.

Exhibit 2.17 shows the graphical interface for the SmartPLS software, with the simple model already drawn. In the following paragraphs, we describe how to set up this model using the SmartPLS program. Before you draw your model, you need to have data that serve as the basis for running the model. The data we will use with the reputation model can be downloaded either as comma-separated value (.csv) or text (.txt) data sets in the download section at the following URL: http://www.pls-sem.com. SmartPLS can use both data file formats (i.e., .csv or .txt). Follow the onscreen instructions to save one of these two files on your hard drive. Click on **Save Target As. . .** to save the data to a folder on your hard drive and then **Close**. Now go to the folder where you previously downloaded and saved the SmartPLS software on your computer. Click on the file that runs SmartPLS (smartpls) and then on the **Run** tab to start the software.

When running SmartPLS for the first time, the program will ask you to enter a product key. The product key is freely available on the SmartPLS website (http://www.smartpls.de) once your account has been activated. Log on to http://www.smartpls.de with your username and password and click on **My Key** in the top-right menu on the webpage. Copy and paste the key into the product key menu in SmartPLS and click on **OK**. SmartPLS will show a welcome screen that (after careful reading) you can close by simply closing the corresponding tab. You are now ready to start using the SmartPLS software.

To create a new project, click on **File → New → Create New Project.** First type a name for the project into the **Project name** box (e.g., **Corporate Reputation**); then click **Next.** You now need to assign a data set to the project, in our case, **full data.csv** (or whatever name you gave to the data you downloaded). To do so, click on the dots tab (. . .) at the right side of the window, find and highlight your data folder, and click **Open**. Once you have specified the data set, click on **Next.** In the screen that follows, you need to specify missing values. Check the box **The indicator data contains missing values,** enter **–99** in the field below, and click on **Finish**.

It is important to note that if you use your own data set for a project using the SmartPLS software, the data must not include any string elements (e.g., respondents' comments to open-ended questions). For example, SmartPLS interprets single dots (such as those produced by IBM SPSS Statistics in case an observation has a system-missing value) as string elements. In our example, the data set does not include any string elements, so this is not an issue. Note also that unlike in other statistical programs such as IBM SPSS Statistics, you can specify only one value for all missing data in SmartPLS. Thus, you have to make sure that all missing values have the same coding (e.g., −99) in your original data set. That is, you need to code all missing values uniformly, regardless of their type (user-defined missing or system missing) and the reason for being missing (e.g., respondent refused to answer, respondent did not know the answer, not applicable).

After completing the specification of the data set and missing values, the new project is created and appears in the **Projects** window that is in the upper left below the menu bar. All previously created SmartPLS projects also appear in this window. Each project can have one or more path models (i.e., the .splsm files) and one or more data sets (i.e., .csv or .txt files). When setting up a new project, SmartPLS will automatically add a model with the same name as the project (in the book example, we use the **Corporate Reputation.splsp**). You can also rename the model by right-clicking on it. In the menu that opens, click on **Rename Resource** and type in the new name for the model. To distinguish our introductory model from the later ones, rename it to **Simple Model** and click on **OK**.

The graphical modeling window on the right is where the user creates a path model. We are starting with a new project (as opposed to working with a saved project), so the modeling window is empty and you can start creating the path model shown in Exhibit 2.17. To do so, first double-click on your new model to get the modeling menu bar to appear at the top of the screen. You can use the options (i.e., 🔲 ◉ ✐) shown in the menu bar at the top. By clicking the **Switch to Insertion Mode** option (◉), you can place new constructs into the modeling window. Each time you left-click in the modeling window, a new construct represented by a red circle will appear. Once you have created all your constructs, left-click on **Switch to Selection Mode** (🔲) to select, resize, or move the latent variables in the modeling window. To connect the latent variables with each other (i.e., to draw path arrows), left-click on the **Switch to Connection Mode** option (✐). Next, left-click on an exogenous (independent) construct and move the cursor on top of the target endogenous (dependent) construct. Now left-click on the endogenous construct, and a path relationship (directional arrow) will be inserted between the two constructs. Repeat the same process and connect all the constructs based on your theory. When you finish, it will look like Exhibit 2.17.

The next step is to name the constructs. To do so, first make sure you are in the Selection Mode (⬚). Move the mouse pointer on the construct in the left upper corner and select it by a left-click. Then, right-click on the selected construct to open a menu with different options and left-click on **Rename Object.** Type the name of your construct in the window of the **Rename Object** box (i.e., *COMP*) and then click **OK.** The name *COMP* will appear under the construct. Follow these steps to name all constructs. Next, you need to assign indicators to each of the constructs. On the left side of the screen, there is an **Indicators** window that shows all the indicators that are in your data set. Start with the *COMP* construct by dragging the first competence indicator *comp_1* from the **Indicators** window and

| Exhibit 2.17 | Initial Corporate Reputation Example |

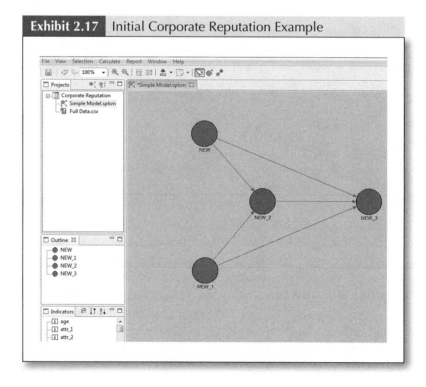

dropping it on the construct (i.e., left-click the mouse and hold the button down, then move it until on top of a construct, then release). After assigning an indicator to a construct, it appears in the graphical modeling window as a yellow rectangle attached to the construct (as reflective). You can move the indicator around, but it will remain attached to the construct (unless you delete it). By right-clicking on the construct and choosing one of the options at the bottom of the menu (e.g., **Align Top**), you can align the indicator(s). Exhibit 2.18 is the example with the data attached and the indicators for construct *COMP* aligned to the top. Assigning an indicator to a construct will also turn the color of the construct from red to blue.

Continue until you have assigned all the indicators to the constructs as shown in Exhibit 2.18. Make sure to save the model by going to **File → Save.** The model will then be saved under its original name (the one you gave it).

Exhibit 2.18	Corporate Reputation Example With Names and Data Assigned

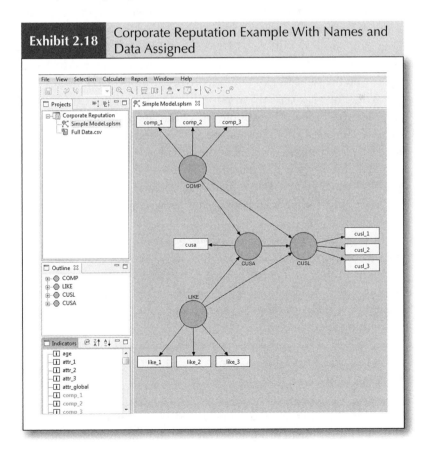

Clicking on the right mouse button while it is placed in the graphical modeling window opens a menu with several modeling options. For example, if you place your mouse over a construct and right-click, you get the **Rename Object** option to rename the construct, or to invert the measurement model of the selected latent variable from reflective to formative measurement, and vice versa (**Invert measurement model**).

Clicking on the right mouse button while the cursor is placed on top of other elements also opens a menu with additional functions. As a further example, if you place the cursor in the **Projects** window and right-click, you can create a new model (**Create New Model**), a new project (**Create New Project**), or **Import Indicator Data.** Moreover, you can select the **Copy, Move, Rename,** and **Remove Resource** options for projects and models that appear in the **Projects** window. For example, the **Copy Resource** option is useful when you would like to modify a PLS path model but want to keep your initial model setup. If you want to use an existing model from the projects window, then double-click with the left mouse button on the path model shown in the **Projects** window, and its graphical representation will appear on the right side of your screen in the modeling window.

You can also directly import the "ready-to-use" project that includes the PLS-SEM example on corporate reputation. The file name is **Corporate_Reputation.splsp.** This project is ready to download on your computer system in the download section at the following URL: http://www.pls-sem.com. Download this file and save it on your computer system. (Note that some operating systems add ".zip" to the original file name. If your computer system does this, you need to delete the ".zip" at the end of the file name after it is downloaded.) Then, press the right mouse button on the **Projects** window and select the option **Import.** SmartPLS allows you to browse your computer and select the downloaded project **Corporate_Reputation.splsp** for import. After successful import, double-click on the model in this project, and the path model as shown in Exhibit 2.18 will appear in a new modeling window.

SUMMARY

- Understand the basic concepts of structural model specification, including mediation, moderation, and higher-order models.

This chapter includes the first three stages in the application of PLS-SEM. Building in an a priori established theory/concept, the model specification starts with the structural model (Stage 1). Each element of the theory/concept represents a construct in the structural model of the PLS path model. Moreover, assumptions for the causal relationships between the elements must be considered. Researchers usually determine hypotheses for the relationships between constructs in the structural model in accordance with their theory/concept. These are the key elements of the structural model (i.e., constructs and their hypothesized relationships), which can also be more complex and contain mediating or moderating relationships. The goal of the PLS-SEM analysis is to empirically test the theory/concept.

- **Explain the differences between reflective and formative measures and be able to specify the appropriate measurement model.** Stage 2 focuses on selecting a measurement model for each theoretical/ conceptual construct in the structural model to obtain reliable and valid measurements. There are two types of measurement models: reflective and formative. The reflective mode has arrows (relationships) pointing from the construct to the observed indicators in the measurement model. If the construct changes, it leads to a simultaneous change of all items in the measurement model. Thus, all indicators are highly correlated. In contrast, the formative mode has arrows pointing from the indicators in the measurement model to the constructs. Hence, all indicators together form the construct, and all relevant elements of the domain must be represented by the selected formative indicators. Since formative indicators represent independent sources of the construct's content, they do not necessarily need to be correlated (in fact, they shouldn't be highly correlated).

Selection of the mode of measurement model and the indicators must be based on theoretical/conceptual reasoning before data collection. A reflective specification would use different indicators than a formative specification of the same construct. One usually uses reflective constructs as target constructs of the theoretically/ conceptually established PLS path model, while formative constructs may be particularly valuable as explanatory sources (independent variables) or drivers of these target constructs. During the data analysis phase, the theoretical/conceptual mode of the measurement models can be empirically tested using the confirmatory tetrad analysis for PLS-SEM.

• **Explain the difference between multi-item and single-item measures and be able to assess when to use each measurement type.** Rather than using multiple items to measure a construct, researchers sometimes choose to use a single item. Single items have practical advantages such as ease of application, brevity, and lower costs associated with their use. However, single-item measures do not offer more for less. From a psychometric perspective, single-item measures are less reliable and to some extent risky from a validity perspective. Nevertheless, some research situations call for or even necessitate the use of single items, for example, when the population being surveyed is limited in size and nonresponse is a major concern. The above issues are important considerations when measuring unobservable phenomena, such as perceptions or attitudes. But single-item measures are clearly appropriate when used to measure observable characteristics such as sales, quotas, profits, and so on.

• **Describe the data collection and examination considerations necessary to apply PLS-SEM.** Stage 3 underlines the need to examine your data after they have been collected to ensure that the results from the methods application are valid and reliable. This stage is important in all types of research but is particularly important when a researcher anticipates using SEM. When empirical data are collected using questionnaires, typically data collection issues must be addressed after the data are collected. The primary issues that need to be examined include missing data, suspicious response patterns (straight lining or inconsistent answers), and outliers. Distributional assumptions are of less concern because of PLS-SEM's nonparametric nature. However, as highly skewed data can cause issues in the estimation of significance levels, researchers should ensure that the data are not too far from normal. As a general rule of thumb, always remember the garbage in, garbage out rule. All your analyses are meaningless if your data are inappropriate.

• **Learn how to develop a PLS path model using the SmartPLS software.** The first three stages of conducting a PLS-SEM analysis are explained by conducting a practical exercise. We discuss how to draw a theoretical/conceptual PLS path model focusing on corporate reputation and its relationship with customer satisfaction and loyalty. We also explain several options that are available in the SmartPLS software. The outcome of the exercise is a PLS path model drawn using the SmartPLS software that is ready to be estimated.

REVIEW QUESTIONS

1. What is a structural model?

2. What is a reflective measurement model?

3. What is a formative measurement model?

4. What is a single-item measure?

5. When do you consider data to be "too non-normal" for a PLS-SEM analysis?

CRITICAL THINKING QUESTIONS

1. How can you decide whether to measure a construct reflectively or formatively?

2. Which research situations favor the use of reflective/formative measures?

3. Discuss the pros and cons of single-item measures.

4. Create your own example of a PLS-SEM (including the structural model with latent variables and the measurement models).

5. Why is it important to carefully analyze your data prior to analysis? What particular problems do you encounter when the data set has relatively large amounts of missing data per indicator (e.g., more than 5% of the data are missing per indicator)?

KEY TERMS

Casewise deletion: an entire observation (i.e., a case or respondent) is removed from the data set because of missing data. It should be used when indicators have more than 5% missing values.

Causal links: are predictive relationships in which the constructs on the left predict the constructs to the right.

Confirmatory tetrad analysis for PLS-SEM (CTA-PLS): is a statistical procedure that allows for empirically testing the measurement model setup (i.e., whether the measures should be specified reflectively or formatively).

Direct effect: is a relationship linking two constructs with a single arrow.

Endogenous latent variables: are constructs considered as dependent in a structural model.

Exogenous latent variables: are constructs that only act as independent variables in a structural model.

Formative measurement: is a type of measurement model setup in which the indicators cause the construct, and arrows point from the indicators to the construct. Also referred to as *Mode B* in PLS-SEM.

HCM: see *Hierarchical component models (HCM).*

Hierarchical component models (HCM): are higher-order structures (mostly second-order) that contain several layers of constructs and involve a higher level of abstraction.

Higher-order models: see *Hierarchical component models (HCM).*

Index: is a set of formative indicators used to measure a construct.

Indicators: are the measured items of a construct.

Indirect effect: is a relationship that involves a sequence of relationships with at least one intervening construct involved.

Inner model: see *Structural model.*

Kurtosis: is a measure of whether the distribution is too peaked (a very narrow distribution with most of the responses in the center).

Mean value replacement: inserts the sample mean for the missing data. Should only be used when indicators have less than 5% missing values.

Measurement models: describe the relationships between the latent variables and their measures. Also referred to as *outer models* in PLS-SEM.

Measurement theory: specifies how constructs should be measured with (a set of) indicators. It determines which indicators to use for construct measurement and the directional relationship between construct and indicators.

Mediating effect: occurs when a third variable or construct intervenes between two other related constructs.

Mode A: see *Reflective measurement.*

Mode B: see *Formative measurement.*

Moderation: see *Moderator effect.*

Moderator effect: occurs when a (latent) variable directly affects the relationship between the exogenous and endogenous latent constructs in the model.

Multigroup analysis: a class of techniques that allows testing for differences between identical models estimated for different groups of data.

Outer models: see *Measurement models.*

Outlier: is an extreme response to a particular question or extreme responses to all questions.

Path model: is a diagram that connects variables/constructs based on theory and logic to visually display the hypotheses that will be tested.

Reflective measurement: is a type of measurement model setup in which measures represent the effects (or manifestations) of an underlying construct. Causality is from the construct to its measures (indicators). Also referred to as *Mode A* in PLS-SEM.

Scale: is a set of reflective indicators used to measure a construct.

Skewness: is the extent to which a variable's distribution is symmetrical around its mean value.

Straight lining: describes a situation in which a respondent marks the same response for a high proportion of the questions.

Structural model: describes the relationships between latent variables. Also referred to as *inner model* in PLS-SEM.

Structural theory: shows how the latent variables are related to each other.

SUGGESTED READINGS

Chin, W. W. (2010). How to write up and report PLS analyses. In V. Esposito Vinzi, W. W. Chin, J. Henseler, & H. Wang (Eds.), *Handbook of partial least squares: Concepts, methods and applications in marketing and related fields* (pp. 655–690). Berlin: Springer.

Esposito Vinzi, V., Chin, W. W., Henseler, J., & Wang, H. (2010). *Handbook of partial least squares: Concepts, methods and applications (Springer handbooks of computational statistics series, vol. II)*. Heidelberg, Dordrecht, London, New York: Springer.

Falk, R. F., & Miller, N. B. (1992). *A primer for soft modeling*. Akron, OH: University of Akron Press.

Garson, G. D. (2012). *Partial least squares*. Asheboro: Statistical Associates.

Haenlein, M., & Kaplan, A. M. (2004). A beginner's guide to partial least squares analysis. *Understanding Statistics, 3*(4), 283–297.

Hair, J. F., Black, W. C., Babin, B. J., & Anderson, R. E. (2010). *Multivariate data analysis*. Englewood Cliffs, NJ: Prentice Hall.

Hair, J. F., Ringle, C. M., & Sarstedt, M. (2011). PLS-SEM: Indeed a silver bullet. *Journal of Marketing Theory and Practice, 19*, 139–151.

Hair, J. F., Wolfinbarger Celsi, M., Money, A. H., Samouel, P., & Page, M. J. (2011). *Essentials of business research methods*. Armonk, NY: Sharpe.

Henseler, J., Ringle, C. M., & Sarstedt, M. (2012). Using partial least squares path modeling in international advertising research: Basic concepts and recent issues. In S. Okazaki (Ed.), *Handbook of research in international advertising* (pp. 252–276). Cheltenham, UK: Edward Elgar.

Lohmöller, J.-B. (1989). *Latent variable path modeling with partial least squares*. Heidelberg: Physica.

Mooi, E. A., & Sarstedt, M. (2011). *A concise guide to market research: The process, data, and methods using IBM SPSS Statistics*. Berlin: Springer.

Roldán, J. L., and Sánchez-Franco, M. J. (2012). Variance-based structural equation modeling: Guidelines for using partial least squares in information systems research. In *Research methodologies, innovations and philosophies in software systems engineering and information systems* (pp. 193–221). Hershey, PA: IGI Global.

Temme, D., Kreis, H., & Hildebrandt, L. (2010). A comparison of current PLS path modeling software: Features, ease-of-use, and performance. In V. Esposito Vinzi, W. W. Chin, J. Henseler & H. Wang (Eds.), *Handbook of partial least squares: Concepts, methods and applications (Springer Handbooks of Computational Statistics Series, vol. II)* (pp. 737–756). Heidelberg, Dordrecht, London, New York: Springer.

Tenenhaus, M., Esposito Vinzi, V., Chatelin, Y.-M., & Lauro, C. (2005). PLS path modeling. *Computational Statistics & Data Analysis, 48*(1), 159–205.

C H A P T E R 3

Path Model Estimation

LEARNING OUTCOMES

1. Learn how PLS-SEM functions and how to run the algorithm.

2. Understand the statistical properties of the PLS-SEM method.

3. Comprehend the options and parameter settings to run the algorithm.

4. Explain how to interpret the results.

5. Apply the PLS-SEM algorithm using the SmartPLS software.

CHAPTER PREVIEW

This chapter covers Stage 4 of the process on how to apply PLS-SEM. Specifically, we focus on the PLS-SEM algorithm and its statistical properties. A basic understanding of the "mechanics" that underlie PLS-SEM, as well as its strengths and weaknesses, is needed to correctly apply the method (e.g., to make decisions regarding software options). Building on these foundations, you will be able to choose the options and parameter settings required to run the PLS-SEM algorithm. After explaining how the PLS model is estimated, we summarize how to interpret the initial results. These will be discussed in much greater detail in Chapters 4 to 6. This chapter closes with an application of the PLS-SEM algorithm to estimate results for the corporate reputation example using the SmartPLS software.

STAGE 4: MODEL ESTIMATION AND THE PLS-SEM ALGORITHM

How the Algorithm Works

The variance-based PLS-SEM algorithm was originally developed by Wold (1975) and later extended by Lohmöller (1989). The algorithm estimates the path coefficients and other model parameters in a way that maximizes the explained variance of the dependent construct(s) (i.e., it minimizes the unexplained variance). This section illustrates how the **PLS-SEM algorithm** works.

To start with, you need to understand the data that are used to run the algorithm. Exhibit 3.1 is a matrix showing the data set for the indicator variables (columns) and observations (rows) in the PLS path model shown in Exhibit 3.2. The measured indicator (x) variables (rectangles in the top portion of Exhibit 3.2) are shown in the row at the top of the matrix. The (Y) constructs (circles in Exhibit 3.2) are shown at the right side of the matrix. For example, there are seven measured indicator variables in this PLS-SEM example, and the variables are identified as x_1 to x_7. Three constructs identified as Y_1, Y_2, and Y_3 are also shown. Note that the Y constructs are not measured variables. The measured x variables are used as raw data input to estimate the Y_1, Y_2, and Y_3 **construct scores** in this example (e.g., for construct Y_1, the scores are data points $Y_{1,1}$ to $Y_{89,1}$) as part of solving the PLS-SEM algorithm.

A **data matrix** like the one in Exhibit 3.1 serves as input for **indicators** in our hypothetical PLS path model (Exhibit 3.2). The data for the measurement model might be obtained from a company database (e.g., the advertising budget, number of employees, profit, etc.), or it could be responses to survey questions. An ID for the observations is listed in the first column to the left under the case label. For example,

Exhibit 3.1				Data Matrix for a PLS-SEM Example					
Case	x_1	x_2	x_3	x_4	x_5	x_6	x_7	Y_1	Y_2	Y_3
1	$x_{1,1}$	$x_{2,1}$	$x_{3,1}$	$x_{4,1}$	$x_{5,1}$	$x_{6,1}$	$x_{7,1}$	$Y_{1,1}$	$Y_{2,1}$	$Y_{3,1}$
...	...	...	...	...	...	...	...	...	...	...
89	$x_{89,1}$	$x_{89,2}$	$x_{89,3}$	$x_{89,4}$	$x_{89,5}$	$x_{89,6}$	$x_{89,7}$	$Y_{89,1}$	$Y_{89,2}$	$Y_{89,3}$

if your sample includes 89 responses (sample size), then the numbers in this column would be 1 to 89 (assuming you use a number as the ID for each respondent/object).

The **minimum sample size** for PLS path model estimation should at least meet the **10 times rule (Chapter 1)**. Researchers should, however, follow more elaborate guidelines, for example, by following the recommendations made by Cohen (1992) in the context of multiple OLS regression analysis (Chapter 1). In this example, the two (formatively measured) exogenous constructs each have two indicators x_1 and x_2 for Y_1, and x_3 and x_4 for Y_2. Moreover, the structural model has two exogenous (independent) constructs Y_1 and Y_2 to explain the single dependent construct Y_3. The maximum number of arrows pointing at a particular latent variable is two. Thus, according to the 10 times rule, $2 \cdot 10 = 20$ represents the minimum number of observations needed to estimate the PLS path model in Exhibit 3.2. Alternatively, following Cohen's (1992) recommendations for multiple OLS regression analysis or running a power analysis using the G*Power program, one would need 52 observations to detect R^2 values of around 0.25, assuming a significance level of 5% and a statistical power of 80% (Chapter 1).

The PLS-SEM algorithm estimates all unknown elements in the PLS path model. The upper portion of Exhibit 3.2 shows the PLS path model with three **latent variables** and seven measured indicator variables. The four indicator variables (x_1, x_2, x_3, and x_4) for the two **exogenous constructs** (Y_1 and Y_2) are modeled as **formative measures** (i.e., relationships from the indicators to the latent variables). In contrast, the three indicator variables (x_5, x_6, and x_7) for the **endogenous construct** (Y_3) are modeled as **reflective measures** (i.e., relationships from the latent variable to the indicators). This kind of setup for the **measurement models** is just an example. Researchers can select between a **reflective** and **formative** measurement model for every construct. For example, alternatively, Y_1 could be modeled as formative while both Y_2 and Y_3 could be modeled as reflective (assuming theory supported this change and it was considered in designing the questionnaire). In Exhibit 3.2, the relationships between the measured indicator variables of the formative constructs Y_1 and Y_2 (i.e., outer weights) are labeled as w_{11}, w_{12}, w_{23}, and w_{24} (the first number is for the construct and the second number is for the arrow; the w stands for weight). Similarly, the relationships between the measured indicator variables of the reflective construct Y_3 (i.e., outer loadings) are labeled as l_{35}, l_{36}, and l_{37} (the l stands for loading). Note that the

Exhibit 3.2	Path Model and Data for Hypothetical PLS-SEM Example (Henseler et al., 2012)

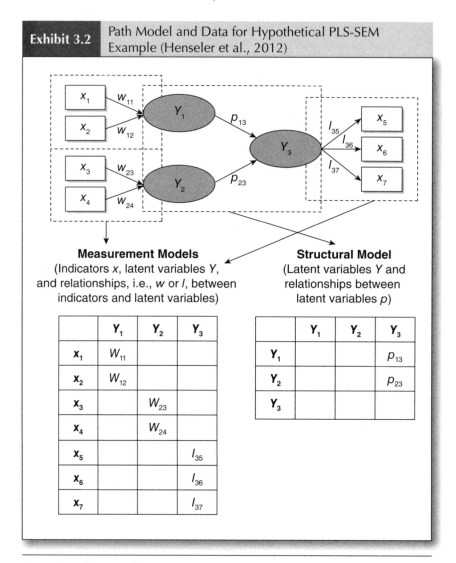

Measurement Models
(Indicators x, latent variables Y, and relationships, i.e., w or l, between indicators and latent variables)

Structural Model
(Latent variables Y and relationships between latent variables p)

	Y_1	Y_2	Y_3
x_1	W_{11}		
x_2	W_{12}		
x_3		W_{23}	
x_4		W_{24}	
x_5			l_{35}
x_6			l_{36}
x_7			l_{37}

	Y_1	Y_2	Y_3
Y_1			p_{13}
Y_2			p_{23}
Y_3			

Source: Henseler, J., Ringle, C. M., and Sarstedt, M. (2012). Using Partial Least Squares Path Modeling in International Advertising Research: Basic Concepts and Recent Issues. In Okazaki, S. (Ed.), *Handbook of Research in International Advertising.* Cheltenham: Edward Elgar Publishing, 252–276.

relationships between constructs and indicator variables are considered weights for formative constructs, whereas the same relationships for reflective constructs are called loadings. Weights and loadings are initially unknown and are estimated by the PLS-SEM algorithm. Similarly, the relationships between the latent variables (i.e., the path coefficients) in the structural model that are labeled as p (Exhibit 3.2) are also initially unknown and estimated as part of solving the PLS-SEM algorithm. The coefficient p_{13} represents the relationship from Y_1 to Y_3, and p_{23} represents the relationship from Y_2 to Y_3.

The PLS-SEM algorithm uses the known elements to estimate the unknown elements of the model. For this task, the algorithm needs to determine the scores of the constructs Y that are used as input for (single and multiple) partial regression models within the path model. Recall that the construct scores were the Y columns on the right side of the matrix in Exhibit 3.1.

After the algorithm calculated the construct scores, the scores are used to estimate each partial regression model in the path model . As a result, we obtain the estimates for all relationships in the measurement models (i.e., the loadings and weights) and the structural model (i.e., the path coefficients). The setup of the partial regression model depends on whether the construct under consideration is modeled as reflective or formative. More specifically, when a formative measurement model is assumed for a construct (e.g., latent variables Y_1 and Y_2 in Exhibit 3.2), the w coefficients (i.e., **outer weights**) are estimated by a partial multiple regression where the latent Y construct (e.g., Y_1) represents a dependent variable and its associated indicator variables x (in case of Y_1, x_1, and x_2) are the independent variables. In contrast, when a reflective measurement model is assumed for a construct (e.g., latent variable Y_3 in Exhibit 3.2), the l coefficients (i.e., **outer loadings**) are estimated through single regressions (one for each indicator variable) of each indicator variable on its corresponding construct.

Structural model calculations are handled as follows. The partial regressions for the structural model specify a construct as the dependent variable (e.g., Y_3 in Exhibit 3.2). This dependent latent variable's direct predecessors (i.e., latent variables with a direct relationship leading to the target construct; here, Y_1 and Y_2) are the independent constructs in a regression used to estimate the path coefficients. Hence, there is a partial regression model for every endogenous latent variable to estimate all the path coefficients in the structural model.

All partial regression models are estimated by the PLS-SEM algorithm's iterative procedures, which include two stages. In the first stage, the construct scores are estimated. Then, in the second stage, the final estimates of the outer weights and loadings are calculated, as well as the structural model's **path coefficients** and the resulting R^2 **values** of the endogenous latent variables. Henseler et al. (2012) provide a detailed description of the stages of the PLS-SEM algorithm.

Statistical Properties

PLS-SEM is an OLS regression-based estimation technique that determines its statistical properties. The method focuses on the **prediction** of a specific set of hypothesized relationships that maximizes the explained variance in the dependent variables, similar to OLS regression models. Therefore, the focus of PLS-SEM is more on prediction than on explanation, which makes PLS-SEM particularly useful for studies on the sources of competitive advantage and success driver studies (Hair, Ringle, & Sarstedt, 2011). Unlike CB-SEM, PLS-SEM does not optimize a unique global scalar function. The lack of a global scalar function and the consequent lack of global goodness-of-fit measures are traditionally considered major drawbacks of PLS-SEM. When using PLS-SEM, it is important to recognize that the term *fit* has different meanings in the contexts of CB-SEM and PLS-SEM. Fit statistics for CB-SEM are derived from the discrepancy between the empirical and the model-implied (theoretical) covariance matrix, whereas PLS-SEM focuses on the discrepancy between the observed (in the case of manifest variables) or approximated (in the case of latent variables) values of the dependent variables and the values predicted by the model in question (Hair et al., 2012a). While a global goodness-of-fit measure for PLS-SEM has been proposed (Tenenhaus, Amato, & Esposito Vinzi, 2004), research shows that the measure is unsuitable for identifying misspecified models (Henseler & Sarstedt, 2012; see Chapter 6 for a discussion of the measure and its limitations). As a consequence, researchers using PLS-SEM rely on measures indicating the model's predictive capabilities to judge the model's quality. These are going to be introduced in Chapters 4 to 6 on the evaluation of measurement models and the structural model.

One of the most important features of PLS-SEM relates to the nature of the construct scores. CB-SEM initially estimates the model parameters without using any case values of the latent variable scores. In contrast, the PLS-SEM algorithm directly and initially computes the construct scores (the scores for Y_1, Y_2, and Y_3 in Exhibit 3.2). The PLS-SEM algorithm treats these scores as perfect substitutes for the indicator variables and therefore uses all the variance from the indicators that can help explain the endogenous constructs. This is because the PLS-SEM approach is based on the assumption that all the measured variance in the model's indicator variables is useful and should be included in estimating the construct scores. As a result, PLS-SEM avoids the indeterminacy problem (difficulty with estimating stable factor scores) and develops more accurate estimates of construct scores compared to CB-SEM. In short, the algorithm calculates the construct scores as exact linear combinations of the associated observed indicator variables—for example, the construct score of Y_3 in Exhibit 3.2 as a linear combination of the indicator variables x_5, x_6, and x_7.

The fact that, in PLS-SEM, latent variables are aggregates of observed indicator variables leads to a fundamental problem. Indicator variables always involve some degree of measurement error. This error is present in the latent variable scores and is ultimately reflected in the path coefficients that are estimated using these scores. The error in the latent variable scores thus induces a bias on the model estimates. The result is that the true path model relationships are frequently underestimated, while the parameters for the measurement models (i.e., the loadings and weights) typically are overestimated. This property (structural model relationships underestimated and measurement model relationships overestimated) is referred to as the **PLS-SEM bias.** Only when the number of observations *and* the number of indicators per latent variable increase to infinity will the latent variable case values approach their true values and the PLS-SEM bias disappear. This characteristic is commonly described as **consistency at large** (Lohmöller, 1989). Infinity is a really big number and implies that this bias never disappears. However, simulation studies show that the PLS-SEM bias is usually at very low levels (Reinartz et al., 2009; Ringle et al., 2009) and is therefore of limited relevance in most empirical settings. This especially holds when the number of constructs, indicators, and relationships (i.e., the **model complexity**) is high and sample size is low, a situation in which the bias produced by CB-SEM is oftentimes substantial, particularly when distributional assumptions are violated. As Rigdon (2012, p. 346) points out, one certainly can construct data sets, simulated from populations based on factor models, where different methods (i.e., PLS-SEM and CB-SEM) produce predictably different results, "but in practice the observed differences are not substantively important."

While estimates produced by PLS-SEM are biased, on average, they also exhibit a higher level of **statistical power** than CB-SEM offers (Hair, Ringle, & Sarstedt, 2011; Reinartz et al., 2009). Consequently, PLS-SEM is better at identifying population relationships and more suitable for exploratory research purposes—a feature that is further supported by the less restrictive requirements of PLS-SEM in terms of model setups, model complexity, and data characteristics (Chapter 1).

Algorithmic Options and Parameter Settings to Run the Algorithm

To estimate a correctly specified PLS path model, **algorithmic options** and **parameter settings** must be selected. The algorithmic options and parameter settings include selecting the structural model path weighting method, the data metric, initial values to start the PLS-SEM algorithm, the stop criterion, and the maximum number of iterations. PLS-SEM allows the user to apply three structural model **weighting schemes:** (1) the centroid weighting scheme, (2) the factor weighting scheme, and (3) the path weighting scheme. While the results differ little across the alternative weighting schemes, path weighting is the recommended approach. This weighting scheme provides the highest R^2 value for endogenous latent variables and is generally applicable for all kinds of PLS path model specifications and estimations. Moreover, when the path model includes higher-order constructs (Chapter 6), researchers should never use the centroid weighting scheme. Henseler et al. (2009) provide further details on the three different weighting schemes available in PLS-SEM.

The PLS-SEM algorithm draws on standardized latent variable scores. Thus, PLS-SEM applications must use **standardized data** for the indicators (more specifically, z-standardization, where each indicator has a mean of 0 and the variance is 1) as input for running the algorithm. This **raw data** transformation is the recommended option (and automatically supported by available software packages such as SmartPLS; Ringle et al., 2005) when starting the PLS-SEM algorithm. When running the PLS-SEM method, the software package standardizes both the raw data of the indicators and the latent variable scores. As a result, the algorithm calculates standardized coefficients between −1 and +1 for every relationship in the structural model and the measurement models. For example, path coefficients close to +1 indicate a strong positive relationship (and vice versa for negative values). The closer the estimated coefficients are to 0, the weaker the relationships. Very low values close to 0 generally are not statistically significant. Checking for significance of relationships is part of evaluating and interpreting the results discussed in Chapters 4 to 6.

The relationships in the measurement model require **initial values** to start the PLS-SEM algorithm. For the first iteration, any nontrivial linear combination of indicators can serve as values for the latent variable scores. In practice, equal weights are a good choice for the initialization of the PLS-SEM algorithm. Therefore, initialization values of +1 are specified for all relationships in the measurement model during the first iteration. In subsequent iterations of the algorithm, these initial values are replaced by path coefficients for the relationships in the measurement model. If all the indicators have the same direction (e.g., are coded so that a low value is less favorable while a high value is more favorable) and all the relationships in the PLS path model have hypothesized positive relationships, the result should be positive coefficients.

An alternative setup, used in the LVPLS (Lohmöller, 1987) and PLS Graph (Chin, 2003) software, assigns the value of +1 to all measurement model relationships except the last one, which obtains the value of −1. While the literature does not provide any reasoning why one should use this alternative kind of setup, the model estimation results can easily be subject to unexpected sign changes in the final estimates and lead to misinterpretation of findings.

The final parameter setting to select is the stopping criterion of the algorithm. The PLS-SEM algorithm is designed to run until the results stabilize. Stabilization is reached when the sum of the outer weights that changes between two iterations is sufficiently low, which means it drops below a predefined limit. A threshold value of $1 \cdot 10^{-5}$ (i.e., **stop criterion**) is recommended to ensure that the PLS-SEM algorithm converges at reasonably low levels of iterative changes in the latent variable scores. One must ensure, however, that the algorithm stops at the predefined stop criterion. Thus, a sufficiently high **maximum number of iterations** must be selected. Since the algorithm is very efficient (i.e., it converges after a relatively low number of iterations even with complex models), the selection of a maximum number of 300 iterations should ensure that **convergence** is obtained at the stop criterion of $1 \cdot 10^{-5}$ (i.e., 0.00001). Prior research has shown that the PLS-SEM algorithm almost always converges (Henseler, 2010). Only under very extreme and artificial conditions, which very seldom occur in practice, is it possible that the algorithm does not converge, which has, however, practically no implications for the results. Exhibit 3.3 summarizes guidelines for initializing the PLS-SEM algorithm.

Results

When the PLS-SEM algorithm converges, the final outer weights are used to compute the final latent variable scores. These scores are then used to run OLS regressions to determine estimates for the path relationships in the structural model. PLS-SEM always provides the outer loadings and outer weights, regardless of the

Exhibit 3.3	Rules of Thumb for Initializing the PLS-SEM Algorithm

- Select the path weighting scheme as the weighting method.
- Use the data metric option that z-standardizes your data input for the PLS-SEM indicator variables (i.e., a mean value of 0, standard deviation of 1).
- Use +1 as the initial value for all outer weights.
- Choose a stop criterion of $1 \cdot 10^{-5}$ (i.e., 0.00001).
- Select a value of at least 300 for the maximum number of iterations.

measurement model setup. With reflectively measured constructs, the outer loadings are single regression results with a particular indicator in the measurement model as a dependent variable (e.g., x_5 in Exhibit 3.2) and the construct as an independent variable (e.g., Y_3 in Exhibit 3.2). In contrast, with formatively measured constructs, the outer weights are resulting coefficients of a multiple regression with the construct as a dependent variable (e.g., Y_1 in Exhibit 3.2) and the indicators as independent variables (e.g., x_1 and x_2 in Exhibit 3.2). The outer loadings or outer weights are computed for all measurement model constructs in the PLS path model. However, outer loadings are primarily associated with the results for the relationships in reflective measurement models, and outer weights are associated with the results for the relationships in formative measurement models.

The estimations for the paths between the latent variables in the structural model are reported as standardized coefficients. In the partial regression models of the structural model, an endogenous latent variable (e.g., Y_3 in Exhibit 3.2) serves as the dependent variable while its direct predecessors serve as independent variables (e.g., Y_1 and Y_2 in Exhibit 3.2). In addition to the coefficients from the estimation of the partial regression models in the structural model (one for each endogenous latent variable), the output includes the R^2 values of each endogenous latent variable in the structural model. The R^2 values are normed between 0 and +1 and represent the amount of explained variance in the construct. For example, an R^2 value of 0.70 for the construct Y_3 in Exhibit 3.2 means that 70% of this construct's variance is explained by the exogenous latent variables Y_1 and Y_2. The goal of the PLS-SEM algorithm is to maximize the R^2 values of the endogenous latent variables and thereby their prediction. Additional criteria must be evaluated to fully understand the results of the PLS-SEM algorithm. These additional criteria are explained in detail in Chapters 4 to 6.

CASE STUDY ILLUSTRATION: PLS PATH MODEL ESTIMATION (STAGE 4)

In order to illustrate and explain PLS-SEM, we will use a single data set throughout the book and the SmartPLS software (Ringle et al., 2005). The data set is from research that attempts to predict corporate reputation and, ultimately, customer loyalty, as introduced in Chapter 2. The data set (i.e., the **Full data.csv** file) and the ready-to-use SmartPLS project (i.e., the Corporate Reputation.splsp file) for this case study are available in the Corporate_Reputation.zip file (http://www.pls-sem.com). Download this file and extract it on your hard drive (e.g., in the C:\SmartPLS\ folder).

Model Estimation

To estimate the corporate reputation model in SmartPLS, you need to create a new project, import the indicator data (i.e., **Full data .csv**), and draw the model as explained in the case study of Chapter 2. Alternatively, you can import the SmartPLS project file for this chapter (i.e., **Corporate Reputation.splsp**). The procedures to import projects into the SmartPLS software are explained in Chapter 2. Once this is done, you need to click on **Calculate,** which you can find at the top of the SmartPLS screen. The menu that shows up provides several algorithms to select from. For estimating the PLS path model, the **PLS Algorithm** is the one to choose. Alternatively, you can left-click on the wheel symbol in the tool bar. A combo box will open and you can select the **PLS Algorithm** from four algorithms (i.e., **PLS Algorithm, FIMIX-PLS, Bootstrapping,** and **Blindfolding**) as displayed in Exhibit 3.4. The other algorithms are useful for different analyses, which we explain in the later chapters.

After selecting the PLS Algorithm function, the dialog box in Exhibit 3.5 appears. None of the indicator variables in the simple corporate reputation model has more than 5% missing values (specifically, the maximum number of missing values [four missing values; 1.16%] is in *cusl_2;* see Chapter 2). Thus, mean value replacement

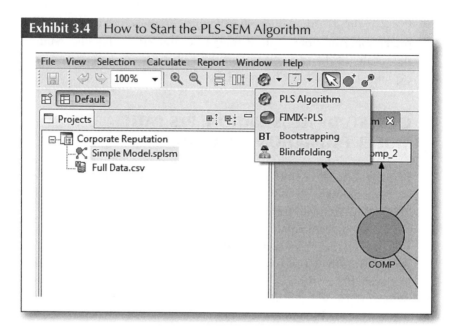

Exhibit 3.4 How to Start the PLS-SEM Algorithm

can be used. Choose the corresponding option under **Missing Value Algorithm** and check the box **Apply Missing Value Algorithm** (Exhibit 3.5).

The PLS-SEM algorithm needs four parameter settings to run it. The **Path Weighting Scheme** is selected for the inner weights estimation, and standardized data are selected for the data metric (**Mean 0, Var 1**). The PLS-SEM algorithm stops when the maximum number of **300** iterations or the stop criterion of **1.0E-5** (i.e., 0.00001) has been reached. The final parameter setting is for **Initial Weights.** Per default, SmartPLS uses a value of 1.0 for all measurement model relationships to initialize the PLS-SEM algorithm. After clicking on **Finish,** the PLS-SEM algorithm starts and the resulting model estimates are obtained (Exhibit 3.6).

Occasionally, the algorithm does not start and a message appears indicating a singular data matrix. There are two potential reasons for this issue. First, one indicator is a constant and thus has zero variance. Second, an indicator is entered twice or is a linear combination of another indicator (e.g., one indicator is a multiple of another such as sales in units and sales in thousands of units). Under these circumstances, PLS-SEM cannot estimate the model, and the researcher has to modify the model by excluding the problematic indicator(s).

Exhibit 3.5	PLS-SEM Algorithm Settings

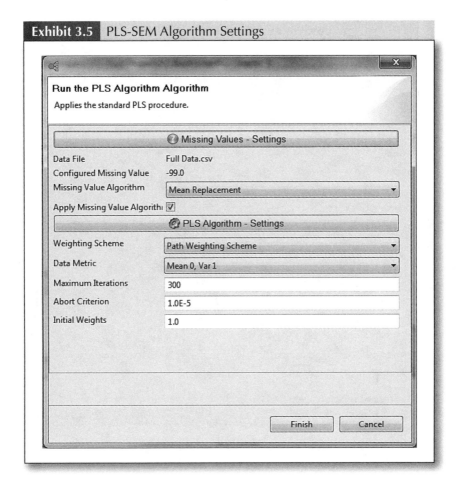

Estimation Results

After the estimation of the model, SmartPLS provides three key results in the modeling window. These are (1) the outer loadings and/or outer weights for the measurement models (there are only outer loadings and no outer weights in this simple model as it only includes reflectively measured constructs), (2) the path coefficients for the structural model relationships, and (3) the R^2 values of the latent endogenous variables CUSA and CUSL (Exhibit 3.6).

The structural model results enable us to determine, for example, that CUSA has the strongest effect on CUSL (0.504), followed by LIKE (0.342) and COMP (0.009). Moreover, the three constructs explain 56.2% of the variance of the endogenous construct CUSL

Exhibit 3.6   PLS-SEM Results

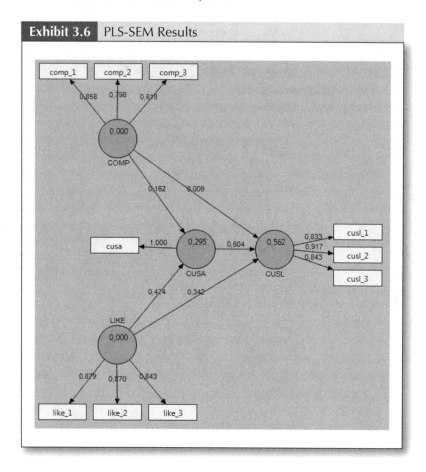

($R^2 = 0.562$), as indicated by the value in the circle. *COMP* and *LIKE* also jointly explain 29.5% of the variance of *CUSA*. In addition to examining the sizes of the path coefficients, we must also determine if they are statistically significant. Based on their sizes, it would appear that the relationships *CUSA* → *CUSL* and *LIKE* → *CUSL* are significant. But it seems very unlikely that the hypothesized path relationship *COMP* → *CUSL* (0.009) is significant. As a rule of thumb, for sample sizes of up to about 1,000 observations, path coefficients with standardized values above 0.20 are usually significant and those with values below 0.10 are usually not significant. Nevertheless, making definite statements about a path coefficient's significance requires determining the coefficient estimates' standard error, which is part of more detailed structural model results evaluations presented in Chapters 5 and 6.

On the basis of the estimated path coefficients and their significance, the researcher can determine whether the conceptual model/ theoretical hypotheses are substantiated empirically. Moreover, by examining the relative sizes of the significant path relationships, it is possible to make statements about the relative importance of the exogenous latent variables in predicting an endogenous latent variable. In our simple example, *CUSA* and *LIKE* are both moderately strong predictors of *CUSL*, whereas *COMP* does not predict *CUSL* at all.

In addition to the results displayed in the modeling window (Exhibit 3.6), SmartPLS offers another way to examine the PLS-SEM outcomes. The task bar option at the top of the screen labeled **Report** enables you to obtain results reports in **HTML** and **LaTeX** format files, which can be saved on your computer. Alternatively, you can open the **Default Report** by going to **Report → Default Report** (note that the default report cannot be saved). On the left-hand side of the default report (Exhibit 3.7), several results tables can be selected such as the **Outer Loadings** and **Outer Weights** tables (menu **PLS → Calculation Results** in the default report). It is important to note that the results for outer loadings and outer weights are provided by the software for all measurement models, regardless of whether they are reflective or formative. If you have reflective measurement models, you interpret the outer loadings results. In contrast, if you have formative measurement models, then you primarily interpret the outer weights results (note, however, that loadings also provide a means to evaluate formative measurement models; see Chapter 5). The default report provides various other results menus of which the **Stop Criterion Changes** is of initial interest. Here we can see the number of iterations the PLS-SEM algorithm ran. We will discuss these and further menus of the default report in later chapters.

Exhibit 3.7 shows the default report for the path coefficients. The results parallel those shown in Exhibit 3.6 (but show one more decimal place). The **Toggle Zero Values** button $\boldsymbol{\mathsf{S}}$ in the task bar of the default report in SmartPLS was used to improve the readability of the results table. The table reads from the row to the column. For example, the value 0.5045 in the *CUSA* row and the *CUSL* column is the standardized path coefficient of the relationship from *CUSA* to *CUSL*. After clicking on the results table on the right-hand side, you can press "CTRL" and "A" on your computer keyboard to mark the entire results table. This selection can then be copied with the keys "CTRL" and "C." Finally, you can open a spreadsheet program such

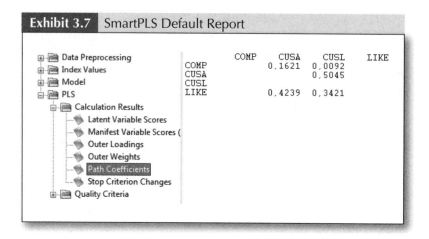

Exhibit 3.7	SmartPLS Default Report

as Microsoft Office Excel or OpenOffice CALC and paste the results table into this application by using the "CTRL" and "V" keys. Using this process, you can copy selected SmartPLS results and save them in a spreadsheet application for writing your final report.

SUMMARY

• **Learn how PLS-SEM functions and how to run the algorithm.** The PLS-SEM algorithm uses the empirical data for the indicators and iteratively determines the construct scores, the path coefficients, indicator loadings and weights, and the R^2 values. Specifically, after determining the scores for every construct, the algorithm estimates all remaining unknown relationships in the PLS path model. The algorithm first obtains the measurement model results, which are the relationships between the constructs and their indicator variables. Then, the algorithm calculates the path coefficients, which are the relationships between the constructs in the structural model, along with the R^2 values of endogenous constructs. All results are standardized, meaning that, for example, path coefficients can be compared with each other.

• **Understand the statistical properties of the PLS-SEM method.** PLS-SEM is an OLS regression-based method, which implies that those statistical properties known from OLS also apply to PLS-SEM. PLS-SEM focuses on the prediction of a specific set of hypothesized relationships that maximizes the explained variance of the dependent variable. The initial key results of the PLS path model estimation are the construct scores. These scores are treated as perfect substitutes for the indicator variables in the measurement models and therefore use all the variance that can help explain the endogenous constructs. Moreover, they facilitate estimating all relationships in the PLS path model. The estimation of these relationships is, however, subject to the PLS-SEM bias, which means that measurement model results are usually overestimated while structural model results are usually underestimated. However, under conditions commonly encountered in research situations, this bias in negligible. Moreover, the parameter estimation efficiency of PLS-SEM delivers high levels of statistical power compared with CB-SEM. Consequently, PLS-SEM better identifies population relationships and is better suited for exploratory research purposes—a feature that is further supported by the method's less restrictive requirements in terms of model setups, model complexity, and data characteristics.

• **Comprehend the options and parameter settings to run the algorithm.** To apply the PLS-SEM algorithm, researchers need to specify several parameter settings. The decisions include selecting the structural model weighting scheme, the data metric, initial values to start the PLS-SEM algorithm, the stop criterion, and the maximum number of iterations. The path weighting scheme maximizes the R^2 values of the endogenous constructs, so that option should be selected. For the data metric, it usually is advantageous to z-standardize the data (i.e., each indicator has mean 0 and variance 1) as standardized PLS-SEM results are easier to interpret. Most software applications offer an option to automatically standardize the input data. Finally, the initial values (e.g., +1) for the relationships in the measurement model, the stop criterion (a small number such as $1 \cdot 10^{-5}$), and a sufficiently large maximum number of iterations (e.g., 300) should be selected.

The PLS-SEM algorithm runs until convergence is achieved or the maximum number of iterations has been reached. The resulting construct scores are then used to estimate all partial regression models in the structural model and the measurement models to obtain the final model estimates.

• **Explain how to interpret the results.** The PLS-SEM method estimates the standardized outer loadings, outer weights, and structural model path coefficients. The indicator loadings and indicator weights are computed for any measurement model in the PLS path model. When reflective measurement models are used, the researcher interprets the outer loadings, whereas outer weights are the primary criterion when formative measurement models are interpreted (note, however, that the loadings also play a role in formative measurement model assessment). For the structural model, the standardized coefficients of the relationships between the constructs are provided as well as the R^2 values for the endogenous constructs. Other more advanced PLS-SEM evaluation criteria used in assessing the results are introduced in Chapters 4 to 6.

• **Apply the PLS-SEM algorithm using the SmartPLS software.** The corporate reputation example and the empirical data available with this book enable you to apply the PLS-SEM algorithm using the SmartPLS software. Selected menu options guide the user in choosing the algorithmic options and parameter settings required for running the PLS-SEM algorithm. The SmartPLS results reports enable the user to check if the algorithm converged (i.e., the stop criterion was reached and not the maximum number of iterations) and to evaluate the initial results for the outer weights, outer loadings, structural model path coefficients, and R^2 values. Additional diagnostic measures for more advanced analyses are discussed in later chapters.

REVIEW QUESTIONS

1. What are the parameter settings and algorithmic options that you would use (e.g., weighting scheme)?

2. Describe how the PLS-SEM algorithm functions.

3. What are meaningful stopping rules for the PLS-SEM algorithm?

4. What are the key results provided after convergence of the PLS-SEM algorithm?

CRITICAL THINKING QUESTIONS

1. What do you need to consider for initializing the PLS-SEM algorithm (i.e., initial values)?

2. Does the PLS-SEM bias represent a crucial problem in PLS-SEM applications? Explain why.

3. What are the advantages and disadvantages of the PLS-SEM algorithm compared with CB-SEM?

4. What feature makes the PLS-SEM method particularly useful for exploratory research?

KEY TERMS

Algorithmic options: offer different ways to run the PLS-SEM algorithm by, for example, selecting between alternative starting values, stop values, weighting schemes, and maximum number of iterations.

Consistency at large: describes an improvement of precision of PLS-SEM results when both the number of indicators per measurement model and the number of observations increase.

Construct scores: are columns of data (vectors) for each latent variable that represent a key result of the PLS-SEM algorithm. The length of every vector equals the number of observations in the data set used.

Constructs: see *Latent variables.*

Convergence: is reached when the results of the PLS-SEM algorithm do not change much. In that case, the PLS-SEM algorithm stops when a prespecified stop criterion (i.e., a small number such as 0.00001) that indicates the minimal changes of PLS-SEM computations has been reached. Thus, convergence has been accomplished when the PLS-SEM algorithm stops because the prespecified stop criterion has been reached and not the maximum number of iterations.

Data matrix: includes the empirical data that are needed to estimate the PLS path model. The data matrix must have one column for every indicator in the PLS path model. The rows represent the observations with their responses to every indicator on the PLS path model.

Endogenous: see *Latent variables.*

Exogenous: see *Latent variables.*

Formative measures: see *Measurement models.*

Indicators: are available data (e.g., responses to survey questions or collected from company databases) that are used in measurement models to measure the latent variables; in SEM, indicators are often called manifest variables.

Initial values: are the values for the relationships between the latent variables and the indicators in the first iteration of the PLS-SEM algorithm. Since the user usually has no idea which indicators are more important and which indicators are less important per measurement model, an equal weight for every indicator in the PLS path model usually serves well for the initialization of the PLS-SEM algorithm. In accordance, all relationships in the measurement models have an initial value of +1.

Latent variables (endogenous, exogenous): are the (unobserved) theoretical or conceptual elements in the structural model. A latent variable that only explains other latent variables (only outgoing relationships in the structural model) is called exogenous, while latent variables with at least one incoming relationship in the structural model are called endogenous.

Maximum number of iterations: is needed to ensure that the algorithm stops. The goal is to reach convergence (*convergence*). But if convergence cannot be reached, the algorithm should stop after a certain number of iterations. This maximum number of iterations (e.g., 300) should be sufficiently high to allow the PLS-SEM algorithm to converge.

Measurement models (formative, reflective): are used to establish latent variables by certain indicator variables. Measurement models are also called outer models in PLS-SEM. A reflective measurement model has relationships from the latent variable to its indicators. In contrast, formative measurement models have relationships from the indicators to the latent variable.

Minimum sample size: see *Ten times rule.*

Model complexity: indicates how many latent variables, structural model relationships, and indicators in reflective and formative measurement models exist in a PLS path model. Even though PLS-SEM virtually has no limits of model complexity, knowledge about the most complex OLS regression is needed to determine the minimum sample size (*ten times rule*).

Outer loadings: are the results of single regressions of each indicator variable on their corresponding construct. Loadings are of primary interest in the evaluation of reflective measurement models but are also interpreted when formative measures are involved.

Outer weights: are the results of a multiple regression of a construct on its set of indicators. Weights are the primary criterion to assess each indicator's relative importance in formative measurement models.

Parameter settings: see *Algorithmic options.*

Path coefficients: are the relationships between the latent variables in the structural model.

PLS-SEM algorithm: is the heart of the method. Based on the PLS path model and the indicator data available, the algorithm estimates the scores of all latent variables in the model, which in turn serve for estimating all path model relationships.

PLS-SEM bias: refers to PLS-SEM's property that structural model relationships are slightly underestimated and relationships in the measurement models are slightly overestimated. While researchers must accept that their results are affected to some extent by the PLS-SEM bias, this bias is negligible in most settings encountered in empirical research.

Prediction: is the primary goal of the PLS-SEM method. The higher the R^2 value (R^2 *values*) of endogenous constructs (*latent variables*), the better their prediction by the PLS path model.

R^2 values: are the amount of explained variance of endogenous *latent variables* in the *structural model*. The higher the R^2 values, the better the construct is explained by the latent variables in the structural model that point at it via structural model path relationships. High R^2 values also indicate that the values of the construct can be well predicted via the PLS path model.

Raw data: are the unstandardized observations in the *data matrix* that is used for the PLS path model estimation.

Reflective measure: see *Measurement models.*

Standardized data: have a mean value of 0 and a standard deviation of 1 (*z*-standardization). The PLS-SEM method usually uses standardized *raw data*. Most software tools automatically standardize the raw data when running the PLS-SEM algorithm.

Statistical power: is the ability of the SEM method to identify significant relationships that in fact exist.

Stop criterion: see *Convergence.*

Structural model: represents the theoretical or conceptual element of the path model. The structural model (also called inner model in PLS-SEM) includes the latent variables and their path relationships.

Ten times rule: One way to determine the minimum sample size specific to the PLS path model that one needs for model estimation (i.e., 10 times the number of independent variables of the most complex OLS regression in the structural or formative measurement model). The 10 times rule should be seen only as a rough estimate of the minimum sample size. Rather, researchers should revert to recommendations such as those presented by Cohen (1992) in his "Power Primer" article or run a power analysis specific to the model at hand.

Weighting scheme: describes a particular method to determine the relationships in the *structural model* when running the *PLS-SEM algorithm*. Standard options are the centroid, factor, and path weighting scheme. The final results do not differ much, and one should use the path weighting scheme as a default option since it maximizes the R^2 *values* of the PLS path model estimation.

SUGGESTED READINGS

Dijkstra, T. K. (2010). Latent variables and indices: Herman Wold's basic design and partial least squares. In V. Esposito Vinzi, W. W. Chin, J. Henseler & H. Wang (Eds.), *Handbook of partial least squares: Concepts, methods and applications* (Springer Handbooks of Computational Statistics Series, vol. II) (pp. 23–46). Heidelberg, Dordrecht, London, New York: Springer.

Hair, J. F., Ringle, C. M., & Sarstedt, M. (2011). PLS-SEM: Indeed a silver bullet. *Journal of Marketing Theory and Practice, 19,* 139–151.

Henseler, J., Ringle, C. M., & Sarstedt, M. (2012). Using partial least squares path modeling in international advertising research: Basic concepts and recent issues. In S. Okazaki (Ed.), *Handbook of research in international advertising* (pp. 252–276). Cheltenham, UK: Edward Elgar.

Henseler, J., Ringle, C. M., & Sinkovics, R. R. (2009). The use of partial least squares path modeling in international marketing. *Advances in International Marketing, 20,* 277–320.

Jöreskog, K. G., & Wold, H. (1982). The ML and PLS techniques for modeling with latent variables: Historical and comparative aspects. In H. Wold & K. G. Jöreskog (Eds.), *Systems under indirect observation,* Part I (pp. 263–270). *Amsterdam: North-Holland.*

Lohmöller, J. B. (1989). *Latent variable path modeling with partial least squares.* Heidelberg: Physica.

Reinartz, W., Haenlein, M., & Henseler, J. (2009). An empirical comparison of the efficacy of covariance-based and variance-based SEM. *International Journal of Research in Marketing, 26*(4), 332–344.

Rigdon, E. E. (2005). Structural equation modeling: Nontraditional alternatives. In B. Everitt & D. Howell (Eds.), *Encyclopedia of statistics in behavioral science* (Vol. 4, pp. 1934–1941). New York: Wiley.

Vilares, M. J., Almeida, M. H., & Coelho, P. S. (2010). Comparison of likelihood and PLS estimators for structural equation modeling: A simulation with customer satisfaction data. In V. Esposito Vinzi, W. W. Chin, J. Henseler & H. Wang (Eds.), *Handbook of partial least squares: concepts, methods and applications* (Springer Handbooks of Computational Statistics Series, vol. II) (pp. 289–305). Heidelberg, Dordrecht, London, New York: Springer.

CHAPTER 4

Assessing PLS-SEM Results Part I

Evaluation of Reflective Measurement Models

LEARNING OUTCOMES

1. Gain an overview of Stage 5 of the process for using PLS-SEM, which deals with the evaluation of measurement models.

2. Describe Stage 5a: evaluating reflectively measured constructs.

3. Use the SmartPLS software to assess reflectively measured constructs in the corporate reputation example.

CHAPTER PREVIEW

Having learned how to create and estimate a PLS path model, we now focus on understanding how to assess the quality of the results. Initially, we summarize the primary criteria used for PLS path model evaluation and their systematic application. Then, we focus on the evaluation of **reflective measurement models.** The PLS path model of corporate reputation is a practical application enabling you to review the relevant measurement model evaluation criteria and the appropriate reporting of results. This provides a foundation for the overview of **formative measurement models** in Chapter 5 and how to evaluate **structural model** results, which is covered in Chapter 6.

OVERVIEW OF STAGE 5: EVALUATION OF MEASUREMENT MODELS

Model estimation delivers empirical measures of the relationships between the indicators and the constructs (measurement models), as well as between the constructs (structural model). The empirical measures enable us to compare the theoretically established measurement and structural models with reality, as represented by the sample data. In other words, we can determine how well the theory fits the data.

Unlike with CB-SEM, a single goodness-of-fit criterion is not available in PLS-SEM. In this context, it is important to recognize that the term *fit* has different meanings in the contexts of CB-SEM and PLS-SEM. Fit statistics for CB-SEM are derived from the discrepancy between the empirical and the model-implied (theoretical) covariance matrix, whereas PLS-SEM focuses on the discrepancy between the observed (in the case of manifest variables) or approximated (in the case of latent variables) values of the dependent variables and the values predicted by the model in question. As a consequence, researchers using PLS-SEM rely on measures indicating the model's predictive capabilities to judge the model's quality. More precisely, the evaluation of the measurement and structural model results in PLS-SEM builds on a set of nonparametric **evaluation criteria** and uses procedures such as bootstrapping and blindfolding.

The systematic application of these criteria follows a two-step process, as shown in Exhibit 4.1. The process involves separate assessments of the measurement models (Stage 5 of the procedure for using PLS-SEM) and the structural model (Stage 6).

Initially, model assessment focuses on the measurement models. Examination of PLS-SEM estimates enables the researcher to evaluate the **reliability** and **validity** of the construct measures. Specifically, multivariate measurement involves using several variables to indirectly measure a concept, such as customer loyalty (*CUSL*) in the PLS-SEM example of corporate reputation (Chapter 2).

The logic of using several individual variables to measure a concept is that the measure will be more accurate. The anticipated improved accuracy is based on the assumption that using several variables (indicators) to measure a single concept is more likely to represent all the different aspects of the concept. Moreover, using several variables to more accurately represent the concept results in a more valid measurement of it. The underlying nature of multivariate

Exhibit 4.1 Systematic Evaluation of PLS-SEM Results

Stage 5: Evaluation of the Measurement Models

Stage 5a: Reflective Measurement Models	*Stage 5b: Formative Measurement Models*
• Internal consistency (composite reliability) • Indicator reliability • Convergent validity (average variance extracted) • Discriminant validity	• Convergent validity • Collinearity among indicators • Significance and relevance of outer weights

Stage 6: Evaluation of the Structural Model
• Coefficients of determination (R^2)   • Predictive relevance (Q^2)   • Size and significance of path coefficients   • f^2 effect sizes   • q^2 effect sizes

analysis facilitates the use of multivariate measurements in research and thereby improves the accuracy of research findings.

There are many sources of measurement error in social sciences research, including poorly worded questions in a survey, misunderstanding of the scaling approach, and incorrect application of a statistical method, all of which lead to random and/or systematic errors. Indeed, all measurements used in multivariate analysis are likely to contain some measurement error. The objective, therefore, is to reduce the measurement error as much as possible. Multivariate measurement enables researchers to more precisely identify measurement error and therefore account for it in research findings.

Measurement error is the difference between the true value of a variable and the value obtained by a measurement. More specifically, the measured value x_m equals the true value x_t plus a measurement error e = ε_r + ε_s, whereby the error can have a random source (random error ε_r), which threatens reliability, or a systematic source (systematic error ε_s), which threatens validity. This relationship can be expressed as follows:

$$x_m = x_t + \varepsilon_r + \varepsilon_s.$$

In Exhibit 4.2, we explain the difference between reliability and validity by comparing a set of three targets. In this analogy, repeated measurements (e.g., of a customer's satisfaction with a specific service) are compared to arrows shot at a target. To measure each true score, we have five measurements (indicated by the black circles). The average value of the circles is indicated by a cross. Validity is indicated when the cross is close to the bull's-eye at the target center. The closer the average value (black cross in Exhibit 4.2) to the true score, the higher the validity. If several arrows are fired, reliability is the distances between the circles. If all the circles are close together, the measure is reliable, even though the circles are not necessarily near the bull's-eye. This corresponds to the upper left box where we have a scenario in which the measure is reliable but not valid. In the upper right box, both reliability and validity are shown. In the lower left box, though, we have a situation in which the measure is neither reliable nor valid. In short, the repeated measurements (circles) are scattered quite widely and the average value (cross) is not close to the bull's-eye. However, even if the average value would match the true score (i.e., if the cross were in the bull's-eye), we would still not consider the measure valid. The reason is that an unreliable measure can never be valid because there is no way we can distinguish the systematic error from the random error (Mooi & Sarstedt, 2011). If we repeated the measurement, say, five more times, the random error would likely shift the cross to a different position. Thus, reliability is a necessary condition for validity. This is also why the not reliable/valid scenario in the lower right box is not possible.

When evaluating the measurement models, we must distinguish between reflectively and formatively measured constructs (Chapter 2). The two approaches are based on different concepts and therefore require consideration of different evaluative measures. Reflective measurement models are assessed on their internal consistency reliability and validity. The specific measures include the composite reliability (as a means to assess the internal consistency reliability), convergent validity, and discriminant validity. The criteria for reflective measurement models cannot be universally applied to formative measurement models. With formative measures, the first step is to ensure **content validity** before collecting the data and estimating the PLS path model. After model estimation, formative measures are assessed for their convergent validity, the significance and relevance and the presence of **collinearity** among indicators.

Exhibit 4.2	Comparing Reliability and Validity (Mooi & Sarstedt, 2011)

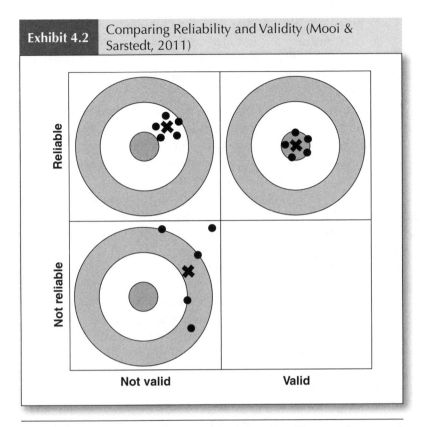

Not valid   **Valid**

Source: Mooi, E., and Sarstedt, M. (2011). *A concise guide to market research* (p. 35). New York: Springer. With kind permission of Springer Science+Business Media.

As implied by its name, a **single-item construct** (Chapter 2) is not represented by a multi-item measurement model. Thus, the criteria for the assessment of measurement models are not applicable to single-item constructs. To evaluate the reliability and validity of single-item measures, researchers must rely on proxies or different forms of validity assessment. For example, researchers can assess a single-item variable by means of criterion validity. This is done by correlating the single-item measure with an established criterion variable and comparing the resulting correlation with the correlation that results if the predictor construct is measured by a multi-item scale (e.g., Diamantopoulos et al., 2012). In terms of reliability, researchers can use the correction for attenuation formula to derive a proxy for single-item reliability (e.g., Sarstedt & Wilczynski, 2009).

These procedures require that both the multi-item measure and the single-item measure are included in the same survey. Thus, these analyses are of primary interest when researchers want to assess in a pretest whether in the main study, a multi-item scale can be replaced with a single-item measure of the same construct.

The structural model estimates are not examined until the reliability and validity of the constructs have been established. If assessment of reflective (i.e., Stage 5a) and formative (i.e., Stage 5b) measurement models provides evidence of the measures' quality, the structural model estimates are evaluated in Stage 6 (Exhibit 4.1; Chapter 6). PLS-SEM assessment of the structural model involves the model's ability to predict. Hence, after reliability and validity are established, the primary evaluation criteria for PLS-SEM results are the **coefficients of determination (R^2 values)** as well as the level and significance of the **path coefficients.**

Assessment of PLS-SEM outcomes can be extended to more advanced analyses (e.g., examining the mediating and/or moderating effects, considering [unobserved] heterogeneity, multigroup testing, common method variance, and others). The objective of these additional analyses is to extend and further differentiate the findings from the basic PLS path model estimation (Chapters 7 and 8). Some of these advanced analyses are necessary to obtain a complete understanding of PLS-SEM results (e.g., checking for the presence of unobserved heterogeneity and significantly different subgroups), while others are optional.

The primary rules of thumb on how to evaluate PLS-SEM results are shown in Exhibit 4.3. In the following sections, we provide an overview of the process for assessing reflective measurement models (Stage 5a). Chapter 5 addresses evaluation of formative measurement models, while Chapter 6 deals with the structural model evaluation.

STAGE 5A: ASSESSING RESULTS OF REFLECTIVE MEASUREMENT MODELS

Assessment of reflective measurement models includes composite reliability to evaluate internal consistency, individual indicator reliability, and average variance extracted (AVE) to evaluate convergent validity. In addition, the Fornell-Larcker criterion and cross loadings are used to assess discriminant validity. In the following sections, we address each criterion for the assessment of reflective measurement models.

Exhibit 4.3	Rules of Thumb for Evaluating PLS-SEM Results

- A single goodness-of-fit criterion is not available to evaluate PLS-SEM estimations. Instead, nonparametric evaluation criteria based on bootstrapping and blindfolding are used.

- Begin the evaluation process by assessing the quality of the reflective and formative measurement models (specific rules of thumb follow later in this chapter for reflective measurement models and in Chapter 5 for formative measurement models).

- If the measurement characteristics of constructs are acceptable, continue with the assessment of the structural model results. Path estimates should be statistically significant and meaningful. Moreover, endogenous constructs in the structural model should have high levels of explained variance—R^2 (Chapter 6 presents specific guidelines).

- Advanced analyses that extend and differentiate initial PLS-SEM findings may be necessary to obtain a correct and complete understanding of the results (Chapters 7 and 8).

Internal Consistency Reliability

The first criterion to be evaluated is typically **internal consistency reliability.** The traditional criterion for internal consistency is **Cronbach's alpha,** which provides an estimate of the reliability based on the intercorrelations of the observed indicator variables. Cronbach's alpha assumes that all indicators are equally reliable (i.e., all the indicators have equal outer loadings on the construct). But PLS-SEM prioritizes the indicators according to their individual reliability. Moreover, Cronbach's alpha is sensitive to the number of items in the scale and generally tends to underestimate the internal consistency reliability. As such, it may be used as a conservative measure of internal consistency reliability. Due to Cronbach alpha's limitations in the population, it is more appropriate to apply a different measure of internal consistency reliability, which is referred to as **composite reliability** (ρ_c). This type of reliability takes into account the different **outer loadings** of the indicator variables and is calculated using the following formula:

$$\rho_c = \frac{\left(\sum_i l_i\right)^2}{\left(\sum_i l_i\right)^2 + \sum_i \mathrm{var}(e_i)},$$

whereby l_i symbolizes the standardized outer loading of the indicator variable i of a specific construct, e_i is the measurement error of indicator variable i, and $var(e_i)$ denotes the variance of the measurement error, which is defined as $1 - l_i^2$.

The composite reliability varies between 0 and 1, with higher values indicating higher levels of reliability. It is generally interpreted in the same way as Cronbach's alpha. Specifically, composite reliability values of 0.60 to 0.70 are acceptable in exploratory research, while in more advanced stages of research, values between 0.70 and 0.90 can be regarded as satisfactory (Nunally & Bernstein, 1994). Values above 0.90 (and definitely > 0.95) are not desirable because they indicate that all the indicator variables are measuring the same phenomenon and are therefore unlikely to be a valid measure of the construct. Specifically, such composite reliability values occur if one uses semantically redundant items by slightly rephrasing the very same question. As the use of redundant items has adverse consequences for the measures' content validity (e.g., Rossiter, 2002) and may boost error term correlations (Drolet & Morrison, 2001 ; Hayduk and Littvay, 2001), researchers are well advised not to engage in this practice. Finally, composite reliability values below 0.60 indicate a lack of internal consistency reliability.

Convergent Validity

Convergent validity is the extent to which a measure correlates positively with alternative measures of the same construct. Using the domain sampling model, indicators of a reflective construct are treated as different approaches to measure the same construct. Therefore, the items that are indicators (measures) of a specific construct should converge or share a high proportion of variance. To establish convergent validity, researchers consider the outer loadings of the indicators, as well as the average variance extracted (AVE).

High outer loadings on a construct indicate that the associated indicators have much in common, which is captured by the construct. This characteristic is also commonly called **indicator reliability**. At a minimum, all indicators' outer loadings should be statistically significant. Because a significant outer loading could still be fairly weak, a common rule of thumb is that the (standardized) outer loadings should be 0.708 or higher. The rationale behind this rule can be understood in the context of the square of a standardized indicator's outer loading, referred to as the **communality** of an item. The square of a standardized indicator's outer loading represents how much of the variation in an item is explained by the construct and is described as the variance extracted from the item. An established rule of thumb is that a latent variable should explain a substantial part of each indicator's variance, usually at least 50%. This also implies that the variance shared between the construct and its indicator is larger than the measurement error variance. This means that an indicator's outer loading should be above 0.708 since that number squared (0.708^2) equals 0.50. Note that in most instances, 0.70 is considered close enough to 0.708 to be acceptable.

Researchers frequently observe weaker outer loadings in social science studies, especially when newly developed scales are used (Hulland, 1999). Rather than automatically eliminating indicators when their outer loading is below 0.70, researchers should carefully examine the effects of item removal on the composite reliability, as well as on the construct's content validity. Generally, indicators with outer loadings between 0.40 and 0.70 should be considered for removal from the scale only when deleting the indicator leads to an increase in the composite reliability (or the average variance extracted; see next section) above the suggested threshold value. Another consideration in the decision of whether to delete an indicator is the extent to which its removal affects content validity. Indicators with weaker outer loadings are sometimes retained on the basis of their contribution to content validity. Indicators with very low outer loadings (below 0.40) should, however, always be eliminated from the scale (Hair, Ringle, & Sarstedt, 2011). Exhibit 4.4 illustrates the recommendations regarding indicator deletion based on outer loadings.

A common measure to establish convergent validity on the construct level is the **average variance extracted** (**AVE**). This criterion is defined as the grand mean value of the squared loadings of the indicators associated with the construct (i.e., the sum of the squared loadings divided by the number of indicators). Therefore, the AVE is equivalent to the **communality** of a construct. Using the same logic as that used with the individual indicators, an AVE value of 0.50 or higher indicates that, on average, the construct explains more than half of the variance of its indicators. Conversely, an AVE of less than 0.50 indicates that, on average, more error remains in the items than the variance explained by the construct.

The AVE of each reflectively measured construct should be evaluated. In the example introduced in Chapter 2, an AVE estimate is

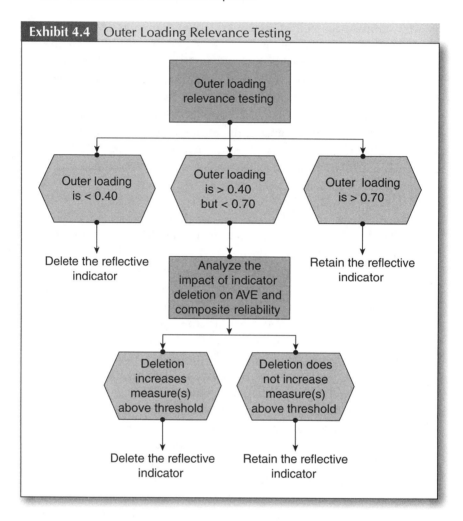

Exhibit 4.4 Outer Loading Relevance Testing

needed only for constructs *COMP, CUSL,* and *LIKE.* For the single-item construct *CUSA,* the AVE is not an appropriate measure since the indicator's outer loading is fixed at 1.00.

Discriminant Validity

Discriminant validity is the extent to which a construct is truly distinct from other constructs by empirical standards. Thus, establishing discriminant validity implies that a construct is unique and captures phenomena not represented by other constructs in the model. Two measures of discriminant validity have been proposed.

One method for assessing discriminant validity is by examining the **cross loadings** of the indicators. Specifically, an indicator's outer loading on the associated construct should be greater than all of its loadings on other constructs (i.e., the cross loadings). The presence of cross loadings that exceed the indicators' outer loadings represents a discriminant validity problem. This criterion is generally considered rather liberal in terms of establishing discriminant validity (Hair, Ringle, & Sarstedt, 2011). That is, it is very likely to indicate that two or more constructs exhibit discriminant validity.

The **Fornell-Larcker criterion** is a second and more conservative approach to assessing discriminant validity. It compares the square root of the AVE values with the latent variable correlations. Specifically, the square root of each construct's AVE should be greater than its highest correlation with any other construct. (Note: This criterion can also be stated as the AVE should exceed the squared correlation with any other construct.) The logic of this method is based on the idea that a construct shares more variance with its associated indicators than with any other construct.

Exhibit 4.5 illustrates this concept. In the example, the AVE values of the constructs Y_1 and Y_2 are 0.55 and 0.65. The AVE values are obtained by squaring each outer loading, obtaining the sum of the three squared outer loadings, and then calculating the average value. For example, with respect to construct Y_1, 0.60, 0.70, and 0.90 squared are 0.36, 0.49, and 0.81. The sum of these three numbers is 1.66 and the average value is therefore 0.55 (i.e., 1.66/3). The correlation between constructs Y_1 and Y_2 (as indicated by the double-headed arrow linking the two constructs) is 0.80. Squaring the correlation of 0.80 indicates that 64% (i.e., the squared correlation; $0.80^2 = 0.64$) of each construct's variation is explained by the other construct. Therefore, Y_1 explains less variance in its indicator measures x_1 to x_3 than it shares with Y_2, which implies that the two constructs (Y_1 and Y_2), which are conceptually different, are not sufficiently different in terms of their empirical standards. Thus, in this example, discriminant validity is not established.

The analysis and presentation of the Fornell-Larcker criterion is illustrated in Exhibit 4.6—for a PLS path model with two reflective constructs (i.e., Y_1 and Y_2), one formative construct (i.e., Y_3), and a single-item construct (i.e., Y_4). The first consideration is that only reflective constructs are evaluated using the Fornell-Larcker criterion. Therefore, constructs Y_3 and Y_4 are exceptions to this

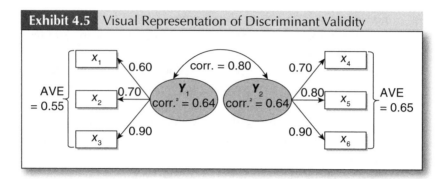

Exhibit 4.5 Visual Representation of Discriminant Validity

type of evaluation since the AVE value is not a meaningful criterion for formative and single-item measures. Looking only at constructs Y_1 and Y_2, note that the square root of each construct's AVE is on the diagonal. The nondiagonal elements represent the correlations between the latent variables. To establish discriminant validity, the square root of each construct's AVE must be larger than its correlation with other constructs. To evaluate the reflective construct Y_2 in Exhibit 4.6, one would compare all correlations in the row of Y_2 and the column of Y_2 with its square root of the AVE. In the case study illustration of the corporate reputation path model later in this chapter, the actual estimated values for this type of analysis are provided.

In Exhibit 4.7, we summarize the criteria used to assess the reliability and validity of reflective construct measures. If the criteria

Exhibit 4.6 Fornell-Larcker Criterion Analysis

	Y_1	Y_2	Y_3	Y_4
Y_1	$\sqrt{AVE_{Y_1}}$			
Y_2	$CORR_{Y_1Y_2}$	$\sqrt{AVE_{Y_2}}$		
Y_3	$CORR_{Y_1Y_3}$	$CORR_{Y_2Y_3}$	Formative measurement model	
Y_4	$CORR_{Y_1Y_4}$	$CORR_{Y_2Y_4}$	$CORR_{Y_3Y_4}$	Single-item construct

Exhibit 4.7	Rules of Thumb for Evaluating Reflective Measurement Models

- Internal consistency reliability: composite reliability should be higher than 0.708 (in exploratory research, 0.60 to 0.70 is considered acceptable). Consider Cronbach's alpha as a conservative measure of internal consistency reliability.
- Indicator reliability: the indicator's outer loadings should be higher than 0.708. Indicators with outer loadings between 0.40 and 0.70 should be considered for removal only if the deletion leads to an increase in composite reliability and AVE above the suggested threshold value.
- Convergent validity: the AVE should be higher than 0.50.
- Discriminant validity:
  o An indicator's outer loadings on a construct should be higher than all its cross loadings with other constructs.
  o The square root of the AVE of each construct should be higher than its highest correlation with any other construct (Fornell-Larcker criterion).

are not met, the researcher may decide to remove single indicators from a specific construct in an attempt to more closely meet the criteria. However, removing indicators should be carried out with care since the elimination of one or more indicators may improve the reliability or discriminant validity but at the same time decrease the measurement's content validity.

CASE STUDY ILLUSTRATION—REFLECTIVE MEASUREMENT MODELS

Running the PLS-SEM Algorithm

We continue working with our PLS-SEM example on corporate reputation. In Chapter 3, we explained how to estimate the PLS path model and how to obtain the results by opening the default report in the SmartPLS software. Recall that to do so, you must first load the simple corporate reputation model and then run the model by clicking on the icon at the top or by using the pull-down menu by going to

Exhibit 4.8	Default Report in SmartPLS

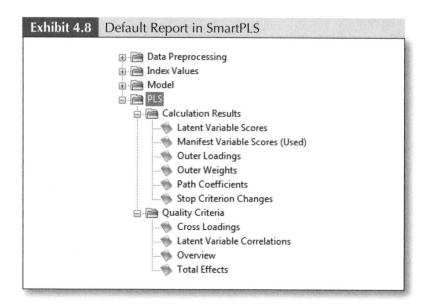

Calculate → **PLS Algorithm.** To obtain the report, left-click on the **Report** pull-down menu at the top of the screen and then on **Default Report.** Exhibit 4.8 summarizes the contents of the default report.

Before analyzing the results, you need to quickly check if the algorithm converged (i.e., the stop criterion of the algorithm was reached and not the maximum number of iterations). To do so, go to **PLS → Calculation Results → Stop Criterion Changes.** You will then see the table shown in Exhibit 4.9, which shows the number of iterations of the PLS-SEM algorithm. This number should be lower than the maximum number of iterations (e.g., 300) that you defined in the PLS-SEM algorithm parameter settings (Chapter 2). At the bottom left side of the table, you will see that the algorithm converged after Iteration 4.

If the PLS-SEM algorithm does not converge in less than 300 iterations (the setting in the software), the algorithm could not find a stable solution. This kind of situation almost never occurs. But if it does occur, there are two possible causes of the problem: (1) the selected stop criterion is at a level that is so small (e.g., 1.0E-25) that small changes in the coefficients of the measurement models prevent the PLS-SEM algorithm from stopping, or (2) the data are abnormal and need to be carefully checked. For example, data problems may occur if the sample size

Exhibit 4.9	Stop Criterion Table in SmartPLS

	comp_1	comp_2	comp_3	cusa	cusl_1	cusl_2	cusl_3	like_1	like_2	like_3
Iteration 0	1,0000	1,0000	1,0000	1,0000	1,0000	1,0000	1,0000	1,0000	1,0000	1,0000
Iteration 1	0,5357	0,3407	0,3284	1,0000	0,3680	0,4207	0,3651	0,4190	0,3775	0,3594
Iteration 2	0,5361	0,3404	0,3282	1,0000	0,3687	0,4202	0,3649	0,4184	0,3779	0,3597
Iteration 3	0,5361	0,3404	0,3282	1,0000	0,3687	0,4202	0,3649	0,4184	0,3779	0,3597
Iteration 4	0,5361	0,3404	0,3282	1,0000	0,3687	0,4202	0,3649	0,4184	0,3779	0,3597

is too small or if an indicator has many identical values (i.e., the same data points, which results in insufficient variability).

When your model converges, you need to examine the following PLS-SEM calculation results tables from the **Default Report** for reflective measurement model assessment: **Outer Loadings** (under **PLS → Calculation Results**) and the **Latent Variable Correlations** and **Overview** tabs under **PLS → Quality Criteria** (Exhibit 4.8). Other information in the report is examined in Chapters 5 and 6, when we extend the simple path model by including formative measures and examine the structural model results.

Reflective Measurement Model Evaluation

The simple corporate reputation model has three latent variables with reflective measurement models (i.e., *COMP, CUSL,* and *LIKE*) as well as a single-item construct (*CUSA*). For the reflective measurement models, we need the estimates for the relationships between the reflective latent variables and their indicators (i.e., outer loadings). Exhibit 4.10 displays the **Default Report** of the SmartPLS software and the results table for the outer loadings. Note that the "toggle zeros" button in the task bar (top left of screen) of the default report in SmartPLS was used to improve the readability of the results table. All outer loadings of the reflective constructs *COMP, CUSL,* and *LIKE* are well above the threshold value of 0.708. The indicator *comp_2* (outer loading: 0.7985) has the smallest indicator reliability with a value of 0.638 (0.7985^2), while the indicator *cusl_2* (outer loading: 0.9173) has the highest indicator reliability with a value of 0.841 (0.9173^2). Thus, all of the indicators for the three reflective constructs are well above the minimum acceptable level for outer loadings.

To evaluate the measures' composite reliability values, left-click on the **Overview** tab under the **PLS → Quality Criteria** menu

(Exhibit 4.11). The composite reliability values of 0.8646 (*COMP*), 0.8991 (*CUSL*), and 0.8986 (*LIKE*) demonstrate that all three reflective constructs have high levels of internal consistency reliability. Note that the composite reliability value of the single-item variable *CUSA* is 1.00. But this cannot be interpreted as evidence that the construct exhibits perfect reliability.

Convergent validity assessment builds on the AVE value as the evaluation criterion. In this example, the AVE values of *COMP* (0.6806), *CUSL* (0.7484), and *LIKE* (0.7471) are well above the required minimum level of 0.50. Thus, the measures of the three reflective constructs have high levels of convergent validity.

Exhibit 4.10 Outer Loadings

- Data Preprocessing
- Index Values
- Model
- PLS
  - Calculation Results
    - Latent Variable Scores
    - Manifest Variable Scores (Used)
    - Outer Loadings
    - Outer Weights
    - Path Coefficients
    - Stop Criterion Changes
  - Quality Criteria

	COMP	CUSA	CUSL	LIKE
comp_1	0.8577			
comp_2	0.7985			
comp_3	0.8176			
cusa		1.0000		
cusl_1			0.8328	
cusl_2			0.9173	
cusl_3			0.8428	
like_1				0.8793
like_2				0.8702
like_3				0.8430

Exhibit 4.11 Overview of Model Quality Criteria

- Data Preprocessing
- Index Values
- Model
- PLS
  - Calculation Results
  - Quality Criteria
    - Cross Loadings
    - Latent Variable Correlations
    - Overview
    - Total Effects

	AVE	Composite Reliability	R Square	Cronbachs Alpha
COMP	0.6806	0.8646		0.7760
CUSA	1.0000	1.0000	0.2946	1.0000
CUSL	0.7484	0.8991	0.5620	0.8310
LIKE	0.7471	0.8986		0.8310

Finally, the Fornell-Larcker criterion and the cross loadings allow checking for discriminant validity. According to the Fornell-Larcker criterion, the square root of the AVE of each construct should be higher than the construct's highest correlation with any other construct in the model (this notion is identical to comparing the AVE with the squared correlations between the constructs). You can find the **Latent Variable Correlations** under **PLS → Quality Criteria** in the **Default Report.** You might want to copy and paste the entire correlation matrix in a spreadsheet program such as Microsoft Excel. Next, replace the unit values on the diagonal with the square root of the AVE values. In Excel, you can calculate the square root by means of the SQRT function. For example, for *COMP*, simply type "=SQRT(0.6806)" in any cell and press return.

Exhibit 4.12 shows the final results of the Fornell-Larcker criterion assessment with the square root of the reflective constructs' AVE on the diagonal and the correlations between the constructs in the lower left triangle. For example, the reflective construct *COMP* has a value of 0.825 for the square root of its AVE, which needs to be compared with all correlation values in the column of *COMP*. Note that for *CUSL*, you need to consider the correlations in both row and column. Overall, the square roots of the AVEs for the reflective constructs *COMP* (0.825), *CUSL* (0.865), and *LIKE* (0.864) are all higher than the correlations of these constructs with other latent variables in the path model.

Alternatively, one can check the cross loadings (click on **Cross Loadings** under **PLS → Quality Criteria** in the **Default Report**). Discriminant validity is established when an indicator's loading on a construct is higher than all of its cross loadings with other constructs. Exhibit 4.13 shows the loadings and cross loadings for every indicator. For example, the indicator *comp_1* has

Exhibit 4.12	Fornell-Larcker Criterion			
	COMP	*CUSA*	*CUSL*	*LIKE*
COMP	0.825			
CUSA	0.436	*Single-item construct*		
CUSL	0.450	0.689	0.865	
LIKE	0.645	0.528	0.615	0.864

Exhibit 4.13	Cross Loadings

	COMP	CUSA	CUSL	LIKE
comp_1	0.8577	0.4643	0.4645	0.6071
comp_2	0.7985	0.2856	0.3038	0.4601
comp_3	0.8176	0.2724	0.2959	0.4971
cusa	0.4356	1.0000	0.6892	0.5284
cusl_1	0.4304	0.5362	0.8328	0.5570
cusl_2	0.3960	0.6546	0.9173	0.5734
cusl_3	0.3413	0.5933	0.8428	0.4612
like_1	0.6022	0.5104	0.5612	0.8793
like_2	0.5227	0.4336	0.5303	0.8702
like_3	0.5443	0.4199	0.4987	0.8430

(Data Preprocessing, Index Values, Model, PLS, Calculation Results, Quality Criteria, Cross Loadings, Latent Variable Correlations, Overview, Total Effects)

the highest value for the loading with its corresponding construct
COMP (0.8577), while all cross loadings with other constructs
are considerably lower (e.g., comp_1 on CUSA: 0.4643). The
same finding holds for the other indicators of COMP as well as
the indicators measuring CUSL and LIKE. Overall, cross loadings as well as the Fornell-Larcker criterion provide evidence for
the constructs' discriminant validity.

Exhibit 4.14 summaries the results of the reflective measurement
model assessment (rounded to three decimal places). As can be seen,
all model evaluation criteria have been met, providing support for the
measures' reliability and validity.

Exhibit 4.14	Results Summary for Reflective Measurement Models					
Latent Variable	Indicators	Loadings	Indicator Reliability	Composite Reliability	AVE	Discriminant Validity?
COMP	comp_1	0.858	0.736	0.865	0.681	Yes
	comp_2	0.796	0.634			
	comp_3	0.818	0.669			
CUSL	cusl_1	0.833	0.694	0.899	0.748	Yes
	cusl_2	0.917	0.841			
	cusl_3	0.843	0.711			
LIKE	like_1	0.880	0.774	0.899	0.747	Yes
	like_2	0.870	0.755			
	like_3	0.843	0.712			

SUMMARY

• **Gain an overview of Stage 5 of the process for using PLS-SEM, which deals with the evaluation of measurement models.** Unlike with CB-SEM, researchers using PLS-SEM cannot draw on a global goodness-of-fit measure to evaluate the overall model fit. In fact, the concept of "fit" cannot be fully transferred to PLS-SEM, which focuses on prediction. In the evaluation of PLS-SEM results, a two-step approach (Stages 5 and 6) needs to be conducted that starts with evaluating the quality of the measurement models (Stage 5). Each type of measurement model (i.e., reflective or formative) has specific evaluation criteria. With reflective measurement models, reliability and validity must be assessed (Stage 5a). In contrast, evaluation of formative measurement models (Stage 5b) involves testing the measures' convergent validity and the significance and relevance of the indicators as well as collinearity among them. Satisfactory outcomes for the measurement model are a prerequisite for evaluating the relationships in the structural model (Stage 6), which includes testing the significance of path coefficients and the coefficient of determination (R^2 value). Depending on the specific model and the goal of the study, researchers may want to use additional advanced analyses (e.g., mediating effects, moderating effects, multigroup analysis, unobserved heterogeneity, impact-performance matrix analysis, or common methods variance).

• **Describe Stage 5a: Evaluating reflectively measured constructs.** The goal of reflective measurement model assessment is to ensure the reliability and validity of the construct measures and therefore provide support for the suitability of their inclusion in the path model. The key criteria include indicator reliability, composite reliability, and convergent validity. In addition, discriminant validity must be achieved, which means that every reflective construct must share more variance with its own indicators than with other constructs in the path model. Reflective constructs are appropriate for PLS-SEM analyses if they meet all these requirements.

• **Use the SmartPLS software to assess reflectively measured constructs in the corporate reputation example.** The case study illustration uses the path model on corporate reputation and the data introduced in Chapter 2. The SmartPLS software provides all relevant results for the evaluation of the measurement models. Tables and figures for this example demonstrate how to correctly report and interpret the PLS-SEM results. This hands-on example not only summarizes the concepts that have been introduced before but also provides additional insights for their practical application.

REVIEW QUESTIONS

1. What is indicator reliability and what is the critical value for this criterion?

2. What is composite reliability and what is the critical value for this criterion?

3. What is average variance extracted and what is the critical value for this criterion?

4. Explain the idea behind discriminant validity and how it can be established.

CRITICAL THINKING QUESTIONS

1. Why are the criteria for reflective measurement model assessment not applicable to formative measures?

2. How do you evaluate single-item constructs? Why is internal consistency reliability a meaningless criterion when evaluating single-item constructs?

3. Should researchers rely purely on statistical evaluation criteria to establish a final set of indicators to use in the path model? Discuss the trade-off between statistical analyses and content validity.

KEY TERMS

AVE: see *Average variance extracted.*

Average variance extracted: a measure of convergent validity. It is the degree to which a latent construct explains the variance of its indicators; see *communality (construct).*

Coefficient of determination: a measure of the proportion of an endogenous construct's variance that is explained by its predictor constructs.

Collinearity: arises when two indicators are highly correlated. When more than two indicators are involved, it is called multicollinearity.

Communality (construct): see *Average variance extracted.*

Communality (item): see *Indicator reliability.*

Composite reliability: a measure of internal consistency reliability, which, unlike Cronbach's alpha, does not assume equal indicator loadings. Should be above 0.70 (in exploratory research, 0.60 to 0.70 is considered acceptable).

Content validity: is a subjective but systematic evaluation of how well the domain content of a construct is captured by its indicators.

Convergent validity: is the extent to which a measure correlates positively with alternative measures of the same construct.

Cronbach's alpha: a measure of internal consistency reliability that assumes equal indicator loadings. In the context of PLS-SEM, composite reliability is considered a more suitable criterion of reliability. However, Cronbach's alpha still represents a conservative measure of internal consistency reliability.

Cross loadings: an indicator's correlation with other constructs in the model.

Discriminant validity: extent to which a construct is truly distinct from other constructs, in terms of how much it correlates with other constructs, as well as how much indicators represent only a single construct.

Evaluation criteria: are used to evaluate the quality of the measurement models and the structural model results in PLS-SEM based on a set of nonparametric evaluation criteria and procedures such as bootstrapping and blindfolding.

Formative measurement model: a measurement model specification in which it is assumed that the construct is caused by the assigned indicators.

Fornell-Larcker criterion: a measure of discriminant validity that compares the square root of each construct's average variance extracted with its correlations with all other constructs in the model.

Indicator reliability: is the square of a standardized indicator's outer loading. It represents how much of the variation in an item is explained by the construct and is referred to as the variance extracted from the item; see *Communality (item)*.

Internal consistency reliability: is a form of reliability used to judge the consistency of results across items on the same test. It determines whether the items measuring a construct are similar in their scores (i.e., if the correlations between the items are large).

Outer loadings: are the estimated relationships in reflective measurement models (i.e., arrows from the latent variable to its indicators). They determine an item's absolute contribution to its assigned construct.

Path coefficients: are estimated path relationships in the structural model (i.e., between the constructs in the model). They correspond to standardized betas in a regression analysis.

R^2 value: see *Coefficient of determination*.

Reflective measurement model: a measurement model specification in which it is assumed that the indicators are caused by the underlying construct.

Reliability: is the consistency of a measure. A measure is reliable (in the sense of test-retest reliability) when it produces consistent outcomes under consistent conditions. The most commonly used measure of reliability is the *internal consistency reliability*.

ρ_c value: see *Composite reliability*.

Single-item construct: a construct that has only a single item measuring it. Since the construct is equal to its measure, the indicator loading is 1.00, making conventional reliability and convergent validity assessments inappropriate.

Structural model: describes the relationships between latent variables. Also referred to as inner model in PLS-SEM.

Validity: is the extent to which a construct's indicators jointly measure what they are supposed to measure.

SUGGESTED READINGS

Boudreau, M.-C., Gefen, D., & Straub, D. W. (2001). Validation in information systems research: A state-of-the-art assessment. *MIS Quarterly*, *25*(1), 1–16.

Chin, W. W. (2010). How to write up and report PLS analyses. In V. Esposito Vinzi, W. W. Chin, J. Henseler, & H. Wang (Eds.), *Handbook of partial least squares: Concepts, methods and applications in marketing and related fields* (pp. 655–690). Berlin: Springer.

Chin, W. W. (1998). The partial least squares approach to structural equation modeling. In G. A. Marcoulides (Ed.), *Modern Methods for Business Research* (pp. 295–358). Mahwah: Erlbaum.

Gefen, D., Rigdon, E. E., & Straub, D. W. (2011). Editor's comment: An update and extension to SEM guidelines for administrative and social science research. *MIS Quarterly, 35*(2), iii–xiv.

Götz, O., Liehr-Gobbers, K., & Krafft, M. (2010). Evaluation of structural equation models using the partial least squares (PLS) approach. In V. Esposito Vinzi, W. W. Chin, J. Henseler & H. Wang (Eds.), *Handbook of partial least squares: Concepts, methods and applications* (Springer Handbooks of Computational Statistics Series, vol. II) (pp. 691–711). Heidelberg, Dordrecht, London, New York: Springer.

Hair, J. F., Ringle, C. M., & Sarstedt, M. (2011). PLS-SEM: Indeed a silver bullet. *Journal of Marketing Theory and Practice, 19,* 139–151.

Hair, J. F., Ringle, C. M., & Sarstedt, M. (2013). Partial least squares structural equation modeling: Rigorous applications, better results and higher acceptance. *Long Range Planning, 46*(1/2), forthcoming.

Hair, J. F., Sarstedt, M., Ringle, C. M., & Mena, J. A. (2012). An assessment of the use of partial least squares structural equation modeling in marketing research. *Journal of the Academy of Marketing Science, 40,* 414–433.

Hulland, J. (1999). Use of partial least squares (PLS) in strategic management research: a review of four recent studies. *Strategic Management Journal, 20*(2), 195–204.

Henseler, J., Ringle, C. M., & Sinkovics, R. R. (2009). The use of partial least squares path modeling in international marketing. *Advances in International Marketing, 20,* 277–320.

Ringle, C. M., Sarstedt, M., & Straub, D. W. (2012). A critical look at the use of PLS-SEM in *MIS Quarterly*. *MIS Quarterly, 36,* iii–xiv.

Straub, D., Boudreau, M. C., & Gefen, D. (2004). Validation guidelines for IS positivist research. *Communications of the Association for Information Systems, 13,* 380–427.

Tenenhaus, M., Esposito Vinzi, V., Chatelin, Y. M., & Lauro, C. (2005). PLS path modeling. *Computational Statistics & Data Analysis, 48*(1), 159–205.

CHAPTER 5

Assessing PLS-SEM Results Part II

Evaluation of the Formative Measurement Models

LEARNING OUTCOMES

1. Explain the criteria used for the assessment of formative measurement models.

2. Understand the basic concepts of bootstrapping for significance testing in PLS-SEM and apply it.

3. Use the SmartPLS software to apply the formative measurement model assessment criteria and learn how to properly report the results of the practical example on corporate reputation.

CHAPTER PREVIEW

Having learned how to evaluate reflective measurement models in the previous chapter (Stage 5a of applying PLS-SEM), our attention now turns to the assessment of formative measurement models (Stage 5b of applying PLS-SEM). The internal consistency perspective that underlies reflective measurement model evaluation cannot be applied to formative models since formative measures do not necessarily covary. Thus, any attempt to purify formative indicators based on correlation patterns can have negative consequences for a construct's content validity. This notion especially holds for PLS-SEM, which assumes that the formative indicators fully capture the content domain of the construct under consideration. Therefore, instead of employing measures such as composite reliability or AVE, researchers should rely on other criteria to assess the quality of formative measurement models.

The chapter begins with an introduction to the criteria needed to evaluate formative measures. This includes a discussion of the bootstrapping routine that facilitates significance testing of PLS-SEM estimates, including formative indicator weights. These criteria are then applied to the corporate reputation model that is extended for this purpose. While the simple model contains only three reflectively measured constructs as well as a single-item construct, the extended model additionally includes four driver constructs of corporate reputation that are measured using formative indicators. This chapter concludes the evaluation of measurement models. In Chapter 6, we move to the evaluation of the structural model (Stage 6 of applying PLS-SEM).

STAGE 5B: ASSESSING RESULTS OF FORMATIVE MEASUREMENT MODELS

Many researchers incorrectly use **reflective measurement model** evaluation criteria to assess the quality of formative measures in PLS-SEM—as revealed by the review of PLS-SEM studies in the strategic management and marketing disciplines by Hair et al. (2012a, 2012b). However, the statistical evaluation criteria for reflective measurement scales cannot be directly transferred to **formative measurement models** where indicators are likely to represent the construct's independent causes and thus do not necessarily correlate highly. Furthermore, formative indicators are assumed to be error free (Diamantopoulos, 2006; Edwards & Bagozzi, 2000), which means the internal consistency reliability concept is inappropriate. Moreover, assessing convergent and discriminant validity using criteria similar to those associated with reflective measurement models is not meaningful when formative indicators and their weights are involved (Chin, 1998). Instead, researchers should focus on establishing **content validity** before empirically evaluating formatively measured constructs. This requires ensuring that the formative indicators capture all (or at least major) facets of the construct. In creating formative constructs, content validity issues are addressed by the **content specification** in which the researcher clearly specifies the domain of content the indicators are intended to measure. Researchers must include a comprehensive set of indicators that fully exhausts the formative construct's domain. Failure to consider all facets of the construct (i.e., relevant formative indicators) entails an exclusion of important parts of the construct itself. In this context, experts' assessment helps safeguard that proper sets of formative indicators have been used. In addition to specific reasons for operationalizing the construct as formative (Chapter 2), researchers should conduct a thorough literature review and ensure a reasonable theoretical grounding when developing measures (Diamantopoulos & Winklhofer, 2001; Jarvis et al., 2003). The evaluation of PLS-SEM results may include reviewing these aspects.

In this chapter, we focus on assessing the empirical PLS-SEM results of formative measurement models following the procedure outlined in Exhibit 5.1. The first step involves assessing the formative measurement model's convergent validity by correlating the formatively measured construct with a reflective measure of the same construct (Step 1). At the indicator level, the question arises as to whether each indicator indeed delivers a contribution to the formative index by carrying the intended meaning. There are two situations in which researchers should critically examine whether a particular indicator should enter the construct or not: First, an indicator's information could be redundant if it exhibits high correlations with other indicators of the same construct. This requires examining collinearity among the indicators (Step 2). Second, an indicator may not significantly contribute to the construct both relatively and absolutely. This can be assessed by examining the (statistical) significance and relevance of the formative indicators (Step 3).

To start with, we consider the convergent validity of formative measurement models, which ensures that the entire domain of the formative construct and all of its relevant facets have been covered by the selected indicators. Next, the assessment of individual indicator validity involves examining potential collinearity issues among the indicators. Last, we answer the question of whether each indicator contributes to forming the index, both absolutely and relatively, by assessing the significance and relevance of the indicators. The key elements displayed in Exhibit 5.1 are addressed in detail, and critical values for the results assessment of each analysis are provided. Moreover, we suggest alternative approaches for situations in which requirements cannot be met in empirical applications.

Exhibit 5.1	Formative Measurement Models Assessment Procedure

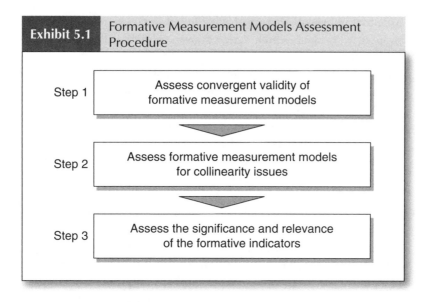

Step 1 — Assess convergent validity of formative measurement models

Step 2 — Assess formative measurement models for collinearity issues

Step 3 — Assess the significance and relevance of the formative indicators

Step 1: Assess Convergent Validity

Convergent validity is the extent to which a measure correlates positively with other measures (indicators) of the same construct. When evaluating formative measurement models, we have to test whether the formatively measured construct is highly correlated with a reflective measure of the same construct. This type of analysis is also known as **redundancy analysis** (Chin, 1998). The term *redundancy analysis* stems from the information in the model being redundant in the sense that it is included in the formative construct and again in the reflective one. Specifically, one has to use the formatively measured construct as an exogenous latent variable predicting an endogenous latent variable operationalized through one or more reflective indicators (Exhibit 5.2). The strength of the path coefficient linking the two constructs is indicative of the validity of the designated set of formative indicators in tapping the construct of interest. Ideally, a magnitude of 0.90 or at least 0.80 and above is desired (Chin, 1998) for the path between $Y_I^{formative}$ and $Y_I^{reflective}$, which translates into an R^2 value of 0.81 or at least 0.64. If the analysis exhibits lack of convergent validity (i.e., the R^2 value of $Y_I^{reflective} < 0.64$), then the formative indicators of the construct $Y_I^{formative}$ do not contribute at a sufficient level to its intended content. The formative constructs need to be theoretically/conceptually refined by exchanging and/or adding indicators.

Note that to execute this approach, the reflective latent variable must be specified in the research design phase and included in data collection for the research.

To identify suitable reflective measures of the construct, researchers can draw on scales from prior research, many of which are reviewed in scale handbooks (e.g., Bearden, Netemeyer, & Haws, 2011; Bruner, James, & Hensel, 2001). Including sets of reflective multi-item measures is not always desirable, however, since they increase the survey length. Long surveys are likely to result in respondent fatigue, decreased response rates, and an increased number of missing values. Furthermore, established reflective measurement instruments may not be available, and constructing a new scale is difficult and time-consuming.

An alternative is to use a global item that summarizes the essence of the construct the formative indicators purport to measure (Sarstedt et al., in press). For the PLS-SEM example on corporate reputation in Chapter 3, an additional statement, "Please assess to which degree [the company] acts in socially conscious ways," was developed and measured on a scale of 0 (*not at all*) to 10 (*extremely*). This question can be used as an endogenous single-item construct to validate the formative measurement of corporate social responsibility (*CSOR*). Later in this chapter, we explain how to access the full data set for this PLS-SEM example on corporate reputation and how to conduct this procedure. Note that while situations that allow for inclusion of single-item measures are rather rare in research (Chapter 2), using a single item for validation purposes is a compromise to balance the problems of questionnaire length and the need to validate formative constructs.

Exhibit 5.2	Redundancy Analysis for Convergent Validity Assessment

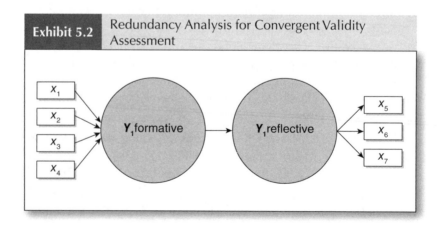

Step 2: Assess Formative Measurement Models for Collinearity Issues

Unlike reflective indicators, which are essentially interchangeable, high correlations are not expected between items in formative measurement models. In fact, high correlations between two formative indicators, also referred to as **collinearity**, can prove problematic from a methodological and interpretational standpoint. Note that when more than two indicators are involved, this situation is called *multicollinearity*. For ease of use, however, we only refer to collinearity in the following discussion.

The most severe form of collinearity occurs if two (or more) formative indicators are entered in the same block of indicators with exactly the same information in them (i.e., they are perfectly correlated). This situation may occur because the same indicator is entered twice or because one indicator is a linear combination of another indicator (e.g., one indicator is a multiple of another indicator such as sales in units and sales in thousand units). Under these circumstances, PLS-SEM cannot estimate one of the two coefficients (technically, a singular matrix occurs during the model estimation; Chapter 3). Collinearity problems may also appear in the structural model (Chapter 6) if, for example, redundant indicators are used as single items to measure two (or more) constructs. If this occurs, researchers need to eliminate the redundant indicators. While prefect collinearity occurs rather seldom, high levels of collinearity are much more common.

High levels of collinearity between formative indicators are a crucial issue because they have an impact on the estimation of weights and their statistical significance. More specifically, in practice, high levels of collinearity often affect the results of analyses in two respects. First, collinearity boosts the standard errors and thus reduces the ability to demonstrate that the estimated weights are significantly different from zero. This issue is especially problematic in PLS-SEM analyses based on smaller sample sizes where standard errors are generally larger due to sampling error. Second, high collinearity can result in the weights being incorrectly estimated, as well as in their signs being reversed. The following example (Exhibit 5.3) illustrates sign reversal due to high correlations between two formative indicators.

On examining the correlation matrix in Exhibit 5.3, note that indicators x_1 and x_2 are both positively correlated with construct Y_1 (0.38 and 0.14, respectively) but have a higher intercorrelation (0.68). Although both bivariate correlations of the indicators are positive with

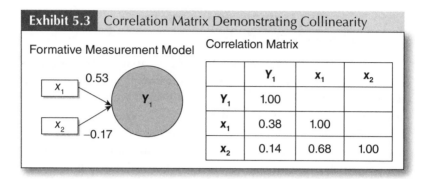

Exhibit 5.3 Correlation Matrix Demonstrating Collinearity

Formative Measurement Model Correlation Matrix

	Y_1	x_1	x_2
Y_1	1.00		
x_1	0.38	1.00	
x_2	0.14	0.68	1.00

the construct Y_1 in this situation, and the two indicators are positively intercorrelated, when the final parameter estimates are computed in the last stage of the algorithm (Chapter 3), the outer weight of x_1 is positive (0.53), whereas the outer weight of x_2 is negative (–0.17). This demonstrates a situation where high collinearity reverses the signs of the weaker indicator (i.e., the indicator less correlated with the construct).

How to Assess Collinearity and Deal With Critical Levels

To assess the level of collinearity, researchers should compute the **tolerance.** The tolerance represents the amount of variance of one formative indicator not explained by the other indicators in the same block. For example, in a block of formative indicators, the tolerance for the first indicator x_1 can be obtained in two steps:

1. Take the first formative indicator x_1 and regress it on all remaining indicators in the same block. Calculate the proportion of variance of x_1 associated with the other indicators $(R^2_{x_1})$.

2. Compute the tolerance for indicator x_1 (TOL_{x_1}) using $1 - R^2_{x_1}$. For example, if the other indicators explain 75% of the first indicator's variance (i.e., $R^2_{x_1} = 0.75$), the tolerance for x_1 is 0.25 $(TOL_{x_1} = 1.00 - 0.75 = 0.25)$.

A related measure of collinearity is the **variance inflation factor** (**VIF**), defined as the reciprocal of the tolerance (i.e., $VIF_{x_1} = 1/TOL_{x_1}$). Therefore, a tolerance value of 0.25 for x_1 (TOL_{x_1}) translates into a VIF value of $1/0.25 = 4.00$ for x_1 (VIF_{x_1}). The term VIF is derived from the square root of the VIF ($\sqrt{VIF}$) being the degree to which the standard error has been increased due to the presence of collinearity. In the example above, a VIF value of 4.00 therefore implies that the standard error has been doubled ($\sqrt{4} = 2.00$) due to collinearity.

The tolerance and VIF are both provided in the regression analysis output of most popular software packages such as R, IBM SPSS Statistics, and Statistica. Especially when nonsignificant weights occur, researchers should pay close attention to these collinearity diagnostic measures. In the context of PLS-SEM, a tolerance value of 0.20 or lower and a VIF value of 5 and higher respectively indicate a potential collinearity problem (Hair, Ringle, & Sarstedt, 2011). These levels indicate that 80% of an indicator's variance is accounted for by the remaining formative indicators associated with the same construct. Besides the VIF, one may also consider using the condition index (CI) to assess the presence of critical collinearity levels in formative measurement models (Götz, Liehr-Gobbers, & Krafft, 2010).

If the level of collinearity is very high (as indicated by a tolerance value of 0.20 or lower and a VIF value of 5 or higher), one should consider removing one of the corresponding indicator(s). However, this requires that the remaining indicators still sufficiently capture the construct's content from a theoretical perspective. Constructing higher-order constructs (Chapter 7) or combining the collinear indicators into a single (new) composite indicator (i.e., an index)—for example, by using their average values, their weighted average value, or their factor scores—are other options for treating collinearity problems. However, the latter step is not without problems because the individual effects of the indicators become confounded, which can have adverse consequences for the content validity of the index.

Exhibit 5.4 displays the process to assess collinearity in formative measurement models based on the VIF. Outer weights in formative measurement models should be analyzed for their significance and relevance only if collinearity is not at a critical level. When this is not the case and collinearity issues cannot be treated, one cannot use and interpret the results of the outer weights in formative measurement models. As a consequence, the formative measurement has to be dismissed. That is, the results of the analysis must not be interpreted and the operationalization of the construct has to be reconsidered.

| Exhibit 5.4 | Collinearity Assessment in Formative Measurement Models Using the VIF |

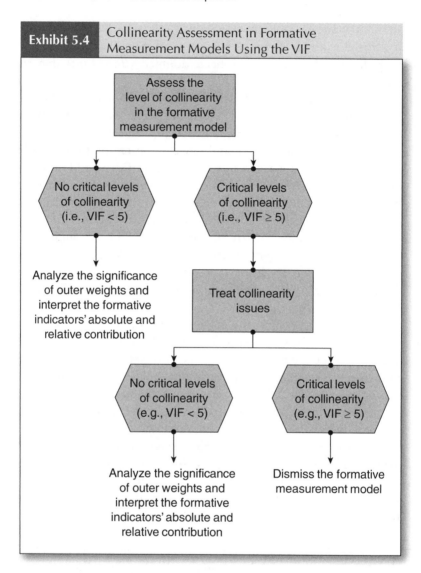

Step 3: Assess the Significance and Relevance of the Formative Indicators

Another important criterion for evaluating the contribution of a formative indicator, and thereby its relevance, is its **outer weight.** The outer weight is the result of a multiple regression (Hair et al., 2010) with the latent variable scores as the dependent variable and the formative indicators as the independent variables (see PLS-SEM algorithm in Chapter 3). Since the construct itself is formed by its underlying formative indicators as a linear combination of the indicator scores and the outer weights in the formative measurement model, running such a multiple regression analysis yields an R^2 value of 1.0 (i.e., no error variance; 100% of the construct is explained by the indicators). The values of the outer weights can be compared with each other and can therefore be used to determine each indicator's **relative contribution** to the construct, or its relative importance. The estimated values of outer weights in formative measurement models are frequently smaller than the outer loadings of reflective indicators. The key question that arises is whether formative indicators truly contribute to forming the construct. To answer this question, we must test if the outer weights in formative measurement models are significantly different from zero by means of the bootstrapping procedure (note that bootstrapping also plays a crucial role in the evaluation of the structural model path coefficients; Chapter 6).

In bootstrapping, subsamples are randomly drawn (with replacement) from the original set of data. Each subsample is then used to estimate the model. This process is repeated until a large number of random subsamples have been created, typically about 5,000. The parameter estimates (in this case, the indicator weights) estimated from the subsamples are used to derive standard errors for the estimates. With this information, t values are calculated to assess each indicator weight's significance. We explain bootstrapping in more detail later in this chapter.

It is important to note that the values of the formative indicator weights are influenced by other relationships in the model (see the PLS-SEM algorithm in Chapter 3). Hence, the exogenous formative construct(s) can have different contents and meanings depending on the endogenous constructs used as outcomes. This is also known as **interpretational confounding** and represents a situation in which the empirically observed meaning between the construct and its measures differs from the theoretically imposed meaning (Kim, Shin, & Grover, 2010). Such outcomes are not desirable since they limit the generalizability of the results (Bagozzi, 2007). Therefore, comparing formative constructs across several PLS path models with different setups (e.g., different endogenous latent variables) should be approached with caution.

*Implications of the Numbers of Indicators Used
on the Outer Weights*

With larger numbers of formative indicators used to measure a construct, it becomes more likely that one or more indicators will have low or even nonsignificant outer weights. Unlike reflective measurement models, where the number of indicators has little bearing on the measurement results, formative measurement has an inherent limit to the number of indicators that can retain a statistically significant weight (Cenfetelli & Bassellier, 2009). Specifically, when indicators are assumed to be uncorrelated, the maximum possible outer weight is $1/\sqrt{n}$, where n is the number of indicators. For example, with 2 (or 5 or 10) uncorrelated indicators, the maximum possible outer weight is $1/\sqrt{2} = 0.707$ (or $1/\sqrt{5} = 0.447$ or $1/\sqrt{10} = 0.316$). Similarly, just as the maximum possible outer weight declines with the number of indicators, the average value of outer weights significantly declines with larger numbers of items. Thus, it becomes more likely that additional formative indicators will become nonsignificant.

To deal with the potential impact of a large number of indicators, Cenfetelli and Bassellier (2009) propose grouping indicators into two or more distinct constructs. This approach of course requires the indicators groups to be conceptually aligned and that the grouping make sense from a theoretical and conceptual perspective. For example, the indicators of the *performance* construct, which we introduce as a driver construct of corporate reputation later in this chapter (see Exhibit 5.13), could be grouped into two sets, as shown in Exhibit 5.5. The indicator items "[the company] is a very well-managed company" (*perf_1*) and "[the company] has a clear vision about the future" (*perf_5*) could be used as reflective indicators of a separate construct called *management competence*. Similarly, the indicators "[the company] is an economically stable company" (*perf_2*), "I assess the business risk for [the company] as modest compared to its competitors" (*perf_3*), and "I think that [the company] has growth potential" (*perf_4*) could be used as reflective indicators of a second construct labeled *economic performance*. An alternative is to create a formative-formative hierarchical component model (Chapter 7). The second-order component itself (*performance*) is then formed by the formatively measured first-order components (*management competence* and *economic performance*) that were previously identified in the grouping process (Exhibit 5.5).

Exhibit 5.5   Example of a Second-Order Construct

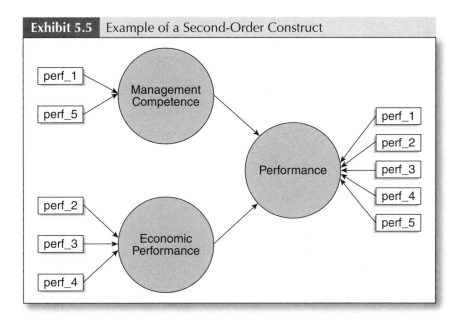

Nonsignificant indicator weights should not automatically be interpreted as indicative of poor measurement model quality. Rather, researchers should also consider a formative indicator's **absolute contribution** to (or **absolute importance** for) its construct—that is, the information an indicator provides without considering any other indicators. The absolute contribution is given by the formative indicator's **outer loading,** which is always provided along with the indicator weights. Different from the outer weights, the outer loadings stem from single regressions of each indicator on its corresponding construct (which in PLS-SEM is equivalent to the bivariate correlation between each indicator and the coonstruct).

When an indicator's outer weight is nonsignificant but its outer loading is high (i.e., above 0.50), the indicator should be interpreted as absolutely important but not as relatively important. In this situation, the indicator would generally be retained. But when an indicator has a nonsignificant weight and the outer loading is below 0.50, the researcher should decide whether to retain or delete the indicator by examining its theoretical relevance and potential content overlap with other indicators of the same construct.

If the theory-driven conceptualization of the construct strongly supports retaining the indicator (e.g., by means of expert assessment), it should be kept in the formative measurement model. But, if the conceptualization does not strongly support an indicator's inclusion, the nonsignificant indicator should most likely be removed from further analysis. In contrast, if the outer loading is low and nonsignificant, there is no empirical support for the indicator's relevance in providing content to the formative index (Cenfetelli & Bassellier, 2009). Therefore, such an indicator should be removed from the formative measurement model.

Eliminating formative indicators that do not meet threshold levels in terms of their contribution has, from an empirical perspective, almost no effect on the parameter estimates when reestimating the model. Nevertheless, formative indicators should never be discarded simply on the basis of statistical outcomes. Before removing an indicator from the formative measurement model, you need to check its relevance from a content validity point of view. Again, omitting a formative indicator means that you omit some of the construct's content. Exhibit 5.6 summarizes the decision-making process for keeping or deleting formative indicators.

In summary, the evaluation of formative measurement models requires establishing the measures' convergent validity, assessing the indicators' collinearity, and analyzing the indicators' relative and absolute contributions, including their significance. Exhibit 5.7 summarizes the rules of thumb for evaluating formative measurement models.

BOOTSTRAPPING PROCEDURE

Concept

PLS-SEM does not assume the data are normally distributed, which implies that parametric significance tests used in regression analyses cannot be applied to test whether coefficients such as outer weights, outer loadings, and path coefficients are significant. Instead, PLS-SEM relies on a nonparametric bootstrap procedure (Davison & Hinkley, 1997; Efron & Tibshirani, 1986) to test coefficients for their significance.

In **bootstrapping**, a large number of subsamples (i.e., **bootstrap samples**) are drawn from the original sample with replacement. Replacement means that each time an observation is drawn at random from the sampling population, it is returned to the sampling population before the next observation is drawn (i.e., the

Exhibit 5.6	Decision-Making Process for Keeping or Deleting Formative Indicators

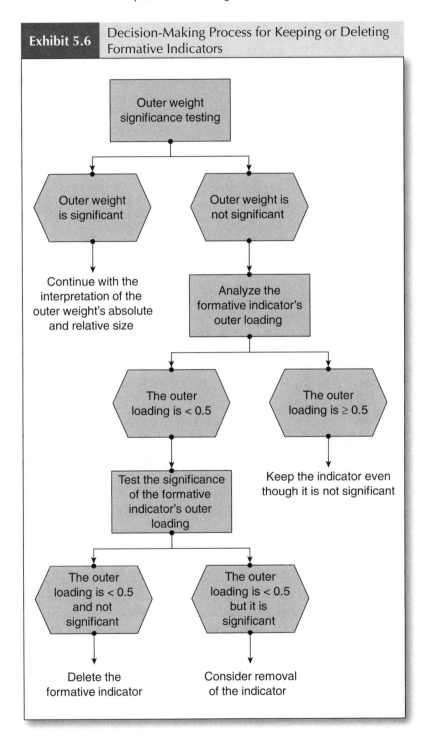

Exhibit 5.7	Rules of Thumb for the Evaluation of Formative Measurement Indicators

- Assess the formative construct's convergent validity by examining its correlation with an alternative measure of the construct, using reflective measures or a global single item (redundancy analysis). The correlation between the constructs should be 0.80 or higher.
- Collinearity of indicators: Each indicator's tolerance (VIF) value should be higher than 0.20 (lower than 5). Otherwise, consider eliminating indicators, merging indicators into a single index, or creating higher-order constructs to treat collinearity problems.
- Examine each indicator's outer weight (relative importance) and outer loading (absolute importance) and use bootstrapping to assess their significance.
- When an indicator's weight is significant, there is empirical support to retain the indicator.
- When an indicator's weight is not significant but the corresponding item loading is relatively high (i.e., > 0.50), the indicator should generally be retained.
- If both the outer weight and outer loading are nonsignificant, there is no empirical support to retain the indicator and it should be removed from the model.

population from which the observations are drawn always contains all the same elements). Therefore, an observation for a certain subsample can be selected more than once or may not be selected at all for subsample. The number of bootstrap samples should be high but must be at least equal to the number of valid observations in the data set. As a rule, 5,000 bootstrap samples are recommended.

Exhibit 5.8 illustrates how the bootstrap technique works. It is important to note that the size of each bootstrap sample must be explicitly specified. The accepted guideline is that each bootstrap sample should have the same number of observations (usually termed **bootstrap cases** in PLS-SEM software's bootstrap modules) as the original sample. For example, if the original sample has 130 valid (!) observations, then each of the 5,000 bootstrap samples should contain 130 cases. Otherwise, the significance testing results are systematically biased. Note that when using casewise replacement to treat missing values, it is crucial to be aware of the final number of observations used for model estimation.

Exhibit 5.8 The PLS-SEM Bootstrap Routine

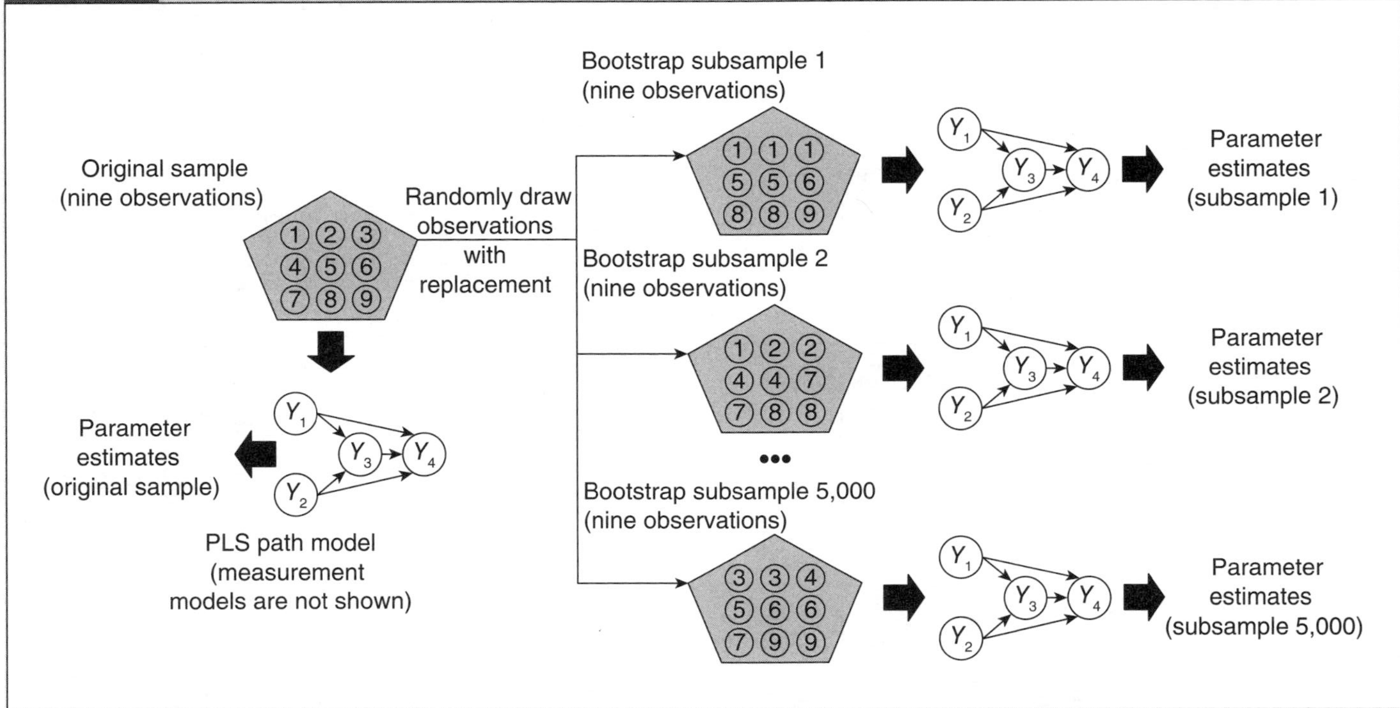

The bootstrap samples are used to estimate the PLS path model. That is, when using 5,000 bootstrap samples, 5,000 PLS path models are estimated. The estimates of the coefficients form a bootstrap distribution, which can be viewed as an approximation of the sampling distribution. Based on this distribution, it is possible to determine the standard error and the standard deviation of the estimated coefficients. We refer to the estimated bootstrap standard error by using se^*, whereby the asterisk denotes that the estimated standard error has been obtained by using the bootstrap method. The bootstrap distribution can be viewed as a reasonable approximation of an estimated coefficient's distribution in the population, and its standard deviation can be used as proxy for the parameter's standard error in the population.

For example, the bootstrap method allows for the statistical testing of the hypothesis that a specific outer weight w_1 is in fact zero in the population. Using the standard error derived from the bootstrap distribution, a Student's t test can be calculated to test whether w_1 is significantly different from zero (i.e., $H_0: w_1 = 0$ and $H_1: w_1 \neq 0$) using the following formula:

$$t = \frac{w_1}{se^*_{w_1}},$$

where w_1 is the weight obtained from the original model estimation using the original set of empirical data, and $se^*_{w_1}$ is the bootstrap standard error of w_1.

As indicated by its name, the test statistic follows a t distribution with **degrees of freedom** (*df*) (which is the number of values in the final calculation of the test statistic that are free to vary) equal to the number of observations minus 1. As a general rule, the t distribution is well approximated by the normal (Gaussian) distribution for more than 30 observations. As the number of observations usually exceeds this threshold, the normal (Gaussian) quantiles can be used to determine **critical t values** (or **theoretical t values**) for significance testing. Therefore, when the size of the resulting **empirical t value** is above 1.96, we can assume that the path coefficient is significantly different from zero at a significance level of 5% ($\alpha = 0.05$; two-tailed test). The critical t values for significance levels of 1% ($\alpha = 0.01$; two-tailed test) and 10% ($\alpha = 0.10$; two-tailed test) probability of error are 2.57 and 1.65, respectively.

An important consideration in the use of bootstrapping in PLS-SEM is that the signs of the latent variable scores are indeterminate (Wold, 1985). This **sign indeterminacy** of latent variable scores may, however, result in arbitrary sign changes in the bootstrap estimates of the coefficients, compared with the estimates obtained from the original sample. Such occurrence of sign changes "pulls" the mean value of bootstrap results (e.g., for an outer weight w_1) toward zero and inflates the corresponding bootstrap standard error $(se_{w_1}^*)$ upward, thereby decreasing the t value.

Three options for dealing with sign changes have been proposed: the **no sign change option,** the **individual-level sign change option,** and the **construct-level sign change option.** *No sign change* simply means to not do anything and to accept the negative impact of sign changes on the results for the empirical t value. The *individual-level sign change* option reverses signs if an estimate for a bootstrap sample results in a different sign compared with that resulting from the original sample. Thus, the signs in the measurement and structural models of each bootstrap sample are made consistent with the signs in the original sample to avoid sign change–related problems. A third option, the *construct-level sign change*, considers a group of coefficients (e.g., all outer weights) simultaneously and compares the signs of the original PLS path model estimation with those of a bootstrapping subsample. If the majority of signs need to be reversed in a bootstrap run to match the signs of the model estimation using the original sample, all signs are reversed in that bootstrap run. Otherwise, no signs are changed. As such, the construct-level sign change is a compromise between the two extremes of no sign changes and individual-level sign changes: Some signs are changed for improvement, but the results do not 100% match the signs of the original model estimation.

In practice, the results of the three different options usually do not differ much, provided that the original estimates are not close to zero. However, if the original estimates are close to zero, the sign reversal may systematically reduce the bootstrapping standard error. We recommend using the no sign change option because it results in the most conservative outcome. If coefficients are significant under the no sign change option, they will also be significant when using the alternative options. Otherwise, the individual sign change option should be used since it provides the highest t values when comparing the three sign change options. If the result still is not significant, you cannot reject the null hypothesis and conclude that the coefficient is not significant. However, if the result is not significant when using the no sign option but significant when using the individual sign change option, you should use the construct-level change option as a good compromise between the two settings. Exhibit 5.9 illustrates how to proceed if the recommended no sign change option delivers a nonsignificant outcome.

Bootstrap Confidence Intervals

Instead of just reporting the significance of a parameter, it is valuable to also report the **bootstrap confidence interval** that provides additional information on the stability of a coefficient estimate. The confidence interval is the range into which the true population parameter will fall assuming a certain level of confidence (e.g., 95%). In a PLS-SEM context, we also talk about bootstrap confidence intervals because the construction of the interval is based on the standard errors obtained from the bootstrapping procedure. How is this kind of significance testing applied in PLS-SEM? For example, if an outer weight w_1 has a bootstrap standard error ($se^*_{w_1}$), then the corresponding approximate $1 - \alpha$ (two-tailed) confidence interval is

$$w_1 \pm z_{1-\alpha/2} \cdot se^*_{w_1},$$

where $z_{1-\alpha/2}$ stems from the standard normal (z) distribution table. If the probability of error is 5% (i.e., $\alpha = 0.05$), then $z_{1-\alpha/2} = z_{0.975} = 1.96$. Thus, the lower bound of the bootstrap confidence interval is $w_1 - 1.96 \cdot se^*_{w_1}$, and the upper bound is $w_1 + 1.96 \cdot se^*_{w_1}$. You can write down the resulting values directly in this way: $[w_1 - 1.96 \cdot se^*_{w_1}; w_1 + 1.96 \cdot se^*_{w_1}]$. A null hypothesis H_0 that w_1 equals zero (i.e., H_0: $w_1 = 0$) in the population is rejected at a given level α, if the corresponding ($1 - \alpha$) bootstrap confidence interval does *not* include zero. In other words, if a confidence interval for an estimated coefficient such as an outer weight w_1 does not include zero, the hypothesis that w_1 equals zero is rejected, and we assume a significant effect. In addition to the significance testing aspect, the range of the confidence interval provides the researcher with an indication of how stable the estimate is. If the confidence interval of a coefficient is wider, then its stability is lower.

Exhibit 5.9	Recommended Use of Bootstrap Sign Change Options

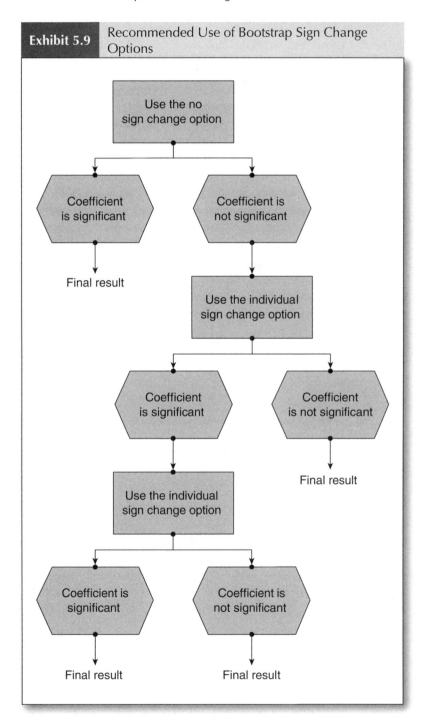

For example, assume that an outer weight of an indicator in a formative measurement model has the value 0.25 and a bootstrap standard error of 0.08. For a probability of error of 1% (i.e., $\alpha = 0.01$), the $z_{1-\alpha/2} = z_{0.995} = 2.57$, and the lower bound has a value of 0.25 − 2.57 · 0.08 = 0.044, while the upper bound has a value of 0.25 + 2.57 · 0.08 = 0.455. Thus, the bootstrap confidence interval is [0.044; 0.455]. Since zero does not fall in this confidence interval, we conclude that the outer weight of 0.25 is significant at the 1% probability of error level.

Extensions of this significance testing approach include the bias-corrected bootstrap confidence interval as suggested by Gudergan, Ringle, Wende, and Will (2008) and further described by Henseler et al. (2009) and Sarstedt, Henseler, and Ringle (2011). Since the bootstrap confidence intervals and the bias-corrected bootstrap intervals usually do not differ much, interested readers are referred to these sources for further details. Exhibit 5.10 summarizes the rules of thumb for significance testing using the bootstrap routine in PLS-SEM.

Exhibit 5.10   Rules of Thumb for the Bootstrap Routine

- The number of bootstrap samples must be larger than the number of valid observations in the original data set but should be higher; generally, 5,000 bootstrap samples are recommended.
- The number of observations (or cases) of each bootstrapping sub-sample must be exactly as large as the number of valid observations in the original data set.
- The bootstrap routine provides the standard error of an estimated coefficient. This information allows you to determine the empirical t value. As the t distribution is well approximated by the normal distribution for more than 30 observations, the quantiles from a normal distribution can generally be used for significance testing. Popular critical (theoretical) t values for a two-tailed test are 1.65 ($\alpha = 0.10$), 1.96 ($\alpha = 0.05$), or 2.57 ($\alpha = 0.01$). If the empirical t value is higher than the critical t value at a selected α level, then the coefficient is significantly different from zero.
- Use the no sign change option to obtain the most conservative empirical t values when running the bootstrap routine.
- Consider reporting bootstrap confidence intervals.

CASE STUDY ILLUSTRATION—EVALUATION OF FORMATIVE MEASUREMENT MODELS

Extending the Simple Path Model

The simple path model introduced in Chapter 2 described the relationships between the two dimensions of corporate reputation (i.e., competence and likeability) as well as the two outcome variables, customer satisfaction and loyalty. While the simple model is useful to explain how corporate reputation affects customer satisfaction and customer loyalty, it does not indicate how companies can manage (i.e., improve) their corporate reputation effectively.

Schwaiger (2004) identified four driver constructs of corporate reputation that companies can steer by means of corporate-level marketing activities. Specifically, the driver constructs of corporate reputation are (1) the quality of a company's products and services as well as its quality of customer orientation (*QUAL*), (2) its economic and managerial performance (*PERF*), (3) a company's corporate social responsibility (*CSOR*), and (4) its attractiveness (*ATTR*). All four driver constructs are related to the competence and likeability dimensions of corporate reputation. Exhibit 5.11 shows the constructs and their relationships, which represent the extended structural model for our PLS-SEM example in the remaining chapters of the text. To summarize, the extended corporate reputation model has three main conceptual/theoretical components: (1) the target constructs of interest (namely, *CUSA* and *CUSL*); (2) the two corporate reputation dimensions, *COMP* and *LIKE*, that represent key determinants of the target constructs; and (3) the four exogenous driver constructs (i.e., *ATTR, CSOR, PERF,* and *QUAL*) of the two corporate reputation dimensions.

While the endogenous latent variables on the right-hand side in Exhibit 5.11 include a single-item construct (i.e., *CUSA*) and reflective constructs (i.e., *COMP, CUSA,* and *LIKE*), the four new driver constructs (i.e., exogenous latent variables) on the left-hand side of the exhibit (i.e., *ATTR, CSOR, PERF,* and *QUAL*) have formative measurement models in accordance with their role in the reputation model (Schwaiger, 2004). Specifically, the four new constructs are measured by a total of 21 formative indicators that have been derived from literature research, qualitative studies, and quantitative pretests (for more details, see Schwaiger, 2004). Exhibit 5.12 shows a complete list of the formative indicators and the corresponding survey questions.

| Exhibit 5.11 | The Conceptual/Theoretical Model |

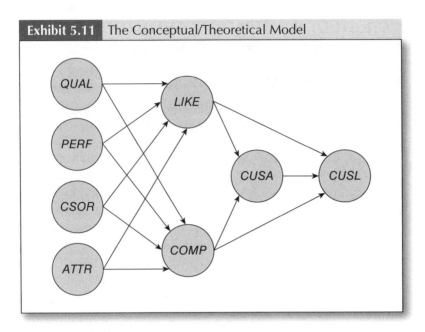

Again, we use a data set with 344 observations for our empirical PLS-SEM analyses. Unlike in the simple model that we used in the prior chapters, we now also have to consider the formative measurement models when deciding on the minimum sample size required to estimate the model. The maximum number of arrowheads pointing at a particular construct occurs in the measurement model of *QUAL*. All other formatively measured constructs have fewer indicators. Similarly, there are fewer arrows pointing at each of the endogenous constructs in the structural model. Therefore, when building on the 10 times rule of thumb, we would need 8 · 10 = 80 observations. Alternatively, following Cohen's (1992) recommendations for multiple OLS regression analysis or running a power analysis using the G*Power program, one would need 84 observations to detect R^2 values of around 0.25, assuming a significance level of 5% and a statistical power of 80% (Chapter 1).

The SmartPLS project and data files for the extended corporate reputation model can be downloaded at http://www.pls-sem.com (i.e., Corporate_Reputation_Extended.zip). Click with the right mouse button on **Corporate_Reputation_Extended.zip** and save the file on your hard drive. Then, extract the **Corporate_Reputation_Extended.zip** file (e.g., in the folder C:\SmartPLS\). The name of the SmartPLS project file is **Corporate Reputation Extended.splsp**, whereby .splsp

Exhibit 5.12	Indicators of the Formative Measurement Models

	Quality (QUAL)
qual_1	The products/services offered by [the company] are of high quality.
qual_2	In my opinion [the company] tends to be an innovator, rather than an imitator with respect to [industry].
qual_3	I think that [the company]'s products/services offer good value for money.
qual_4	The services [the company] offers are good.
qual_5	Customer concerns are held in high regard at [the company].
qual_6	[The company] seems to be a reliable partner for customers.
qual_7	I regard [the company] as a trustworthy company.
qual_8	I have a lot of respect for [the company].
	Performance (PERF)
perf_1	[The company] is a very well-managed company.
perf_2	[The company] is an economically stable company.
perf_3	I assess the business risk for [the company] as modest compared to its competitors.
perf_4	I think that [the company] has growth potential.
perf_5	[The company] has a clear vision about the future of the company.
	Corporate Social Responsibility (CSOR)
csor_1	[The company] behaves in a socially conscious way.
csor_2	I have the impression that [the company] is forthright in giving information to the public.
csor_3	I have the impression that [the company] has a fair attitude toward competitors.
csor_4	[The company] is concerned about the preservation of the environment.

(Continued)

Exhibit 5.12	(Continued)
csor_5	I have the feeling that [the company] is not only concerned about profits.
	Attractiveness (ATTR)
attr_1	In my opinion [the company] is successful in attracting high-quality employees.
attr_2	I could see myself working at [the company].
attr_3	I like the physical appearance of [the company] (company, buildings, shops, etc.).

stands for a project that can be directly imported into the SmartPLS software (Ringle, Wende, & Will, 2005). Run the SmartPLS software and click on **File → Import** in the menu. When the Import box appears on the screen, click on **Next** and then on **Browse** to locate and import **Corporate Reputation Extended.splsp** as described in detail in Chapter 2. Thereafter, a new project appears with the name **Corporate Reputation Extended** in the SmartPLS **Projects** window on the left-hand side. This project contains several models (.splsm files) and the data set **Full Data.csv.** Highlight **Corporate Reputation Extended** and click on the option that expands all (· ▣↕). Several files will be shown. The files include **Base Model.splsm, Convergent Validity ATTR. splsm, Convergent Validity CSOR.splsm,** and so forth, plus a data file called **Full Data.csv.** Next, double-click on **Base Model.splsm,** and the extended PLS path model for the corporate reputation example opens as displayed in Exhibit 5.13.

Alternatively, if you want to practice using the SmartPLS software, you can create the extended model by yourself. Following the description in Chapter 2, we use the SmartPLS software to extend the simple model. For this purpose, right-click on the **Corporate Reputation** project in the **Projects** window and select the option **Copy Resource** (Exhibit 5.14). A menu opens and gives you the option to select a name for the copy of the existing project; for example, type in the name **Corporate Reputation Extended** or something similar. By clicking on **OK**, SmartPLS will copy the initial project under the new name in the project folder window. Unfold the **Corporate Reputation Extended** project by clicking on the plus symbol in the **Projects** window (to the left of your new file name). You will then see the same files in the **Corporate Reputation Extended** project as were in the

Exhibit 5.13 Extended Model in SmartPLS

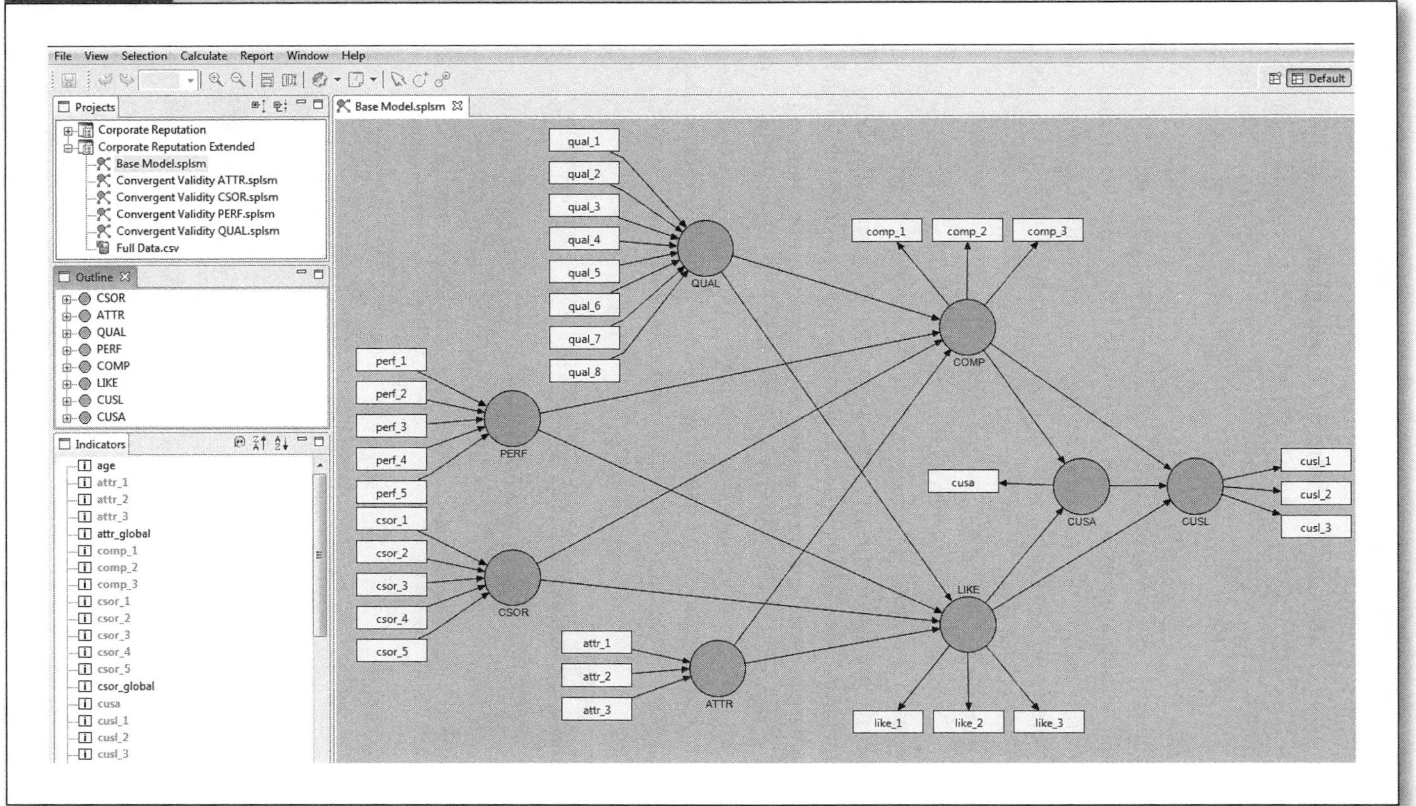

Corporate Reputation project: (1) the SmartPLS model **Simple Model .splsm** and (2) the data set **Full Data.csv.**

Next, rename the **Simple Model.splsm** file as **Base Model .splsm.** After clicking with the right mouse button on the **Simple Model.splsm** file in the **Corporate Reputation Extended** project (→ SmartPLS **Projects** window), a dialog with several options opens (Exhibit 5.14). Select the **Rename Resource** option in this dialog and enter **Base Model,** and then click **OK** (the file extension .splsm will automatically be added to your new model name). After unfolding the **Corporate Reputation Extended** project in the **Projects** window, you will find that **Simple Model.splsm** has been renamed as **Base Model.splsm.** Moreover, you will see the **Full Data.csv** file in the new project.

Now, you can start extending the simple PLS path model on corporate reputation. Double-click on the **Base Model.splsm** file in the **Corporate Reputation Extended** project—which is the copy of the **Simple Model.splsm** file—and the existing PLS path model elements will open it in the **Modeling** window. Click on the **Modeling** window and select everything by pressing on the CTRL and A keys on your keyboard. Move all existing PLS path model elements further to the right-hand side of the **Modeling** window (simply left-click and hold down anywhere on the model, and move your mouse to the right).

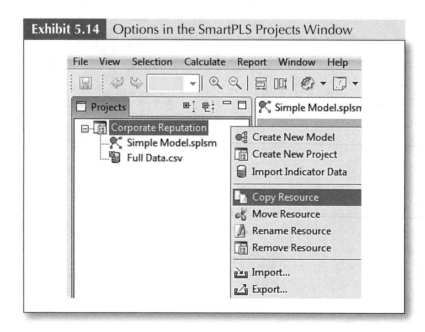

Exhibit 5.14 Options in the SmartPLS Projects Window

Note that if your simple model filled the screen, you may wish to reduce the model size by clicking on the minus sign at the top left of the **Modeling** window. Next, click the 💣 button in the menu (i.e., **Switch to Insertion Mode**)—alternatively, press the CTRL and 2 keys on your keyboard—and place four additional constructs into the **Modeling** window. Refer to Exhibit 5.13 to see where to place the new constructs. Right-click on any of the constructs, and a dialog box opens with several options (Exhibit 5.15). The **Rename Object** option allows you to rename each construct in accordance with the extended model setup shown in Exhibit 5.13.

Then, draw the path relationships between the constructs. Click the 🔗 button in the menu (i.e., **Switch to Connection Mode**)—alternatively, press the CTRL and 3 keys on your keyboard—and connect the new constructs with the existing ones in the **Modeling** window as shown in Exhibit 5.13. To draw path relationships, you need to first click on the starting constructs and then on the target construct.

Finally, drag and drop the corresponding indicators from the **Indicators** window to each of the constructs. Initially, the indicators will be associated with the constructs as reflective indicators. To change the measurement model setup to formative, right-click on the construct again and select **Invert Measurement Model** (Exhibit 5.15).

Exhibit 5.15	Options in the SmartPLS Modeling Window

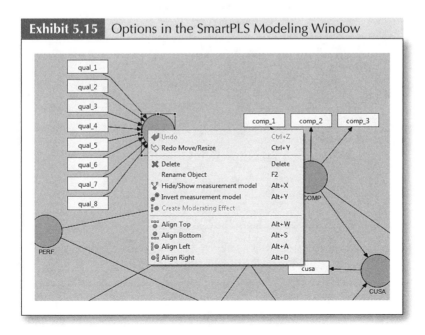

Doing so will switch the indicators from reflective to formative. The final model in your SmartPLS **Modeling** window should look similar to the one shown in Exhibit 5.13. At this point, be sure to save your newly drawn full model.

Once the model is set up, we click on **Calculate → PLS Algorithm** and run PLS-SEM using the options presented in Chapter 3 (i.e., path weighting scheme, 300 iterations, abort criterion: 1.0E-5) and as displayed in Exhibit 5.16. Just like the reduced data set that we used in the previous chapters, the **Full Data.csv** data set has almost no missing values. Only the indicators *cusl_1* (three missing values; 0.87% of all responses on this indicator), *cusl_2* (four missing values; 1.16% of all responses on this indicator), *cusl_3* (three missing values; 0.87% of all responses on this indicator), and *cusa* (one missing value; 0.29% of all responses on this indicator) have missing

Exhibit 5.16 Settings to Start the PLS-SEM Algorithm

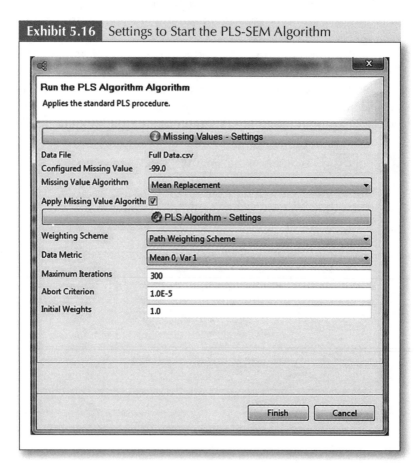

values. Since the number of missing values is relatively small (i.e., less than 5% missing values per indicator; Chapter 2), we use mean value replacement instead of casewise deletion to treat the missing values when running the PLS-SEM algorithm (Exhibit 5.16).

When the PLS-SEM algorithm terminates, go to **Report → Default Report** and check whether the algorithm converged (Chapter 3). For this example, the PLS-SEM algorithm will stop when the maximum number of **300** iterations or the stop criterion of **1.0E-5** (i.e., 0.00001) has been reached. Go to **PLS → Calculation Results → Stop Criterion Changes** in the default report to determine how the algorithm stopped. If the algorithm stopped based on the stop criterion and not the number of iterations, then continue with the measurement model evaluation. If the algorithm stopped based on the number of iterations (which is, however, practically never the case), the calculation results can't be reliably interpreted and the model setup and/or data need to be reconsidered.

The results presentation in the **Modeling** window gives you a first overview of the outcomes. As shown in Exhibit 5.17, you see the standardized outer weights for the formative measurement models (e.g., *QUAL*), standardized outer loadings for the reflective measurement models (e.g., *CUSL*), and a 1.000 for the relationship between the *CUSA* construct and its single-item measure. In the latter case, the outer relationship is always 1 regardless of whether the mode of the single-item construct is formative or reflective. Moreover, the standardized path relationships between the constructs in the structural model are shown as well as the R^2 values for the endogenous latent variables (i.e., the values in the circles). Note that a value of 0.000 in the circles does not denote zero R^2 values. Instead, it means there are no R^2 values since those constructs are exogenous latent variables in the structural model (sources and not targets), which, by definition, have no R^2 value.

Reflective Measurement Model Evaluation

An important characteristic of PLS-SEM is that the model estimates always depend on the model under consideration. For instance, eliminating or adding certain indicators or constructs will also have an effect on the model estimates in different parts of the

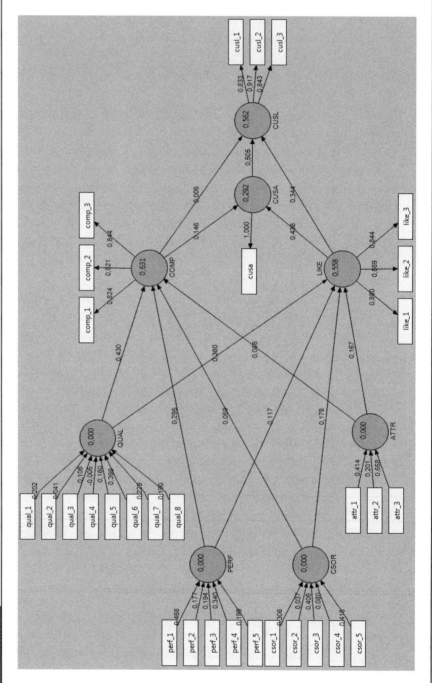

Exhibit 5.17 PLS-SEM Results

model. Since we extended the initial model by adding four constructs, we need to reassess the reflective measurement models according to the criteria presented in Chapter 4. To examine the results, open the default report (**Report → Default Report**) and check the results under **PLS → Quality Criteria → Overview**. Exhibit 5.18 shows the results presentation in the SmartPLS software. To improve the readability, we used the ⓢ button in the menu bar (top left) to toggle zero values in the results table and the ⁺ᵇ button (top left) to reduce the decimals of the displayed results. The information in the exhibit reveals that all reflectively measured constructs have AVE values of 0.688 and higher, which is considerably above the critical value of 0.5 (Chapter 4). In addition, all composite reliability values are well above the critical threshold of 0.70.

Looking at the indicator loadings (**PLS → Calculation Results → Outer Loadings** in the default report) reveals that all reflective indicators have loadings of 0.821 and higher, as shown in Exhibit 5.19 (zero values have been toggled). It is important to note that PLS software applications such as SmartPLS always provide outer loadings and outer weights for all constructs in the PLS path model, regardless of whether they are measured reflectively or formatively. Thus, Exhibit 5.19 displays the outer loadings for both the reflective and formative constructs. For the reflective measurement model evaluation, however, one is only interested in the outer loadings of the reflective constructs (i.e., *COMP, LIKE,* and *CUSL*).

Exhibit 5.18	Results for Reflective Measurement Model Evaluation Criteria

	AVE	Composite Reliability	R Square	Cronbachs Alpha
ATTR				
COMP	0.688	0.869	0.631	0.776
CSOR				
CUSA	1.000	1.000	0.292	1.000
CUSL	0.748	0.899	0.562	0.831
LIKE	0.747	0.899	0.558	0.831
PERF				
QUAL				

Data Preprocessing
Index Values
Model
PLS
  Calculation Results
    Latent Variable Scores
    Manifest Variable Scores (Used)
    Outer Loadings
    Outer Weights
    Path Coefficients
    Stop Criterion Changes
  Quality Criteria
    Cross Loadings
    Latent Variable Correlations
    Overview
    Total Effects

Exhibit 5.19   PLS-SEM Results for Outer Loadings

		ATTR	COMP	CSOR	CUSA	CUSL	LIKE	PERF	QUAL
⊞ Data Preprocessing	attr_1	0.755							
⊞ Index Values	attr_2	0.506							
⊞ Model	attr_3	0.891							
⊟ PLS	comp_1		0.824						
⊟ Calculation Results	comp_2		0.821						
Latent Variable Scores	comp_3		0.844						
Manifest Variable Scores (Used)	csor_1			0.771					
Outer Loadings	csor_2			0.571					
Outer Weights	csor_3			0.838					
Path Coefficients	csor_4			0.617					
Stop Criterion Changes	csor_5			0.848					
⊟ Quality Criteria	cusa				1.000				
Cross Loadings	cusl_1					0.833			
Latent Variable Correlations	cusl_2					0.917			
Overview	cusl_3					0.843			
Total Effects	like_1						0.880		
	like_2						0.869		
	like_3						0.844		
	perf_1							0.846	
	perf_2							0.690	
	perf_3							0.573	
	perf_4							0.717	
	perf_5							0.638	
	qual_1								0.741
	qual_2								0.570
	qual_3								0.749
	qual_4								0.664
	qual_5								0.787
	qual_6								0.856
	qual_7								0.722
	qual_8								0.627

Last, an analysis of the cross-loadings (**PLS → Quality Criteria → Cross Loadings** in the default report) provides support for the reflective constructs' discriminant validity as each reflective indicator loads highest on the construct it is linked to (Chapter 4). The Fornell-Larcker criterion also suggests that the constructs discriminant well because the square root of the AVE of each reflective construct is larger than the correlations with the remaining constructs in the model (Chapter 4). The SmartPLS default report results for the Fornell-Larcker criterion are shown in Exhibit 5.20. Note that when assessing the Fornell-Larcker criterion in a model that includes formative constructs, one needs to compare the reflective construct's AVE values (more precisely their square root) with *all* latent variable correlations (i.e., also those of formative constructs). However, the AVEs of formatively measured constructs should not be compared with the correlations (in fact, these are not even reported in SmartPLS).

Formative Measurement Model Evaluation

To evaluate the formative measurement models of the extended corporate reputation model, we follow the formative measurement models assessment procedure (Exhibit 5.1). First, we need to examine whether the formative constructs exhibit convergent validity. To do so, we carry out separate redundancy analyses for each construct. The

Exhibit 5.20 Fornell-Larcker Criterion

	ATTR	COMP	CSOR	CUSA	CUSL	LIKE	PERF	QUAL
ATTR	Formative measurement model							
COMP	0.613	**0.829**						
CSOR	0.592	0.596	Formative measurement model					
CUSA	0.416	0.423	0.422	Single-item construct				
CUSL	0.439	0.439	0.417	0.689	**0.865**			
LIKE	0.612	0.638	0.617	0.529	0.615	**0.864**		
PERF	0.665	0.728	0.626	0.425	0.479	0.639	Formative measurement model	
QUAL	0.689	0.763	0.700	0.489	0.532	0.712	0.788	Formative measurement model

Note: The square root of AVE values is shown on the diagonal and printed in bold (reflective constructs only); nondiagonal elements are the latent variable correlations.

original questionnaire contained global single-item measures with generic assessments of the four phenomena—*attractiveness, corporate social responsibility, performance,* and *quality*—that we can use as measures of the dependent construct in the redundancy analyses. Note that when you are designing your own research study that includes formatively measured constructs, you need to include this type of global measure in the survey to be able to conduct this type of test for your formative constructs.

To test convergent validity, we need to create the new models, as shown in Exhibit 5.21. Each model is included in the SmartPLS project file **Corporate Reputation Extended.splsp** that you can download and import into the SmartPLS software. At the www .pls-sem.com website, click with the right mouse button on **Corporate Reputation Extended.splsp** and save the file on your hard drive (e.g., C:\SmartPLS\). Then, run the SmartPLS software and press on **File → Import** in the menu to import the **Corporate Reputation Extended.splsp** as described earlier in this chapter and in Chapter 2. Thereafter, a new project appears with the name **Corporate Reputation Extended** in the SmartPLS **Projects** window on the left-hand side. This project contains several models (.splsm files) and the data set **Full Data.csv.** Besides **Base Model.splsm,** we also see the model files **Convergent Validity ATTR.splsm, Convergent Validity CSOR.splsm, Convergent Validity PERF.splsm,** and **Convergent Validity QUAL.splsm** in the **Projects** window of the SmartPLS software, as displayed in Exhibit 5.13. Each model opens after double-clicking on it.

Alternatively, you can newly create these four models for the convergent validity assessment in the **Corporate Reputation Extended** project in SmartPLS. To do so, select **Corporate Reputation Extended** in the **Project** window (click with the left mouse button) and then click the right mouse button. A box with several options appears (Exhibit 5.14). Select the option **Create New Model.** Thereafter, you can select a name for the new model (e.g., **Convergent Validity ATTR**). After pressing on the **OK** button, the new model (e.g., **Convergent Validity ATTR.splsm**) appears in the **Corporate Reputation Extended** project. When we double-click on this new model (e.g., **Convergent Validity ATTR.splsm**), an empty modeling window appears. Now, we follow the steps explained in the earlier chapters to create one of the models displayed in Exhibit 5.21 (e.g., the first one, **Convergent Validity ATTR.splsm**).

Exhibit 5.21	Convergent Validity Assessment of Formative Measurement Models

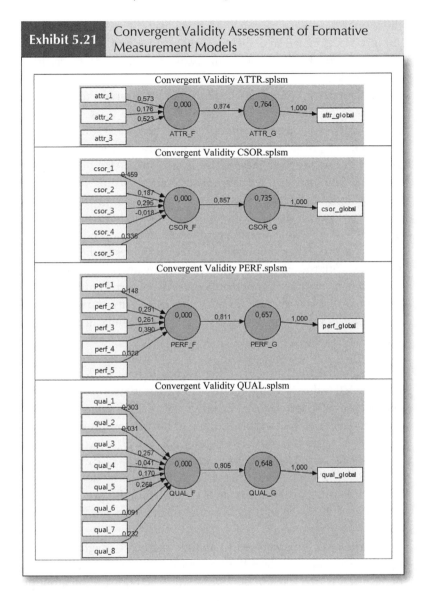

The first box in Exhibit 5.21 shows the results for the redundancy analysis for the *ATTR* construct. The original formative construct is labeled with *ATTR_F*, whereas the global assessment of the company's attractiveness using a single-item construct is labeled with *ATTR_G*. As can be seen, this analysis yields a path coefficient of 0.87, which is above the threshold of 0.80, thus providing support for the formative construct's convergent validity. The redundancy analyses of *CSOR, PERF,* and *QUAL* yield estimates of 0.86, 0.81, and 0.81, respectively. Thus, all formatively measured constructs have sufficient degrees of convergent validity.

In the next step, we check the formative measurement models for collinearity of indicators. The SmartPLS software does not provide users with the tolerance and the VIF values. Statistical software packages such as R, IBM SPSS Statistics, or Statistica, however, present collinearity statistics in their linear regression modules. After importing the indicator data into such a statistical software package, we can run a multiple regression with the formative indicators of a specific formative construct as independent variables and any other indicator, which is not included in that specific measurement model, as the dependent variable (otherwise, it does not matter which indicator serves as the dependent variable). With the exception of the collinearity analysis, the results of the regression analysis do not matter and are not further analyzed. The only result that is important for assessing collinearity issues is the VIF (or tolerance) value. For example, we may use the indicator *cusa_1* as the dependent variable and *attr_1, attr_2,* and *attr_3* as the independent variables in a regression model to obtain the VIF value for the formative indicators of the *ATTR* construct. Exhibit 5.22 displays the resulting VIF values for all formative constructs in the model. We present a step-by-step introduction on how to obtain VIF values using IBM SPSS Statistics in the Download section at http://www.pls-sem.com.

According to the results in Exhibit 5.22, *qual_3* has the highest VIF value (2.269). Hence, VIF values are uniformly below the threshold value of 5. We conclude, therefore, that collinearity does not reach critical levels in any of the formative constructs and is not an issue for the estimation of the PLS path model in the extended example on corporate reputation.

In the next step, we need to analyze the outer weights for their significance and relevance. We first consider the significance of the outer weights by means of bootstrapping. The bootstrapping option in the SmartPLS menu bar allows you to start the dialog for running the bootstrap routine (**Calculate → Bootstrapping**). We keep all information for missing value treatment and the PLS-SEM algorithm as in the initial model estimation and focus on the additional information for running the bootstrapping procedure. The bootstrapping dialog requires selecting an algorithmic option (i.e., the sign change option) and two parameter settings (i.e., cases and samples) as displayed in

Exhibit 5.22 Variance Inflation Factor Results

ATTR		CSOR		PERF		QUAL	
Indicators	VIF	Indicators	VIF	Indicators	VIF	Indicators	VIF
attr_1	1.275	csor_1	1.560	perf_1	1.560	qual_1	1.806
attr_2	1.129	csor_2	1.487	perf_2	1.506	qual_2	1.632
attr_3	1.264	csor_3	1.735	perf_3	1.229	qual_3	2.269
		csor_4	1.556	perf_4	1.316	qual_4	1.957
		csor_5	1.712	perf_5	1.331	qual_5	2.201
						qual_6	2.008
						qual_7	1.623
						qual_8	1.362

Exhibit 5.23. Select the **No Sign Changes** option. The number of cases (i.e., the number observations per subsample that are randomly drawn with replacement from the original sample) must equal the number of valid observations in the original sample. As we use mean replacement to treat missing values, we select 344 cases to bootstrap the PLS-SEM results of the corporate reputation example. Finally, for an initial first run, we may wish to choose a smaller number of boot-strap subsamples (e.g., 500) to be randomly drawn and estimated with the PLS-SEM algorithm since that requires less time. For the final results preparation, however, we recommend using 5,000 bootstrap subsamples, which takes more computer time (Exhibit 5.23).

After running the bootstrap routine, SmartPLS shows the t values for the measurement and structural model estimates derived from the bootstrapping procedure in the graphical modeling window (Exhibit 5.24). The results in Exhibit 5.24 will differ from your results and will change again when rerunning the bootstrapping routine. This is because bootstrapping builds on randomly drawn subsamples, and each time you run the bootstrapping routine, different subsamples will be drawn. The differences become very small, however, if the number of bootstrap-ping subsamples is sufficiently large (e.g., 5,000). We can compare the

Exhibit 5.23	Settings to Start the Bootstrap Routine

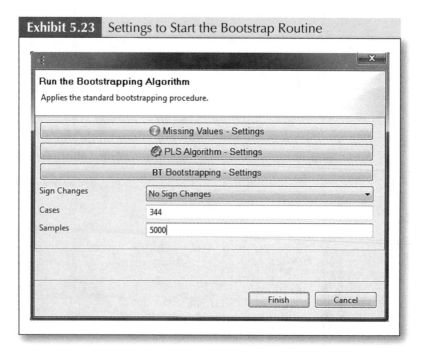

t values shown in Exhibit 5.24 with the critical values from the standard normal distribution to decide whether the coefficients are significantly different from zero. For example, the critical values for significance levels of 1% ($\alpha = 0.01$) and 5% ($\alpha = 0.05$) probability of error are 2.57 and 1.96, respectively. The empirical *t* values in the formative measurement models displayed in Exhibit 5.24 must be higher than the critcal values to establish significant outer weights at a given α level.

By clicking on **Report → Default Report,** we get a more detailed overview of the results. The **Default Report** provides us with the PLS-SEM estimates for each bootstrap sample and an overview of results, including standard errors, mean values, and *t* values. Exhibit 5.25 is an excerpt of the **Default Report** showing the summary report of the bootstrap results for the outer weights (again, your results will look slightly different because bootstrapping is a random process). The original estimate of an outer weight (shown in the second column, Original Sample (O); Exhibit 5.25) divided by the bootstrap standard deviation for that outer weight (displayed in the fourth column, Standard Deviation (STDEV); Exhibit 5.25) results in its empirical *t* value as displayed in the last column in Exhibit 5.25.

Exhibit 5.26 summarizes the results for the formatively measured constructs *ATTR, CSOR, PERF,* and *QUAL* by showing the original outer weights estimates, the *t* values, and the corresponding significance levels (marked with asterisks) as well as the *p* values. The latter are not

Exhibit 5.24 Bootstrap Results

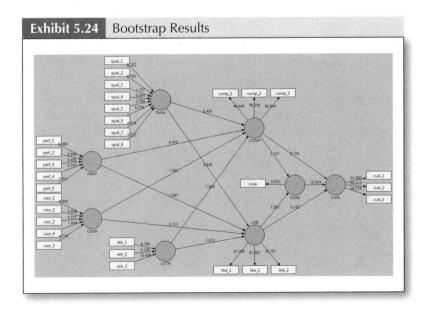

Exhibit 5.25	Bootstrap Results for Outer Weights

directly provided by SmartPLS, but they can be calculated using standard statistical programs or spreadsheet software. For example, in Microsoft Excel, we can use the TDIST function that requires us to specify the empirical t value and the degrees of freedom (df; i.e., the number of bootstrap cases minus one). In addition, we need to specify whether the test is one-tailed or two-tailed. The function has the following general form: TDIST(t value; df; tails). With regard to our example, we can calculate the p value for the weight of $attr\_1$ (two-tailed test) by entering "=TDIST(5.769; 343; 2)" into one of the cells. Finally, Exhibit 5.26 shows the 90% bootstrap confidence intervals for the outer weights that we calculated manually. For example, the indicator $attr\_1$ has an original value of 0.414 and a bootstrap standard error of 0.073. For a significance level of $\alpha = 0.10$, the resulting confidence interval has a lower bound of 0.296 (i.e., $0.414 - 1.65 \cdot 0.073$) and an upper bound of 0.533 (i.e., $0.414 + 1.65 \cdot 0.073$).

Looking at the significance levels, we find that all formative indicators are significant except $csor\_2$, $csor\_4$, $qual\_2$, and $qual\_4$. These four weights remain nonsignificant when using alternative sign change options for running the bootstrapping procedure (i.e., individual sign changes or construct-level changes). We hence consider this finding the final result of our analysis (Exhibit 5.9) based on the logic summarized in the following sentences. The default report of the SmartPLS software also provides their outer loadings and t values in the results table for the outer loadings. Using this information, we note that the lowest outer loading of these four indicators has a value of 0.57, and all t values are clearly above 2.57, which indicate the significance of their outer loading ($p < .01$). Moreover, prior research and theory also provide support for the relevance of these indicators for capturing the corporate social responsibility and quality dimensions of corporate reputation

Exhibit 5.26 Outer Weights Significance Testing Results

Formative Constructs	Formative Indicators	Outer Weights (Outer Loadings)	t Value	Significance Level	p Value	Confidence Intervals[a]
ATTR	attr_1	0.414 (0.755)	5.769	***	.000	[0.296, 0.533]
	attr_2	0.201 (0.506)	3.109	***	.002	[0.094, 0.307]
	attr_3	0.658 (0.891)	10.439	***	.000	[0.554, 0.762]
CSOR	csor_1	0.306 (0.771)	3.659	***	.000	[0.168, 0.445]
	csor_2	0.037 (0.571)	0.536	NS	.573	[−0.077, 0.152]
	csor_3	0.406 (0.838)	4.727	***	.000	[0.264, 0.548]
	csor_4	0.080 (0.617)	1.044	NS	.296	[−0.046, 0.207]
	csor_5	0.416 (0.848)	4.730	***	.000	[0.271, 0.561]
PERF	perf_1	0.468 (0.846)	6.685	***	.000	[0.352, 0.583]
	perf_2	0.177 (0.690)	2.596	**	.012	[0.064, 0.289]
	perf_3	0.194 (0.573)	3.405	***	.001	[0.100, 0.289]

(Continued)

Exhibit 5.26 (Continued)

Formative Constructs	Formative Indicators	Outer Weights (Outer Loadings)	t Value	Significance Level	p Value	Confidence Intervals[a]
	perf_4	0.340 (0.717)	4.783	***	.000	[0.223, 0.458]
	perf_5	0.199 (0.638)	2.904	***	.003	[0.086, 0.311]
QUAL	qual_1	0.202 (0.741)	3.262	***	.001	[0.100, 0.305]
	qual_2	0.041 (0.570)	0.788	NS	.450	[−0.045, 0.127]
	qual_3	0.106 (0.749)	1.707	*	.078	[0.004, 0.208]
	qual_4	−0.005 (0.664)	0.084	NS	.935	[−0.094, 0.085]
	qual_5	0.160 (0.787)	2.792	***	.004	[0.065, 0.254]
	qual_6	0.398 (0.856)	6.275	***	.000	[0.293, 0.503]
	qual_7	0.229 (0.722)	4.018	***	.000	[0.135, 0.323]
	qual_8	0.190 (0.627)	3.223	***	.002	[0.093, 0.287]

Note: NS = not significant.

a. Bootstrap confidence intervals for 10% probability of error ($\alpha = 0.10$).

$*p < .10. **p < .05. ***p < .01.$

(Eberl, 2010; Sarstedt et al., 2013; Schwaiger, 2004; Schwaiger, Sarstedt, & Taylor, 2010). Thus, we retain the indicators in the formative constructs even though their outer weights are not significant.

The analysis of outer weights concludes the evaluation of the formative measurement models. Considering the results from Chapters 4 and 5 jointly, all reflective and formative constructs exhibit satisfactory levels of quality. Thus, we can proceed with the evaluation of the structural model (Chapter 6).

SUMMARY

- **Explain the criteria used for the assessment of formative measurement models.** The statistical evaluation criteria for reflective measurement scales cannot be directly transferred to formative measurement models where indicators are likely to represent the construct's independent causes and thus do not necessarily correlate highly. Researchers must include a comprehensive set of indicators that fully exhausts the formative construct's domain. Failure to consider all facets of the construct (i.e., relevant formative indicators) entails an exclusion of important parts of the construct itself. The evaluation of formative measurement models focuses on examining whether each indicator contributes to forming the index. Hence, the significance and relevance of the indicator weights must be assessed. Nonsignificant indicator weights should not automatically be interpreted as indicating poor measurement model quality. Rather, researchers should also consider a formative indicator's absolute contribution to its construct (i.e., its loading). Only if both weights and loadings are low or even nonsignificant should a formative indicator be deleted. In addition, potential collinearity issues among sets of formative indicators need to be addressed in the measurement model assessment. Last, the measures' convergent validity must ensure that the entire domain of the construct and all of its relevant facets have been covered by the selected formative indicators. By accounting for these issues, one makes sure that the formative construct can be used for the PLS-SEM analysis and that the estimations of outer weights are correctly interpreted.

- **Understand the basic concepts of bootstrapping for significance testing in PLS-SEM and apply it.** PLS-SEM is a distribution-free multivariate data analysis technique and, as such, does not rely on distributional assumptions. As a consequence and different from, for example, OLS regression, PLS-SEM does not initially provide t values to evaluate the estimates' significance. Instead, researchers have to rely on the bootstrapping procedure that provides bootstrap standard errors. These standard errors can, in turn, be used to approximate t values. Bootstrapping is a resampling approach that draws random samples (with replacement) from the data and uses these samples to estimate the path model multiple times under slightly changed data constellations. When running the bootstrapping procedure, researchers should draw 5,000 bootstrap samples with each sample including the same number of cases as there are valid observations in the original data set. The random nature of the bootstrapping procedure might cause arbitrary sign changes in the model estimates that researchers can correct for by using the construct-level or individual-level sign change options. However, choosing the no sign change option is generally recommended because it is the most conservative option.

- **Use the SmartPLS software to apply the formative measurement model assessment criteria and learn how to properly report the results of the practical example on corporate reputation.** Expanding the corporate reputation model example by four formative constructs allows us to continue the SmartPLS application of the previous chapters. The SmartPLS software makes results for the evaluation of the formative measurement models available. Besides the outcomes of the PLS-SEM algorithm, running the bootstrapping routine delivers the results required for testing the significance of formative indicators' outer weights. Tables and figures for the PLS path model example on corporate reputation demonstrate how to correctly report and interpret the PLS-SEM results. This hands-on example not only reinforces the concepts that have been introduced before but also gives additional insights for their practical application.

REVIEW QUESTIONS

1. How do you assess the content validity of formative constructs?

2. Why do you need to consider the significance and relevance of formative indicators?

3. What VIF level indicates critical levels of indicator collinearity?

4. What is the basic idea underlying bootstrapping?

5. Which sign changes procedure, number of cases, and samples should you choose when running the bootstrap procedure?

CRITICAL THINKING QUESTIONS

1. What is the difference between reflective and formatively measured constructs? Explain the difference between outer loadings and outer weights.

2. Why are formative constructs particularly useful as exogenous latent variables in a PLS path model?

3. Why is indicator collinearity an issue in formative measurement models?

4. Critically discuss the following statement: "Nonsignificant indicators should be eliminated from a formative measurement model as they do not contribute to forming the index."

KEY TERMS

Absolute contribution: is the information an indicator variable provides about the formatively measured item, ignoring all other indicators. The absolute contribution is provided by the loading of the indicator (i.e., its bivariate correlation with the formatively measured construct).

Absolute importance: see *Absolute contribution.*

Bootstrap cases: make up the number of observations drawn in every bootstrap run. The number should equal the number of valid observations in the original data set.

Bootstrap confidence interval: provides the lower and upper limit of values within which a true population parameter will fall with a certain probability (e.g., 95%). The construction of the interval relies on bootstrapping standard errors.

Bootstrap samples: make up the number of samples drawn in the bootstrapping procedure that must be higher than the number of bootstrap cases. Generally, 5,000 or more samples are recommended.

Bootstrapping: is a resampling technique that draws a large number of subsamples from the original data (with replacement) and estimates models for each subsample. It is used to determine standard errors of coefficient estimates to assess the coefficient's statistical significance without relying on distributional assumptions.

Collinearity: arises when two indicators are highly correlated. When more than two indicators are involved, it is called multicollinearity.

Construct-level sign change option: is the algorithmic option in bootstrapping that corrects for extreme samples drawn in the resampling runs.

Content specification: is the specification of the scope of the latent variable, that is, the domain of content the set of formative indicators is intended to capture.

Content validity: is a subjective but systematic evaluation of how well the domain content of a construct is captured by its indicators.

Convergent validity: is the degree to which the formatively measured construct correlates positively with an alternative (reflective or single-item) measure of the same construct; see *Redundancy analysis.*

Critical *t* value: is the cutoff or criterion on which the significance of a coefficient is determined. If the *empirical t value* is larger than the critical *t* value, the null hypothesis of no effect is rejected. Typical critical *t* values are 2.57, 1.96, and 1.65 for a significance level of 1%, 5%, and 10%, respectively (two-tailed tests).

Degrees of freedom: is the number of values in the final calculation of the test statistic that are free to vary.

Empirical *t* value: is the test statistic value obtained from the data set at hand (here: the bootstrapping results).

Formative measurement models: are based on a measurement model specification in which it is assumed that the construct is caused by the assigned indicators.

Individual-level sign change option: is an algorithmic option in bootstrapping that corrects for extreme samples drawn in the resampling runs.

Interpretational confounding: is a situation in which the empirically observed meaning between a construct and its measures differs from the theoretically implied meaning.

Multicollinearity: see *Collinearity.*

No sign change option: is an algorithmic option in bootstrapping that, unlike the *construct-level sign change option* and the *individual-level sign change option,* does not correct for extreme samples drawn in the resampling runs.

Outer loadings: are the relationships in reflective measurement models (i.e., from the latent variable to the indicators). They determine an item's *absolute contribution* to its assigned construct.

Outer weights: are the relationships in formative measurement models (i.e., from the indicators to the latent variables). They determine an item's *relative contribution* to its assigned construct.

Redundancy analysis: is a measure of a formative construct's *convergent validity*. It tests whether a formatively measured construct is highly correlated with a reflective measure of the same construct.

Reflective measurement models: are based on a measurement model specification in which it is assumed that the indicators are caused by the underlying construct.

Relative contribution: is the unique importance of each indicator by partializing the variance of the formatively measured construct that is predicted by the other indicators. An item's relative contribution is provided by its weight.

Sign indeterminacy: is a characteristic of PLS-SEM that causes arbitrary sign changes in the bootstrap estimates of path coefficients, loadings, and weights compared with the estimates obtained from the original sample.

Theoretical *t* value: see *Critical t value*.

Tolerance: see *Variance inflation factor (VIF)*.

Variance inflation factor (VIF): quantifies the severity of collinearity among the indicators in a formative measurement model. The VIF is directly related to the tolerance value ($VIF_i = 1/\text{tolerance}_i$).

SUGGESTED READINGS

Albers, S. (2010). PLS and success factor studies in marketing. In V. Esposito Vinzi, W. W. Chin, J. Henseler & H. Wang (Eds.), *Handbook of partial least squares: concepts, methods and applications* (Springer handbooks of computational statistics series, vol. II) (pp. 409–425). New York: Springer.

Cenfetelli, R. T. & Bassellier, G. (2009). Interpretation of formative measurement in information systems research. *MIS Quarterly, 33*(4), 689–708.

Chin, W. W. (2010). How to write up and report PLS analyses. In V. Esposito Vinzi, W. W. Chin, J. Henseler, & H. Wang (Eds.), *Handbook of partial least squares: Concepts, methods and applications in marketing and related fields* (pp. 655–690). Berlin: Springer.

Diamantopoulos, A. (2008). Formative indicators: Introduction to the special issue. *Journal of Business Research, 61*(12), 1201–1202.

Diamantopoulos, A., & Winklhofer, H. M. (2001). Index construction with formative indicators: An alternative to scale development. *Journal of Marketing Research, 38*(2), 269–277.

Gudergan, S. P., Ringle, C. M., Wende, S., & Will, A. (2008). Confirmatory tetrad analysis in PLS path modeling. *Journal of Business Research, 61*(12), 1238–1249.

Hair, J. F., Ringle, C. M., & Sarstedt, M. (2011). PLS-SEM: Indeed a silver bullet. *Journal of Marketing Theory and Practice, 19*, 139–151.

Hair, J. F., Sarstedt, M., Pieper, T., & Ringle, C. M. (in press). Applications of partial least squares path modeling in management journals: A review. *Long Range Planning, 45,* 320–340.

Hair, J. F., Sarstedt, M., Ringle, C. M., & Mena, J. A. (2012). An assessment of the use of partial least squares structural equation modeling in marketing research. *Journal of the Academy of Marketing Science, 40,* 414–433.

Henseler, J., Ringle, C. M., & Sinkovics, R. R. (2009). The use of partial least squares path modeling in international marketing. *Advances in International Marketing, 20,* 277–320.

Petter, S., Straub, D., & Rai, A. (2007). Specifying formative constructs in information systems research. *MIS Quarterly, 31*(4), 623–656.

Ringle, C. M., Sarstedt, M., & Straub, D. W. (2012). A critical look at the use of PLS-SEM in *MIS Quarterly. MIS Quarterly, 36,* iii–xiv.

CHAPTER 6

Assessing PLS-SEM Results Part III

Evaluation of the Structural Model

LEARNING OUTCOMES

1. Assess the path coefficients in the structural model.

2. Evaluate the coefficients of determination (R^2 values).

3. Understand and evaluate the f^2 effect size.

4. Use the blindfolding procedure to assess the predictive relevance (Q^2 value) of the path model.

5. Comprehend heterogeneity and how it may affect PLS-SEM estimates.

6. Understand how to report and interpret the structural model results.

CHAPTER PREVIEW

Chapters 4 and 5 provided insights into the evaluation of reflective and formative measurement models. This chapter continues the analysis and focuses on the structural model that represents the underlying theory/concept of the path model. Assessment of the structural model results enables you to determine how well empirical data support the theory/concept and therefore to decide if your theory/concept has been empirically confirmed. For this purpose, the key results (i.e., the path coefficients and R^2 values) of the structural model are examined first. Thereafter, we provide a cautionary warning regarding a global goodness-of-fit criterion for PLS-SEM as proposed in the literature and as frequently used in prior studies. Finally, we address the critical issue of unobserved heterogeneity in estimates of relationships in the path model that may lead to misleading and incorrect conclusions if not correctly identified. The chapter concludes with a practical application and assessment of the PLS-SEM results of the structural model by means of our corporate reputation example and the SmartPLS software.

STAGE 6: ASSESSING PLS-SEM STRUCTURAL MODEL RESULTS

Once we have confirmed that the construct measures are reliable and valid, the next step addresses the assessment of the structural model results. This involves examining the model's predictive capabilities and the relationships between the constructs. Exhibit 6.1 shows a systematic approach to the assessment of structural model results.

Before we describe these analyses, however, we need to examine the structural model for collinearity (Step 1). The reason is that the estimation of path coefficients in the structural models is based on OLS regressions of each endogenous latent variable on its corresponding predecessor constructs. Just as in a regular multiple regression, the path coefficients might be biased if the estimation involves significant levels of collinearity among the predictor constructs.

When examining the structural model, it is important to understand that PLS-SEM fits the model to the sample data to obtain the best parameter estimates by maximizing the explained variance of the endogenous latent variable(s). This aspect of PLS-SEM is different from CB-SEM, which estimates parameters so that the differences between the sample covariances and those predicted by the theoretical/conceptual model are minimized. As a result, with CB-SEM, the covariance matrix implied by the theoretical/conceptual model is as close as possible to the sample covariance matrix. Goodness-of-fit measures associated with CB-SEM (which are based on the

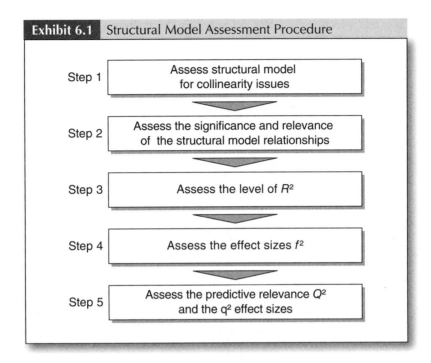

Exhibit 6.1 Structural Model Assessment Procedure

Step 1 — Assess structural model for collinearity issues

Step 2 — Assess the significance and relevance of the structural model relationships

Step 3 — Assess the level of R^2

Step 4 — Assess the effect sizes f^2

Step 5 — Assess the predictive relevance Q^2 and the q^2 effect sizes

difference between the two covariance matrices), such as the chi-square (χ^2) statistic or the various fit indices, are not applicable in a PLS-SEM context.

Instead of applying measures of goodness of fit, the structural model in PLS-SEM is assessed on the basis of heuristic criteria that are determined by the model's predictive capabilities. These criteria, by definition, do not allow for testing the overall goodness of the model fit in a CB-SEM sense. Rather, the model is assumed to be specified correctly and is assessed in terms of how well it predicts the endogenous variables/constructs (see Rigdon, 2012, for a discussion of model fit in CB-SEM vis-à-vis PLS-SEM's prediction orientation). The key criteria for assessing the structural model in PLS-SEM are the significance of the path coefficients (Step 2), the level of the R^2 values (Step 3), the f^2 effect size (Step 4), the predictive relevance (Q^2), and the q^2 effect size (Step 5).

In the following sections, each criterion will be introduced. We also discuss a proposed PLS-SEM global goodness-of-fit criterion and learn that this criterion does *not* actually provide a global goodness-of-fit measure. Finally, we describe why the consideration of heterogeneity is crucial when evaluating a path model and briefly describe approaches for dealing with heterogeneous data structures. These will be described further in Chapter 8.

Step 1: Collinearity Assessment

To assess **collinearity,** we apply the same measures as in the evaluation of formative measurement models (i.e., tolerance and VIF values) in Chapter 5. In doing so, we need to examine each set of predictor constructs separately for each subpart of the structural model. For instance, in the model shown in Exhibit 6.2, Y_1 and Y_2 jointly explain Y_3. Likewise, Y_2 and Y_3 act as predictors of Y_4. Therefore, one needs to check whether there are significant levels of collinearity between each set of predictor variables, that is, Y_1 and Y_2 as well as Y_2 and Y_3.

Analogous to the assessment of formative measurement models, we consider tolerance levels below 0.20 (VIF above 5.00) in the predictor constructs as indicative of collinearity. If collinearity is indicated by the tolerance or VIF guidelines, one should consider eliminating constructs, merging predictors into a single construct, or creating higher-order constructs (Chapter 7) to treat collinearity problems.

Step 2: Structural Model Path Coefficients

After running the PLS-SEM algorithm, estimates are obtained for the structural model relationships (i.e., the path coefficients), which

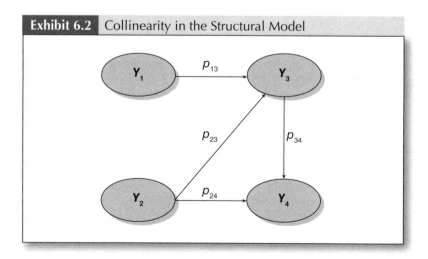

Exhibit 6.2 Collinearity in the Structural Model

represent the **hypothesized relationships** among the constructs. The
path coefficients have **standardized values** between −1 and +1.
Estimated path coefficients close to +1 represent strong positive relationships (and vice versa for negative values) that are almost always
statistically significant (i.e., different from zero in the population). The
closer the estimated coefficients are to 0, the weaker the relationships.
Very low values close to 0 are usually nonsignificant (i.e., not significantly different from zero).

Whether a coefficient is significant ultimately depends on its
standard error that is obtained by means of **bootstrapping.** The bootstrapping routine is applied as in Chapter 5, where we used the procedure to assess whether a formative indicator significantly contributes
to its corresponding construct. The bootstrap standard error allows
computing the **empirical t value.** For example, to estimate the significance of the path coefficient linking constructs Y_1 and Y_3 (i.e., p_{13}; see
Exhibit 6.2), we would enter the original path coefficient estimate
(p_{13}) and the bootstrap standard error ($se^*_{p_{13}}$) in the following formula:

$$t = \frac{p_{13}}{se^*_{p_{13}}}.$$

Analogous to the descriptions in Chapter 5, the t distribution
can be reasonably approximated for sample sizes larger than 30.
Correspondingly, we can use the quantiles from the normal distribution as critical values with which to compare the empirical t
value. When the empirical t value is larger than the **critical value,**
we say that the coefficient is significant at a certain error probability (i.e., significance level). Commonly used critical values for **two-
tailed tests** are 1.65 (significance level = 10%), 1.96 (significance
level = 5%), and 2.57 (significance level = 1%). In marketing,
researchers usually assume a significance level of 5%. This does not
always apply, however, since consumer research studies sometimes
assume a significance level of 1%, especially when experiments are
involved. On the other hand, when a study is exploratory in nature,
researchers often assume a significance level of 10%. Ultimately,
the choice of the significance level depends on the field of study and
the study's objective.

Exhibit 6.3 shows an example of a structural model where the path
relationship p_{14} from Y_1 to Y_4 has a value of 0.25. If the bootstrapping
routine (e.g., for 5,000 subsamples; 450 bootstrap cases) delivers a

standard error of 0.118 for this relationship, the empirical t value is $0.25/0.118 = 2.119$. This value is higher than the theoretical t value of 1.96 for a 5% probability of error. As a result, one can conclude that the relationship from Y_1 to Y_4 is significant at a level of 5%.

Instead of t values, researchers routinely report p values that correspond to the probability of erroneously rejecting the null hypothesis, given the data at hand. Spreadsheet applications such as Microsoft Excel or CALC in OpenOffice enable computation of the exact p **value**. For instance, in Microsoft Excel, you can use the TDIST function that requires you to specify the empirical t value and the **degrees of freedom** (df). In addition, you need to specify whether the test is one-tailed or two-tailed. The function has the following general form: TDIST(t value; df; tails). In our example, for a two-tailed test using an empirical t value of 2.119 and 449 degrees of freedom (i.e., the number of valid observations/bootstrap cases minus one: $450 - 1 = 449$), one would enter the following line in any cell of the Excel spreadsheet: "=TDIST(2.119;449;2)". This yields a p value of 0.035, indicating that the path relationship from Y_1 to Y_4 with a value of 0.25 is significant at a 5% probability of error.

Exhibit 6.3   Path Coefficients in the Structural Model

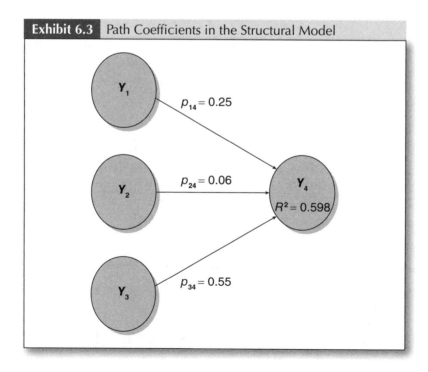

In addition to calculating the t and p values, the bootstrapping **confidence interval** for a prespecified probability of error can be determined. Similar to the approach used in Chapter 5, the confidence interval for p_{14} is given by

$$p_{14} \pm z_{1-\alpha/2} \cdot se^*_{p_{14}},$$

where $z_{1-\alpha/2}$ stems from the standard normal (z) distribution table. For example, when the probability of error is 5% (i.e., $\alpha = 0.05$), $z_{1-\alpha/2} = z_{0.975} = 1.96$. Thus, the lower bound of the bootstrap confidence interval is $p_{14} - 1.96 \cdot se^*_{p_{14}}$, and the upper bound is $p_{14} + 1.96 \cdot se^*_{p_{14}}$. In our example, the structural model path coefficient p_{14} has a value of 0.25 (Exhibit 6.3) and a bootstrapping standard error of 0.118. With a significance level of 5%, the resulting confidence interval has a lower bound of 0.019 (i.e., 0.25 – 1.96 · 0.118) and an upper bound of 0.481 (i.e., 0.25 + 1.96 · 0.118). Thus, the resulting confidence interval is [0.019, 0.481]. The original estimate of the structural model path coefficient with a value of 0.25 is significant if zero does not fall within the confidence interval at the given significance level, which is the case in the example.

When interpreting the results of a path model, we need to test the significance of all structural model relationships. When reporting results, however, we examine the empirical t value, the p value, *or* the bootstrapping confidence interval. There is no need to report all three types of significance testing results since they all lead to the same conclusion.

After examining the significance of relationships, it is important to assess the **relevance of significant relationships**. Many studies do not undertake this important step in their analyses but simply focus on the significance of effects. However, the path coefficients in the structural model may be significant, but their size may be so small that they do not warrant managerial attention. An analysis of the relative importance of relationships is crucial for interpreting the results and drawing conclusions.

The structural model path coefficients can be interpreted relative to one another. If one path coefficient is larger than another, its effect on the endogenous latent variable is greater. More specifically, the individual path coefficients of the path model can be interpreted just as the standardized beta coefficients in an OLS regression. These coefficients represent the estimated change in the endogenous construct for a unit change in the exogenous construct. If the path coefficient is statistically significant (i.e., the coefficient is significantly different from zero in the population), its value indicates the extent to which the exogenous construct is associated with the endogenous construct. The goal of PLS-SEM is to identify not only significant path coefficients in the structural model but significant and relevant effects.

For example, the **significance testing** of the structural model shown in Exhibit 6.3 substantiates that two of the three path relationships are significant. The exogenous constructs Y_1 and Y_3 significantly contribute to explaining the endogenous latent variable Y_4 or, in other words, contribute to explaining the variation in Y_4. On the contrary, Y_2 is not significantly related to Y_4 and therefore does not contribute to explaining Y_4.

Researchers are often interested in evaluating not only one construct's **direct effect** on another but also its **indirect effects** via one or more mediating constructs. The sum of direct and indirect effects is referred to as the **total effect**. The interpretation of total effects is particularly useful in studies aimed at exploring the differential impact of different driver constructs on a criterion construct via several mediating variables. In Exhibit 6.4, for example, constructs Y_1 and Y_3 are linked by a direct effect ($p_{13} = 0.20$). In addition, there is an indirect effect between the two constructs via the mediating construct Y_2. This indirect effect can be calculated as the product of the two effects p_{12} and p_{23} ($p_{12} \cdot p_{23} = 0.80 \cdot 0.50 = 0.40$). The total effect is 0.60, which is calculated as $p_{13} + p_{12} \cdot p_{23} = 0.20 + 0.80 \cdot 0.50 = 0.60$.

Although the direct effect of Y_1 to Y_3 is not very strong (i.e., 0.20), the total effect (both direct and indirect combined) is quite pronounced (i.e., 0.60), indicating the relevance of Y_1 in explaining Y_3. This type of result suggests that the direct relationship from Y_1 to Y_3 is mediated by Y_2. In Chapter 7, we will deal with the question of how to analyze mediating effects.

Step 3: Coefficient of Determination (R^2 Value)

The most commonly used measure to evaluate the structural model is the **coefficient of determination** (R^2 value). This coefficient is a measure of the model's predictive accuracy and is calculated as the squared correlation between a specific endogenous construct's actual and predicted values. The coefficient represents the exogenous latent variables' combined effects on the endogenous latent variable. Because

Exhibit 6.4 Example of Direct, Indirect, and Total Effects

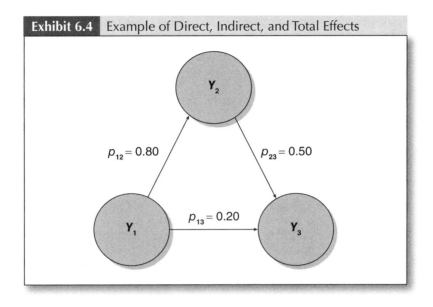

the coefficient is the squared correlation of actual and predicted values, it also represents the amount of variance in the endogenous constructs explained by all of the exogenous constructs linked to it. The R^2 **value** ranges from 0 to 1 with higher levels indicating higher levels of predictive accuracy. It is difficult to provide rules of thumb for acceptable R^2 values as this depends on the model complexity and the research discipline. Whereas R^2 values of 0.20 are considered high in disciplines such as consumer behavior, in success driver studies (e.g., in studies that aim at explaining customer satisfaction or loyalty), researchers expect much higher values of 0.75 and above. In scholarly research that focuses on marketing issues, R^2 values of 0.75, 0.50, or 0.25 for endogenous latent variables can, as a rough rule of thumb, be respectively described as substantial, moderate, or weak (Hair, Ringle, & Sarstedt, 2011; Henseler et al., 2009).

Problems often arise if we use the R^2 value to compare models that are specified differently (but with the same endogenous construct). For example, if we add nonsignificant constructs to a structural model that are slightly correlated with the endogenous latent variable, the R^2 will increase. This type of impact is most noticeable if the sample size is close to the number of exogenous latent variables predicting the endogenous latent variable under consideration. Thus, if we use the R^2 as the only basis for understanding the model's predictive accuracy, there is an inherent bias toward selecting models with many exogenous constructs, including ones that may be only slightly related to the endogenous constructs.

Selecting a model based on the R^2 value is not a good approach. Adding additional (nonsignificant) constructs to explain an endogenous latent variable in the structural model always increases its R^2 value. The more paths pointing toward a target construct, the higher its R^2 value. However, researchers want models that are good at explaining the data (thus, with high R^2 values) but also have fewer exogenous constructs. Such models are called **parsimonious**.

As with multiple regression, the **adjusted R^2 value** (R^2_{adj}) can be used as the criterion to avoid bias toward complex models. This criterion is modified according to the number of exogenous constructs relative to the sample size. The R^2_{adj} value is formally defined as

$$R^2_{adj} = 1 - (1 - R^2) \cdot \frac{n-1}{n-k-1},$$

where n is the sample size and k the number of exogenous latent variables used to predict the endogenous latent variable under consideration. The R^2_{adj} value reduces the R^2 value by the number of explaining constructs and the sample size and thus systematically compensates for adding nonsignificant exogenous constructs merely to increase the explained variance R^2. Note that we cannot interpret the R^2_{adj} just like the regular R^2. Rather, the R^2_{adj} is used for comparing PLS-SEM results involving models with different numbers of exogenous latent variables and/or data sets with different sample sizes. See Sarstedt et al. (2013) for an example application.

For example, let's assume a sample size of 300 observations (i.e., $n = 300$) with regard to the example in Exhibit 6.3. You are interested in comparing the R^2_{adj} values of the endogenous construct Y_4 of this model with an extended model that has one additional exogenous construct Y_0 with a nonsignificant effect on Y_4. Likewise, the extended model relies on fewer observations (i.e., $n = 250$) because of missing values in the indicators of the additionally considered exogenous construct. The consideration of Y_0 slightly increases the R^2 of Y_4 from 0.598 to 0.600. However, a different picture emerges when comparing the adjusted R^2 values, which also take the model complexity and sample sizes into account, for the original situation ($n = 300$) and the extended situation ($n = 250$):

$$R^2_{adj,Original} = 1 - (1 - R^2) \cdot \frac{n-1}{n-k-1}$$

$$= 1 - (1 - 0.598) \cdot \frac{300-1}{300-3-1} = 0.594;$$

$$R^2_{adj,Extended} = 1 - (1 - R^2) \cdot \frac{n-1}{n-k-1}$$

$$= 1 - (1 - 0.600) \cdot \frac{250-1}{250-4-1} = 0.593.$$

Based on the R^2_{adj} values, we would rather opt for the original model. While the differences in (adjusted) R^2 values are not very pronounced in this example, they can vary in different setups that involve comparing models with a great number of exogenous latent variables. Note that one can also use the bootstrapping routine to test for significant differences between (adjusted) R^2 values between two models (for an example, see Sarstedt et al., 2013). However, the standard bootstrapping procedure in SmartPLS does not allow this type of computation.

Step 4: Effect Size f^2

In addition to evaluating the R^2 values of all endogenous constructs, the change in the R^2 value when a specified exogenous construct is omitted from the model can be used to evaluate whether the omitted construct has a substantive impact on the endogenous constructs. This measure is referred to as the f^2 **effect size.** The effect size can be calculated as

$$f^2 = \frac{R^2_{included} - R^2_{excluded}}{1 - R^2_{included}},$$

where $R^2_{included}$ and $R^2_{excluded}$ are the R^2 values of the endogenous latent variable when a selected exogenous latent variable is included in or excluded from the model. The change in the R^2 values is calculated by estimating the PLS path model twice. It is estimated the first time with the exogenous latent variable included (yielding $R^2_{included}$) and the second time with the exogenous latent variable excluded (yielding $R^2_{excluded}$). Guidelines for assessing f^2 are that values of

0.02, 0.15, and 0.35, respectively, represent small, medium, and large effects (Cohen, 1988) of the exogenous latent variable.

For example, in the path model shown in Exhibit 6.3, the $R^2_{included}$ value is 0.598. In contrast, the $R^2_{excluded, Y_1}$ value is 0.525, the $R^2_{excluded, Y_2}$ value is 0.588, and the $R^2_{excluded, Y_3}$ value is 0.455. Consequently, the exogenous constructs Y_1, Y_2, and Y_3 for explaining the endogenous latent variable Y_4 have f^2 effect sizes of 0.182, 0.025, and 0.356, respectively. Hence, the effect size of construct Y_1 on the endogenous latent variable Y_4 is medium, the effect size of construct Y_2 on the endogenous latent variable Y_4 is small, and construct Y_3 has a large effect size. Another application of f^2 effect size computations follows later in this chapter when we work with the example on corporate reputation.

Step 5: Blindfolding and Predictive Relevance Q^2

In addition to evaluating the magnitude of the R^2 values as a criterion of predictive accuracy, researchers should also examine Stone-Geisser's **Q^2 value** (Geisser, 1974; Stone, 1974). This measure is an indicator of the model's **predictive relevance**. More specifically, when PLS-SEM exhibits predictive relevance, it accurately predicts the data points of indicators in reflective measurement models of endogenous constructs and endogenous single-item constructs (the procedure does not apply for formative endogenous constructs). In the structural model, Q^2 values larger than zero for a certain reflective endogenous latent variable indicate the path model's predictive relevance for this particular construct.

The Q^2 value is obtained by using the **blindfolding** procedure for a ceratin omission distance D.=. Blindfolding is a sample reuse technique that omits every dth data point in the endogenous construct's indicators and estimates the parameters with the remaining data points (Chin, 1998; Henseler et al., 2009; Tenenhaus et al., 2005). The omitted data points are considered missing values and treated accordingly when running the PLS-SEM algorithm (e.g., by using mean value replacement). The resulting estimates are then used to predict the omitted data points. The difference between the true (i.e., omitted) data points and the predicted ones is then used as input for the Q^2 measure. Blindfolding is an iterative process that repeats until each data point has been omitted and the model reestimated. The blindfolding procedure is only applied to endogenous constructs that have a reflective measurement model specification as well as to endogenous single-item constructs.

When applying the blindfolding procedure to the PLS-SEM in Exhibit 6.5, the data points in the measurement model of the reflective endogenous construct are estimated by means of a two-step approach. First, the information from the structural model is used to predict the scores of latent variable Y_3. More specifically, after running the PLS-SEM algorithm, the scores of the latent variables Y_1, Y_2, and Y_3 are available. Instead of directly using the Y_3 scores, the blindfolding procedure predicts these scores by using the available information for the structural model (i.e., the latent variable scores of Y_1 and Y_2, as well as the structural model coefficients p_{13} and p_{23}). Specifically, the prediction of Y_3 equals the standardized scores of the following equation: $\hat{Y}_3 = p_{13} \cdot Y_1 + p_{23} \cdot Y_2$, whereby $\hat{Y}_3$ represents the structural model's prediction. These scores differ from the scores of Y_3, which were obtained by applying the PLS-SEM algorithm because they result from the structural model estimates rather than those from the measurement model (Chapter 3).

In the second step, the predicted scores ($\hat{Y}_3$) of the reflective endogenous latent variable are used to predict systematically omitted (or eliminated) data points of the indicators x_5, x_6, and x_7 in the measurement model. The systematic pattern of data point elimination and prediction depends on the **omission distance (D)**, which must be determined to run the blindfolding procedure. An omission distance of 3, for example, implies that every third data point of the indicators x_5, x_6, and x_7 is eliminated in a single blindfolding round. Since the blindfolding procedure has to omit and predict every data point of the indicators used in the measurement

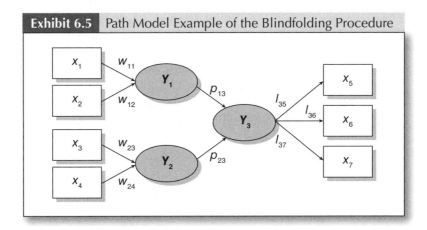

Exhibit 6.5   Path Model Example of the Blindfolding Procedure

model of a reflective endogenous latent variable, it has to include three rounds. Hence, the number of blindfolding rounds always equals the omission distance D.

Exhibit 6.6 shows the application of the blindfolding procedure with respect to the reflective endogenous latent variable Y_3 shown in Exhibit 6.5. For illustrative purposes, the number of observations for the standardized data of indicators x_5, x_6, and x_7 is reduced to seven in the reflective measurement model of construct Y_3. We select an omission distance of 3 in this example, but a higher number between 5 and 10 should be used in most applications (Hair et al., 2012b). Note that [$d1$], [$d2$], and [$d3$] in Exhibit 6.6 are not entries in the data matrix but are used to show how the data elimination pattern is applied to the data points of x_5, x_6, and x_7. For example, the first data point of indicator x_5 has a value of –0.452 and is connected to [$d1$], which indicates that this data point is eliminated in the first blindfolding round. The assignment of the omission distance (e.g., [$d1$], [$d2$], and [$d3$] in Exhibit 6.6) occurs per column. When the assignment of the pattern ends with [$d1$] in the last observation (i.e., Observation 7) in the first column of indicator x_5 (Exhibit 6.6), the procedure continues assigning [$d2$] to the first observation in the second column of indicator x_6.

Exhibit 6.6 displays the assignment of the data omission pattern for the omission distance of 3. It is important to note that the omission distance D has to be chosen so that the number of observations used in the model estimation divided by D is not an integer. If the number of observations divided by D results in an integer, you would always delete the same set of observations in each round from the data matrix. For example, if you have 90 observations, the omission distance must not be 9 or 10 as in, respectively, $90/9 = 10$ and $90/10 = 9$. Rather, you should use omission distances of 7 or 8.

As shown in Exhibit 6.6, the data points [$d1$] are eliminated in the first blindfolding round. The remaining data points are now used to estimate the path model in Exhibit 6.5. A missing value treatment function (e.g., the mean value replacement) is used for the deleted data points when running the PLS-SEM algorithm. These PLS-SEM estimates differ from the original model estimation and from the results of the two following blindfolding rounds. The outcomes of the first blindfolding round are used to first predict the $\hat{Y}_3$ scores of the selected reflective endogenous latent variable. Thereafter, the predicted values of $\hat{Y}_3$ and the estimations of the outer loadings

Exhibit 6.6 Blindfolding Procedure

Observations	Standardized Indicator Data			First Blindfolding Round: Omission of Data Points [d1]		
	Indicators of the Reflective Construct Y_3			Indicators of the Reflective Construct Y_3		
	x_5	x_6	x_7	x_5	x_6	x_7
1	−0.452 [d1]	−0.309 [d2]	−0.152 [d3]		−0.309 [d2]	−0.152 [d3]
2	0.943 [d2]	1.146 [d3]	0.534 [d1]	0.943 [d2]	1.146 [d3]	
3	−0.452 [d3]	−0.309 [d1]	−2.209 [d2]	−0.452 [d3]		−2.209 [d2]
4	0.943 [d1]	−1.036 [d2]	−0.837 [d3]		−1.036 [d2]	−0.837 [d3]
5	0.943 [d2]	−1.036 [d3]	0.534 [d1]	0.943 [d2]	−1.036 [d3]	
6	−1.150 [d3]	−1.036 [d1]	−0.837 [d2]	−1.150 [d3]		−0.837 [d2]
7	1.641 [d1]	−0.309 [d2]	1.220 [d3]		−0.309 [d2]	1.220 [d3]

(Continued)

Exhibit 6.6 (Continued)

	Second Blindfolding Round: Omission of Data Points [d2]			Third Blindfolding Round: Omission of Data Points [d3]		
	Indicators of the Reflective Construct Y_3			Indicators of the Reflective Construct Y_3		
Observations	x_5	x_6	x_7	x_5	x_6	x_7
1	−0.452 [d1]		−0.152 [d3]	−0.452 [d1]	−0.309 [d2]	
2		1.146 [d3]	0.534 [d1]	0.943 [d2]		0.534 [d1]
3	−0.452 [d3]	−0.309 [d1]		0.943 [d1]	−0.309 [d1]	−2.209 [d2]
4	0.943 [d1]		−0.837 [d3]	0.943 [d1]	−1.036 [d2]	
5		−1.036 [d3]	0.534 [d1]	0.943 [d2]		0.534 [d1]
6	−1.150 [d3]	−1.036 [d1]			−1.036 [d1]	−0.837 [d2]
7	1.641 [d1]		1.220 [d3]	1.641 [d1]	−0.309 [d2]	

(i.e., l_{35}, l_{36}, and l_{37}; Exhibit 6.6) in the first blindfolding round allow every single eliminated data point to be predicted in this first round. The second and the third blindfolding rounds follow a similar process.

After the last blindfolding round, each data point of the indicators of a selected reflective endogenous latent variable has been removed and then predicted. Thus, the blindfolding procedure can compare the original values with the predicted values. If the prediction is close to the original value (i.e., there is a small **prediction error**), the path model has a high predictive accuracy. The prediction errors (calculated as the difference between the true values [i.e., the omitted values] and the predicted values), along with a trivial prediction error (defined as the mean of the remaining data), are then used to estimate the Q^2 value (Chin, 1998). Q^2 values larger than 0 suggest that the model has predictive relevance for a certain endogenous construct. In contrast, values of 0 and below indicate a lack of predictive relevance.

It is important to note that the Q^2 value can be calculated by using two different approaches. The **cross-validated redundancy** approach—as described in this section—builds on the path model estimates of both the structural model (scores of the antecedent constructs) and the measurement model (target endogenous construct) of data prediction. Therefore, prediction by means of cross-validated redundancy fits the PLS-SEM approach perfectly. An alternative method, the **cross-validated communality** approach, uses only the construct scores estimated for the target endogenous construct (without including the structural model information) to predict the omitted data points. We recommend using the cross-validated redundancy as a measure of Q^2 since it includes the key element of the path model, the structural model, to predict eliminated data points.

The Q^2 values estimated by the blindfolding procedure represent a measure of how well the path model can predict the originally observed values. Similar to the f^2 effect size approach for assessing R^2 values, the relative impact of predictive relevance can be compared by means of the measure to the q^2 effect size, formally defined as follows:

$$q^2 = \frac{Q^2_{included} - Q^2_{excluded}}{1 - Q^2_{included}}.$$

For example, to determine the q^2 effect size of construct y_1 on the reflective endogenous latent variable Y_3 in Exhibit 6.5, one would compute the PLS-SEM results of the model with construct Y_1 ($Q^2_{included}$) and, thereafter, of the path model without construct Y_1 ($Q^2_{excluded}$). In doing so, one has to use identical values for the omission distance D when computing the results of $Q^2_{included}$ and $Q^2_{excluded}$. As a relative measure of predictive relevance, values of 0.02, 0.15, and 0.35 indicate that an exogenous construct has a small, medium, or large predictive relevance for a certain endogenous construct. An application of q^2 effect size to the reputation model follows later in this chapter.

HETEROGENEITY

Another important aspect of structural model evaluation is the **heterogeneity** of observations, which can be a threat to the validity of PLS-SEM results (e.g., Rigdon, Ringle, Sarstedt, & Gudergan, 2011; Ringle, Sarstedt, & Mooi, 2010; Sarstedt, Schwaiger, & Ringle, 2009) because it can distort the results. Researchers often encounter a situation in which different parameters occur for different subpopulations such as segments of consumers, firms, or countries. If heterogeneity is present in a sample, it means that two or more subgroups exhibit different underlying relationships with the constructs. Researchers often anticipate this possibility and, for example, test to see if the parameters for a model differ between males and females or for different ethnic heritage in cross-cultural research. This is referred to as **observed heterogeneity** because the researcher has information that suggests possible differences in the known subgroups that need to be tested. Because heterogeneity is often present in empirical research, researchers should always consider potential sources of heterogeneity (Hair, Ringle, & Sarstedt, 2011; Hair et al., 2012a), for example, by forming groups of data based on a priori information (e.g., age or gender = observed heterogeneity) and testing separate models for each group. Unfortunately, the presence of heterogeneity in a sample can never be fully known a priori. Consequently, situations arise in which differences related to **unobserved heterogeneity** prevent the PLS path model from being accurately estimated. In many instances, the researcher may not even be aware of the fact that heterogeneity is causing estimation problems. In this case, researchers need to apply approaches that identify and treat unobserved heterogeneity in the sample (e.g., FIMIX-PLS; Rigdon, Ringle, & Sarstedt, 2010; Ringle, Wende, et al., 2010; Sarstedt, Becker, Ringle, & Schwaiger, 2011; Sarstedt & Ringle, 2010). The treatment of observed and unobserved heterogeneity will be explained in more detail in Chapter 8.

GOODNESS-OF-FIT INDEX

Tenenhaus et al. (Tenenhaus et al., 2004; Tenenhaus, Esposito Vinzi, Chatelin, & Lauro, 2005) proposed a PLS **goodness-of-fit index** (GoF) as "an operational solution to this problem as it may be meant as an index for validating the PLS model globally" (Tenenhaus et al., 2005, p. 173). Henseler and Sarstedt (2012) recently challenged the usefulness of the GoF both conceptually and empirically. Their research shows that the GoF does not represent a goodness-of-fit criterion for PLS-SEM. In particular, the GoF is, unlike fit measures in CB-SEM, not able to separate valid models from invalid ones. Since the GoF is also not applicable to formatively measurement models and does not penalize overparametrization efforts, researchers are advised not to use this measure.

Exhibit 6.7 summarizes the key criteria for evaluating structural model results.

CASE STUDY ILLUSTRATION—HOW ARE PLS-SEM STRUCTURAL MODEL RESULTS REPORTED?

We continue with the extended corporate reputation model as introduced in Chapter 5. If you do not have the PLS path model readily available in SmartPLS, download the file **Corporate_Reputation_Extended.zip** from the http://www.pls-sem.com website, save it on your hard drive, and extract the **Corporate Reputation Extended.splsp** and the **Full Data.csv** files from this zip file (e.g., in the folder C:\SmartPLS\). Then, run the SmartPLS software and click on **File → Import** in the menu. When the Import box appears on the screen, click on **Next** and then on **Browse** to locate and import the ready-to-use SmartPLS project **Corporate Reputation Extended.splsp** as described in detail in Chapter 2.

Exhibit 6.7   Rules of Thumb for Structural Model Evaluation

- Examine each set of predictors in the structural model for collinearity. Each predictor construct's tolerance (VIF) value should be higher than 0.20 (lower than 5). Otherwise, consider eliminating constructs, merging predictors into a single construct, or creating higher-order constructs to treat collinearity problems.

- Use bootstrapping to assess the significance of path coefficients. The minimum number of bootstrap samples must be at least as large as the number of valid observations but should be 5,000. The number of cases should be equal to the number of valid observations in the original sample. Critical values for a two-tailed test are 1.65 (significance level = 10%), 1.96 (significance level = 5%), and 2.57 (significance level = 1%). In applications, you should usually consider path coefficients with a 5% or less probability of error as significant.

- PLS-SEM aims at maximizing the R^2 values of the endogenous latent variable(s) in the path model. Thus, the objective is high R^2 values. While the exact interpretation of the R^2 value level depends on the particular model and research discipline, in general, R^2 values of 0.75, 0.50, or 0.25 for the endogenous constructs can be described as respectively substantial, moderate, and weak.

- Use the R^2_{adj} when comparing models with different exogenous constructs and/or different numbers of observations.

- The effect size f^2 allows assessing an exogenous construct's contribution to an endogenous latent variable's R^2 value. The f^2 values of 0.02, 0.15, and 0.35 indicate an exogenous construct's small, medium, or large effect, respectively, on an endogenous construct.

- Predictive relevance: Use blindfolding to obtain cross-validated redundancy measures for each endogenous construct. Make sure the number of observations used in the model estimation divided by the omission distance D is not an integer. Choose D values between 5 and 10. The resulting Q^2 values larger than 0 indicate that the exogenous constructs have predictive relevance for the endogenous construct under consideration. As a relative measure of predictive relevance (q^2), values of 0.02, 0.15, and 0.35 respectively indicate that an exogenous construct has a small, medium, or large predictive relevance for a certain endogenous construct.

- Do not use the GoF.

- Heterogeneity: If theory supports the existence of alternative subgroups of data, carry out PLS-SEM multigroup or moderator analyses. If no theory or information is available about the underlying groups of data, an assessment should be conducted to identify unobserved heterogeneity.

Exhibit 6.8 Results in Modeling Window

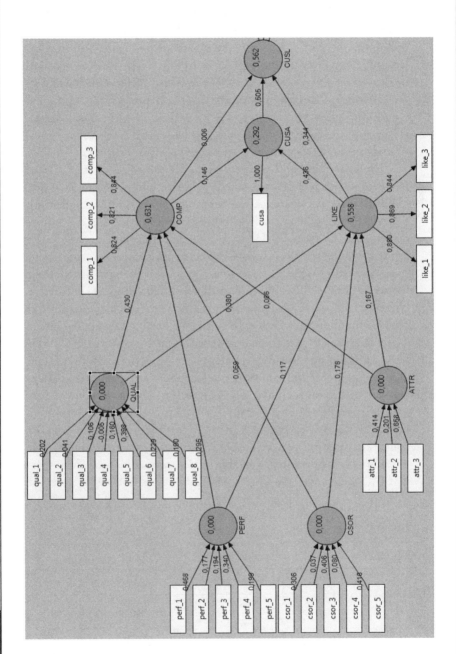

Thereafter, a new project appears with the name **Corporate Reputation Extended** in the SmartPLS **Projects** window on the left-hand side. This project contains several models (.splsm files) and the data set **Full Data.csv**. Highlight **Corporate Reputation Extended** and click on the expand all option (⊞⃗). Several files will be shown. The files include **Base Model.splsm, Convergent Validity ATTR.splsm, Convergent Validity CSOR.splsm,** and so forth, plus a data file called **Full Data.csv.** Next double-click on **Base Model. splsm,** and the extended PLS path model for the corporate reputation example opens as discussed in the previous chapter.

The assessment of the structural model builds on the results from the standard model estimation, the bootstrapping routine, and the blindfolding procedure. After running the PLS-SEM algorithm, SmartPLS shows the key results of the model estimation in the modeling window (Exhibit 6.8). Here we can see the path coefficients as well as the R^2 values of the endogenous constructs (shown in the circles).

For a more detailed assessment, we need to open the default report by going to **Menu → Report → Default Report.** Before we interpret the results, however, we first need to check the structural model for collinearity issues. To do so, we need to extract the latent variable scores from the default report, which you can find under **PLS → Calculation Results → Latent Variable Scores.** These are then used as input for the collinearity assessment in another statistical software program such as R, IBM SPSS Statistics, or Statistica. This analysis parallels that in Chapter 5, where we used the formative indicators as input; here, because we assess the structural model for collinearity issues, we need to make use of the latent variable scores. After importing the latent variable scores into such a statistical software package, we can run a multiple regression with a set of

Exhibit 6.9	Collinearity Assessment				
First Set		Second Set		Third Set	
Constructs	VIF	Constructs	VIF	Constructs	VIF
ATTR	2.122	COMP	1.686	COMP	1.716
CSOR	2.083	LIKE	1.686	LIKE	1.954
PERF	2.889			CUSA	1.412
QUAL	3.487				

predictor constructs as independent variables and any other latent variable, which does not serve as a predictor in this specific analysis, as the dependent variable (otherwise, it does not matter which construct serves as the dependent variable; Chapter 5). The results of the regression analysis do not matter and are not further analyzed. The only result that is important for assessing collinearity issues are the tolerance (VIF) values.

In this example, we run three separate OLS regressions for each part of the model using IBM SPSS Statistics and request collinearity diagnostics. Specifically, we assess the following sets of (predictor) constructs for collinearity: (1) *ATTR, CSOR, PERF,* and *QUAL* as predictors of *COMP* (and *LIKE*); (2) *COMP* and *LIKE* as predictors of *CUSA;* and (3) *COMP, LIKE,* and *CUSA* as predictors of *CUSL.* Exhibit 6.9 shows the VIF values of the analyses. As can be seen, all VIF values are clearly below the threshold of 5. Therefore, collinearity among the predictor constructs is not an issue in the structural model, and we can continue examining the default report.

To start with, we examine the R^2 values of the endogenous latent variables, which are available in the default report (**PLS → Quality Criteria → Overview**). Following our rules of thumb, the R^2 values of *COMP* (0.631), *CUSL* (0.562), and *LIKE* (0.558) can be considered moderate, whereas the R^2 value of *CUSA* (0.292) is rather weak.

Under **PLS → Calculation Results → Path Coefficients,** we find the path coefficients as shown in the modeling window. Looking at the relative importance of the exogenous driver constructs for the perceived competence (*COMP*), one finds that the customers' perception of the company's quality of products and services (*QUAL*) is most important, followed by its performance (*PERF*). In contrast, the perceived attractiveness (*ATTR*) and degree to which the company acts in socially conscious ways (*CSOR*) have very little bearing on the perceived competence. These two drivers are, however, of increased importance for establishing a company's likeability. Moving on in the model, we also find that likeability is the primary driver for the customers' satisfaction and loyalty, as illustrated by the increased path coefficients compared with those of competence.

More interesting, though, is the examination of total effects. Specifically, we can evaluate how strongly each of the four formative driver constructs (*ATTR, CSOR, PERF,* and *QUAL*) ultimately influences the key target variable *CUSL* via the mediating constructs

COMP, LIKE, and *CUSA.* Total effects are shown under **PLS →
Quality Criteria → Total Effects** in the default report. Here we can
see that among the four driver constructs, quality has the strongest
total effect on loyalty (0.2483), followed by corporate social responsibility (0.1053), attractiveness (0.1010), and performance (0.0894).
Therefore, it is advisable for companies to focus on marketing
activities that positively influence the customers' perception of the
quality of their products and services. By also taking the construct's
indicator weights into consideration, we can even identify which
specific element of quality needs to be addressed. Looking at the
outer weights (**PLS → Calculation Results → Outer Weights**) reveals
that *qual_6* has the highest outer weight (0.398). This item relates
to the survey question "[the company] seems to be a reliable partner
for customers." Thus, marketing managers should try to enhance the
customer's perception of the reliability of their products and services
by means of marketing activities.

The analysis of structural model relationships showed that several path coefficients (e.g., *COMP → CUSL*) had rather low values.
To assess whether such relationships are significant, we run the bootstrapping procedure. The extraction of bootstrapping results for the
structural model estimates is analogous to the descriptions in the
context of formative measurement model assessment (Chapter 5).
The calculation option in the SmartPLS menu bar is where you run
the bootstrapping routine (**Menu → Calculate → Bootstrapping;** note
that you may first need to click on **Base Model.splsm** to move from
the default report back to the reputation model). We use mean
replacement in the PLS-SEM algorithm setting and the no sign changes
option, 344 cases, and 5,000 samples in the bootstrapping settings.
The results tables appear if you open the default report directly after
running the bootstrapping routine in the SmartPLS software (**Menu
→ Report → Default Report**). Under **Bootstrapping → Path
Coefficients,** we find the results of each bootstrap run.

Exhibit 6.10 shows the PLS-SEM estimates of the *ATTR →
COMP* and the *ATTR → LIKE* relationships of the first 15 bootstrapping subsamples (your results will differ somewhat from those in
Exhibit 6.10 because bootstrapping is a random process that produces
different results in each run). Note that Exhibit 6.10 displays only a
fraction of the results table. The full table includes the estimates of all
the path coefficients for all 5,000 subsamples. These estimates are
used to compute the bootstrapping mean values, standard deviations,

standard errors, and *t* values of all the path coefficient estimates, shown under **Bootstrapping** → **Path Coefficients (Mean, STDEV, T-Values)**. Bootstrapping results for the total effects can be found under **Bootstrapping** → **Total Effects (Mean, STDEV, T-Values)**.

Exhibit 6.10	Bootstrapping Default Report

Exhibit 6.11 displays the path coefficients, the *t* values and their significance levels, *p* values, and the confidence intervals. Again, the user usually reports either the *t* values and their significance levels or the *p* value or the confidence intervals (note that the significance levels, *p* values, and confidence intervals were determined separately because the SmartPLS software does not provide them as output). We show the entire results for illustrative purposes. We find that all relationships in the structural model are significant, except *ATTR* → *COMP*, *COMP* → *CUSL*, and *CSOR* → *COMP*. These results suggest that companies should concentrate their marketing efforts on enhancing their likeability (by strengthening customers' quality perceptions) rather than their perceived competence to maximize customer loyalty. This is not surprising, considering that customers rated mobile network operators. As their services (provision of network capabilities) are intangible, affective judgments play a much more important role than cognitive judgments for establishing customer loyalty. Furthermore, we learn that *ATTR* and *CSOR* only influence likeability, which is also not surprising since these two driver constructs are also more affective in nature.

Exhibit 6.12 shows the corresponding results for the total effects of the exogenous constructs *ATTR*, *CSOR*, *PERF*, and *QUAL* on the target constructs *CUSA* and *CUSL* (also from **Bootstrapping** → **Total Effects (Mean, STDEV, T-Values)** in the bootstrapping output). The results show that all total effects are significant at least at a 5% level.

Exhibit 6.11 Significance Testing Results of the Structural Model Path Coefficients

	Path Coefficients	t Values	Significance Levels	p Values	90% Confidence Intervals
ATTR → COMP	0.09	1.63	NS	.10	[0.00, 0.17]
ATTR → LIKE	0.17	2.64	***	.01	[0.06, 0.27]
COMP → CUSA	0.15	2.20	**	.03	[0.04, 0.25]
COMP → CUSL	0.01	0.11	NS	.91	[−0.08, 0.09]
CSOR → COMP	0.06	1.09	NS	.28	[−0.03, 0.15]
CSOR → LIKE	0.18	3.17	***	.00	[0.09, 0.27]
CUSA → CUSL	0.51	11.99	***	.00	[0.44, 0.57]
LIKE → CUSA	0.44	7.41	***	.00	[0.34, 0.53]
LIKE → CUSL	0.34	6.31	***	.00	[0.25, 0.43]
PERF → COMP	0.30	4.42	***	.00	[0.18, 0.41]
PERF → LIKE	0.12	1.69	*	.09	[0.00, 0.23]
QUAL → COMP	0.43	6.48	***	.00	[0.32, 0.54]
QUAL → LIKE	0.38	5.76	***	.00	[0.27, 0.49]

Note: NS = not significant.

*$p < .10$. **$p < .05$. ***$p < .01$.

Exhibit 6.12 Significance Testing Results of the Total Effects

	Total Effect	t Values	Significance Levels	p Values	90% Confidence Intervals
ATTR → CUSA	0.09	2.80	***	.01	[0.02, 0.15]
ATTR → CUSL	0.10	2.73	***	.01	[0.02, 0.18]
CSOR → CUSA	0.09	3.16	***	.00	[0.03, 0.14]
CSOR → CUSL	0.11	3.11	***	.00	[0.04, 0.17]
PERF → CUSA	0.09	2.46	**	.01	[0.02, 0.17]
PERF → CUSL	0.09	2.06	**	.04	[0.00, 0.16]
QUAL → CUSA	0.23	6.11	***	.00	[0.16, 0.30]
QUAL → CUSL	0.25	5.72	***	.00	[0.16, 0.33]

$**p < .05. ***p < .01.$

Next, we run the blindfolding procedure to assess the predictive relevance of the path model. You can run the blindfolding procedure by going to **Menu → Calculate → Blindfolding** (note that you may first need to click on **Base Model.splsm** to move from the bootstrapping report back to the reputation model). In the menu that follows, we keep all the information of the missing value treatment and the PLS-SEM algorithm as in the initial model estimation (Chapter 3). We also need to specify the omission distance. Remember not to use an omission distance in which the division of the number of observations used in the model estimation and the distance is an integer. As we have 344 observations, we can choose an omission distance of $D = 7$. Last, we must specify which endogenous constructs should be analyzed in blindfolding. Make sure to select only endogenous latent variables with a reflective measurement model. Although you can select multiple latent variables in the dialog, you need to run the blindfolding routine for one reflective target construct after the other in the current version of the SmartPLS software. In this example, we start the analysis by running the blindfolding algorithm with the *CUSL* construct (Exhibit 6.13).

Exhibit 6.13	Settings to Start the Blindfolding Routine

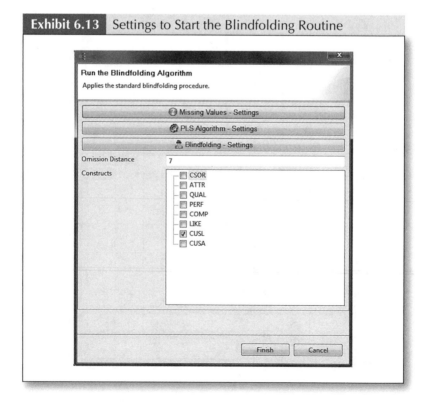

By opening the default report directly after running the blindfolding routine (**Menu → Report → Default Report**), the results appear as shown in Exhibit 6.14. The only results table we need to focus on is the one for the **Construct Crossvalidated Redundancy** estimates. The first part of the results table (as displayed on the right in Exhibit 6.14) presents the summary with the total outcomes of the blindfolding procedure, followed below by the outcomes of each of the seven blindfolding rounds. Although the total results of several latent variables are available, we only use the outcome of the selected one, which is *CUSL*. The results of the other constructs must be extracted in separate blindfolding runs. With respect to *CUSL*, we obtain the sum of the squared observations (SSO) and the sum of the squared prediction errors (SSE). The result in the last column (i.e., 1 – SSE/SSO) is the value of the predictive relevance Q^2. In our path model, the predictive relevance Q^2 of *CUSL* has a value of 0.4178, which implies that the model has predictive relevance for this construct.

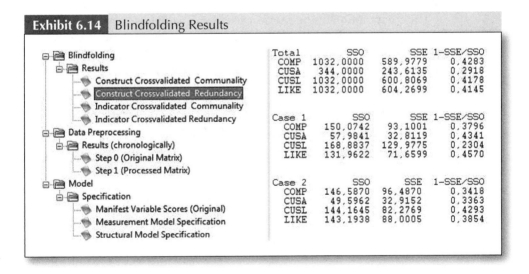

Exhibit 6.14 Blindfolding Results

Exhibit 6.15 provides the Q^2 values (along with the R^2 values) of all endogenous constructs. All Q^2 values are considerably above zero, thus providing support for the model's predictive relevance regarding the endogenous latent variables.

The final assessments address the f^2 and q^2 effect sizes. These must be computed manually because the SmartPLS does not provide them.

To compute the f^2 value of a selected endogenous latent variable, we need the $R^2_{included}$ and $R^2_{excluded}$ values. The $R^2_{included}$ results from the overall model estimation are available from Exhibit 6.15. The $R^2_{excluded}$ value is obtained from a model reestimation after deleting a specific predecessor of that endogenous latent variable. For example, the endogenous latent variable CUSL has an original R^2 value of 0.562 ($R^2_{included}$). If CUSA is deleted from the path model and the model is reestimated, the R^2 of CUSL has a value of only 0.385 ($R^2_{excluded}$). These two values are the inputs for computing the f^2 effect size of CUSA on CUSL:

$$f^2_{CUSA \rightarrow CUSL} = \frac{R^2_{included} - R^2_{excluded}}{1 - R^2_{included}} = \frac{0.562 - 0.385}{1 - 0.562} = 0.404.$$

In accordance with the rules of thumb for the f^2, the effect size can be considered large.

The computation of the q^2 effect size is an analogous procedure. However, instead of the R^2 values, the Q^2 values of the predictive relevance are used as inputs (after running the blindfolding procedure). For example, the endogenous latent variable CUSL has a Q^2 value of 0.418 ($Q^2_{included}$). After deleting CUSA from the path model and reestimating the model with the blindfolding procedure, the Q^2 of CUSL only has a value of 0.285 ($Q^2_{excluded}$). These two values are the inputs for computing the q^2 effect size of CUSA on CUSL:

$$q^2_{CUSA \rightarrow CUSL} = \frac{Q^2_{included} - Q^2_{excluded}}{1 - Q^2_{included}} = \frac{0.418 - 0.285}{1 - 0.418} = 0.229.$$

Following the rules of thumb, the q^2 effect size for this relationship can be considered medium. Exhibit 6.16 summarizes the results of the f^2 and q^2 effect sizes with respect to all the relationships in the model, along with the path coefficients. Target constructs appear in the first row, whereas the predecessor constructs are in the first column. For example, the path coefficient from ATTR to COMP is 0.086; the f^2 (q^2) effect size is 0.011 (0.028).

Exhibit 6.15   Results of R^2 and Q^2 Values

Endogenous Latent Variable	R^2 Value	Q^2 Value
COMP	0.631	0.430
CUSL	0.562	0.418
CUSA	0.292	0.292
LIKE	0.558	0.413

Exhibit 6.16   Summary of Results

	COMP			CUSL		
	Path Coefficients	f^2 Effect Size	q^2 Effect Size	Path Coefficients	f^2 Effect Size	q^2 Effect Size
ATTR	0.086	0.011	0.028			
COMP				0.006	0.000	-0.002
CSOR	0.059	0.005	0.002			
CUSA				0.505	0.404	0.229
LIKE				0.344	0.139	0.077
PERF	0.295	0.076	0.040			
QUAL	0.430	0.144	0.061			

	CUSA			LIKE		
	Path Coefficients	f^2 Effect Size	q^2 Effect Size	Path Coefficients	f^2 Effect Size	q^2 Effect Size
ATTR				0.167	0.029	0.020
COMP	0.146	0.018	0.020			
CSOR				0.178	0.036	0.017
CUSA						
LIKE	0.436	0.161	0.140			
PERF				0.117	0.011	0.007
QUAL				0.380	0.095	0.053

SUMMARY

- **Assess the path coefficients in the structural model.** Two things are important when assessing the PLS-SEM results for the structural model: the significance and the relevance of coefficients. Testing for significance requires application of the bootstrapping routine and examination of t values, p values, or bootstrapping confidence intervals. Next, the relative sizes of path coefficients are compared, as well as the total effects, f^2 effect size, and q^2 effect size. By interpreting these results, you can identify the key constructs with the highest relevance to explain the endogenous latent variable(s) in the structural model.

- **Evaluate the coefficients of determination (R^2 values).** The PLS-SEM method was developed primarily for prediction purposes. The R^2 values (i.e., coefficients of determination) represent the amount of explained variance of the endogenous constructs in the structural model. A well-developed path model to explain certain key target constructs (e.g., customer satisfaction, customer loyalty, or technology acceptance) should deliver sufficiently high R^2 values. The exact interpretation of the R^2 value depends on the particular research discipline. In general, R^2 values of 0.25, 0.50, and 0.75 for target constructs are considered as weak, medium, and substantial, respectively.

- **Understand and evaluate the f^2 effect size.** The f^2 effect size enables you to analyze the relevance of constructs in explaining selected endogenous latent constructs. More specifically, you analyze how much a predictor construct contributes to the R^2 value of a target construct in the structural model. Initially, you estimate the R^2 value with a particular predecessor construct. Without the predecessor construct, the result is a lower R^2 value. On the basis of the difference of the R^2 values for estimating the model with and without the predecessor construct, you obtain the f^2 effect size. Results of 0.02, 0.15, and 0.35 are interpreted as small, medium, and large f^2 effect sizes, respectively.

- **Use the blindfolding procedure for assessing the predictive relevance (Q^2 value) of the path model.** The blindfolding procedure is a resampling technique that systematically deletes and predicts every data point of the indicators in the reflective measurement model of endogenous constructs. By comparing the original values with the predictions, the prediction error of the path model for this particular reflective target construct is obtained. The computation of the Q^2 value for assessing predictive relevance uses this prediction error. The path model has predictive relevance for a selected reflective endogenous construct if the Q^2 value is above zero. In accordance the with f^2 effect size for the R^2 values, you can also compute the q^2 effect size for the Q^2 values. The q^2 effect size of a selected construct and its relationship to an endogenous construct in the structural model uses the same critical values for assessment used for the f^2 effect size evaluation.

- **Comprehend heterogeneity and how it may affect PLS-SEM estimates.** Another important aspect of structural model evaluation is heterogeneity of observations, which can be a threat to the validity of PLS-SEM results. That is, researchers often encounter a situation where different parameters occur for different subpopulations such as segments of consumers, firms, or countries. Heterogeneity can become a crucial issue with misleading interpretations and false conclusions if, for instance, a structural model relationship has a significant positive effect for one group and a significant negative effect for another. On the aggregate data level, this relationship may appear insignificant, whereas on a group level, the relationships are significant. Hence, researchers must examine this issue as another element of the PLS-SEM results evaluation and thus apply techniques for the identification and analysis of heterogeneity in the sample (Chapter 8).

- **Learn how to report and interpret structural model results.** By extending the example on corporate reputation so it includes additional constructs, you can learn to systematically apply the structural model assessment criteria. The SmartPLS software provides all relevant results for the evaluation of the structural model. The tables and figures for this example described in the chapter demonstrate how to correctly interpret and report the PLS-SEM results. The hands-on example not only summarizes the previously introduced concepts but also provides additional insights for practical applications of PLS-SEM.

REVIEW QUESTIONS

1. What are the key criteria for assessing the results of the structural model?

2. Why do you assess the significance of path coefficients?

3. What is an appropriate R^2 value level?

4. Which is the critical Q^2 value to establish predictive relevance?

5. What are the critical values for interpreting the f^2 and q^2 effect sizes?

CRITICAL THINKING QUESTIONS

1. What problems do you encounter in evaluating the structural model results of PLS-SEM? How do you approach this task?

2. Why is the use of the goodness-of-fit index for PLS-SEM not advisable?

3. Why use the bootstrapping routine for significance testing? Explain the algorithm options and parameters you need to select.

4. Explain the f^2 effect size.

5. How does the blindfolding procedure function and what are the consequences of increasing and decreasing the omission distance D? Explain the Q^2 value and the q^2 effect size results.

6. Why is heterogeneity a critical issue that must be addressed when running PLS-SEM?

KEY TERMS

Adjusted R^2 value (R^2_{adj}): is a modified measure of the *coefficient of determination* that takes into account the number of predictor constructs. The statistic is useful for comparing models with different numbers of predictor constructs, different sample sizes, or both.

Blindfolding: is a sample reuse technique that omits part of the data matrix and uses the model estimates to predict the omitted part.

Bootstrapping: is a resampling technique that draws a large number of subsamples from the original data (with replacement) and estimates models for each subsample. It is used to determine standard errors of coefficients in order to assess their statistical significance without relying on distributional assumptions.

Coefficient of determination (R^2): is a measure of the proportion of an endogenous construct's variance that is explained by its predictor constructs.

Collinearity: arises in the context of structural model evaluation when two constructs are highly correlated.

Confidence interval: provides an estimated range of values that is likely to include an unknown population parameter. It is determined by its lower and upper bounds, which depend on a predefined probability of error and the standard error of the estimation for a given set of sample data. When zero does not fall into the confidence interval, an estimated parameter can be assumed to be significantly different from zero for the prespecified probability of error (e.g., 5%).

Critical value: see *Significance testing*.

Cross-validated communality: is used to obtain the Q^2 value based on the prediction of the data points by means of the underlying measurement model (see *Blindfolding*).

Cross-validated redundancy: is used to obtain the Q^2 value based on the prediction of the data points by means of the underlying structural model and measurement model (see *Blindfolding*).

Degrees of freedom: is the number of values in the final calculation of a statistic that are free to vary.

Direct effect: is a relationship linking two constructs with a single arrow between the two.

Empirical *t* value: see *Significance testing*.

f^2 effect size: is a measure used to assess the relative impact of a predictor construct on an endogenous construct.

GoF: see *Goodness of fit index.*

Goodness-of-fit index (GoF): has been developed as an overall measure of model fit for PLS-SEM. However, as the GoF cannot reliably distinguish valid from invalid models and since its applicability is limited to certain model setups, researchers should avoid its use.

Heterogeneity: indicates that significantly different PLS-SEM results are associated with different relevant subgroups (observed or unobserved) in the population.

Hypothesized relationships: are proposed explanations for constructs that define the path relationships in the structural model. The PLS-SEM results enable researchers to statistically test these hypotheses and thereby empirically substantiate the existence of the proposed path relationships.

Indirect effect: a sequence of relationships with at least one intervening construct involved.

Observed heterogeneity: occurs when the sources of heterogeneity are known and can be traced back to observable characteristics such as demographics (e.g., gender, age, income).

Omission distance (D): determines which data points are deleted when applying the blindfolding (see *Blindfolding*) procedure. An omission distance D of 9, for example, implies that every ninth data point, and thus $1/9 = 11.11\%$ of the data in the original data set, are deleted during each blindfolding round. The omission distance should be chosen so that the number of observations used from model estimation divided by D is not an integer. Furthermore, D should be between 5 and 10.

Parsimonious models: are models with as few parameters as possible for a given quality of model estimation results.

Path coefficients: are estimated path relationships for the structural model (i.e., between the latent variables in the model). They correspond to standardized betas in a regression analysis.

Prediction error: measures the difference between the prediction of a data point and its original value in the sample.

Predictive relevance (Q^2): see *Q^2 value.*

p value: is in the context of structural model assessment, the probability of error for assuming that a path coefficient is significantly different from zero. In applications, researchers compare the p value of a coefficient with a significance level selected prior to the analysis to decide whether the path coefficient is statistically significant.

Q^2 **effect size:** is a measure used to assess the relative predictive relevance of a predictor construct on an endogenous construct.

Q^2 **value:** is a measure of predictive relevance based on the *blindfolding* technique.

R^2 **value:** see *Coefficient of determination.*

Relevance of significant relationships: compares the relative importance of predictor constructs to explain endogenous latent constructs in the structural model. Significance is a prerequisite for the relevance, but not all constructs and their significant path coefficients are highly relevant to explain a selected target construct.

Significance testing: is the process of testing whether a certain result likely has occurred by chance. In the context of structural model evaluation, it involves testing whether a path coefficient is truly different from zero in the population. Assuming a specified significance level, we reject the null hypothesis of no effect (i.e., the path coefficient is zero in the population) if the empirical t value (as provided by the data) is larger than the critical value. Commonly used critical values for two-tailed tests (derived from the normal distribution) are 2.57, 1.96, and 1.65 for significance levels of 1%, 5%, and 10%, respectively.

Standard error: is the standard deviation of the sampling distribution of that statistic. Standard errors are important to show how much sampling fluctuation a statistic has.

Standardized values: indicate how many standard deviations an observation is above or below the mean.

Total effect: is the sum of the direct effect and all indirect effects linking two constructs.

Two-tailed tests: see *Significance testing.*

Unobserved heterogeneity: occurs when the sources of heterogeneous data structures are not (fully) known.

SUGGESTED READINGS

Albers, S. (2010). PLS and success factor studies in marketing. In V. Esposito Vinzi, W. W. Chin, J. Henseler & H. Wang (Eds.), *Handbook of partial least squares: concepts, methods and applications* (Springer handbooks of computational statistics series, vol. II) (pp. 409–425). New York: Springer.

Boudreau, M. C., Gefen, D., & Straub, D. W. (2001). Validation in information systems research: A state-of-the-art assessment. *MIS Quarterly, 25*(1), 1–16.

Cenfetelli, R. T., & Bassellier, G. (2009). Interpretation of formative measurement in information systems research. *MIS Quarterly, 33*(4), 689–708.

Chin, W. W. (2010). How to write up and report PLS analyses. In V. Esposito Vinzi, W. W. Chin, J. Henseler, & H. Wang (Eds.), *Handbook of partial least squares: Concepts, methods and applications in marketing and related fields* (pp. 655–690). Berlin: Springer.

Diamantopoulos, A. (2008). Formative indicators: Introduction to the special issue. *Journal of Business Research, 61*(12), 1201–1202.

Diamantopoulos, A., & Winklhofer, H. M. (2001). Index construction with formative indicators: An alternative to scale development. *Journal of Marketing Research, 38*(2), 269–277.

Gefen, D., Rigdon, E. E., & Straub, D. W. (2011). Editor's comment: An update and extension to SEM guidelines for administrative and social science research. *MIS Quarterly, 35*(2), iii–xiv.

Gudergan, S. P., Ringle, C. M., Wende, S., & Will, A. (2008). Confirmatory tetrad analysis in PLS path modeling. *Journal of Business Research, 61*(12), 1238–1249.

Hair, J. F., Ringle, C. M., & Sarstedt, M. (2011). PLS-SEM: Indeed a silver bullet. *Journal of Marketing Theory and Practice, 19*, 139–151.

Hair, J. F., Sarstedt, M., Pieper, T., & Ringle, C. M. (2012a). Applications of partial least squares path modeling in management journals: A review. *Long Range Planning, 45*, 320–340.

Hair, J. F., Sarstedt, M., Ringle, C. M., & Mena, J. A. (2012). An assessment of the use of partial least squares structural equation modeling in marketing research. *Journal of the Academy of Marketing Science, 40*, 414–433.

Henseler, J., Ringle, C. M., & Sinkovics, R. R. (2009). The use of partial least squares path modeling in international marketing. *Advances in International Marketing, 20*, 277–320.

Hulland, J. (1999). Use of partial least squares (PLS) in strategic management research: A review of four recent studies. *Strategic Management Journal, 20*(2), 195–204.

Ringle, C. M., Sarstedt, M., & Straub, D. W. (2012). A critical look at the use of PLS-SEM in *MIS Quarterly*. *MIS Quarterly, 36*, iii–xiv.

Roldán, J. L., and Sánchez-Franco, M. J. (2012). Variance-based structural equation modeling: Guidelines for using partial least squares in information systems research. In *Research methodologies, innovations and philosophies in software systems engineering and information systems* (pp. 193–221). Hershey, PA: IGI Global.

Tenenhaus, M., Esposito Vinzi, V., Chatelin, Y. M., & Lauro, C. (2005). PLS path modeling. *Computational statistics & data analysis, 48*(1), 159–205.

C H A P T E R   7

Advanced Topics in PLS-SEM

LEARNING OUTCOMES

1. Understand how to conduct a PLS-SEM importance-performance matrix analysis (IPMA).

2. Explain mediator analysis and how to execute it using PLS-SEM.

3. Understand higher-order constructs and how to apply this concept in PLS-SEM.

CHAPTER PREVIEW

This chapter addresses several advanced PLS-SEM topics. We begin with an importance-performance matrix analysis (IPMA). Standard PLS-SEM analyses provide information on the relative importance of constructs in explaining other constructs in the structural model. Information on the importance of constructs is relevant for drawing conclusions. However, IPMA extends the results of PLS-SEM by also taking the performance of each construct into account. As a result, conclusions can be drawn on two dimensions (i.e., both importance and performance), which is particularly important to prioritize managerial actions. Consequently, it is preferable to primarily focus on improving the performance of constructs with a large importance regarding their explanation of a certain target construct but that, simultaneously, have a relatively low performance.

Another important topic is mediation. A significant mediator variable may to some extent absorb a cause-effect relationship. Examining mediating variables enables researchers to better understand the relationships between dependent and predictor constructs.

Finally, higher-order constructs enable researchers to include a more general construct that represents several of its subcomponents in a PLS-SEM. The number of potential relationships in the structural model is thus reduced, and the PLS path model becomes more parsimonious and easier to grasp.

IMPORTANCE-PERFORMANCE MATRIX ANALYSIS

Method

A key characteristic of the PLS-SEM method is the extraction of latent variable scores. **Importance-performance matrix analysis (IPMA)** is useful in extending the findings of the basic PLS-SEM outcomes using the latent variable scores (Fornell, Johnson, Anderson, Cha, & Bryant, 1996; Höck, Ringle, & Sarstedt, 2010; Kristensen, Martensen, & Grønholdt, 2000; Slack, 1994; Völckner, Sattler, Hennig-Thurau, & Ringle, 2010). The extension builds on the PLS-SEM estimates of the path model relationships and adds an additional dimension to the analysis that considers the latent variables' average values. For a specific endogenous latent variable representing a key target construct in the analysis, IPMA contrasts the structural model total effects (importance) and the average values of the latent variable scores (performance) to highlight significant areas for the improvement of management activities (or the specific focus of the model). More specifically, the results permit the identification of determinants with a relatively high importance and relatively low performance. These are major areas of improvement that can subsequently be addressed by marketing or management activities.

A basic PLS-SEM analysis identifies the relative **importance** of constructs in the structural model by extracting estimations of the direct, indirect, and total relationships. The IPMA extends these PLS-SEM results with another dimension, which includes the actual **performance** of each construct.

Executing an IPMA first requires identifying a target construct. To complete an IPMA of a particular target construct, the total effects and the performance values are needed. The importance of latent variables for an endogenous target construct—as analyzed by means of an importance-performance matrix—emerges from these variables' total effects (Slack, 1994). In PLS-SEM, the total effects are derived from a PLS path model estimation.

Consider the example in Exhibit 7.1, which shows the PLS-SEM results of a structural model. The information in parentheses (inside each construct) is the performance of each latent variable on a scale from 0 to 100. The standardized path coefficients are beside each of the arrows, representing the strength of the relationships between constructs.

We now use the results to create a results representation for the IPMA of the key target construct Y_4, as shown in Exhibit 7.2. The x-axis represents the total effects of the latent variables Y_1, Y_2, and Y_3 on the target construct Y_4 (i.e., their importance). The y-axis depicts the (rescaled) average construct scores of Y_1, Y_2, and Y_3 (i.e., their performance). We find that Y_1 is a particularly important construct to explain the target construct Y_4. In a ceteris paribus situation, an increase of one point in the performance of Y_1 is expected to increase the performance of Y_4 by the value of the total effect, which is 0.84. At the same time, the performance of Y_1 is relatively low, so there is substantial room for improvement. Consequently, in the PLS path model example, construct Y_1 is the most relevant for managerial actions.

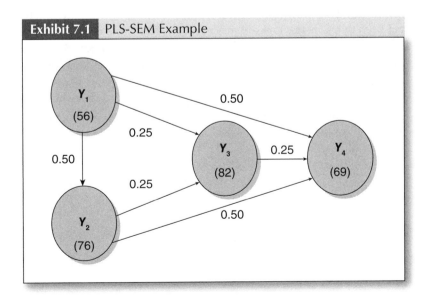

Exhibit 7.1   PLS-SEM Example

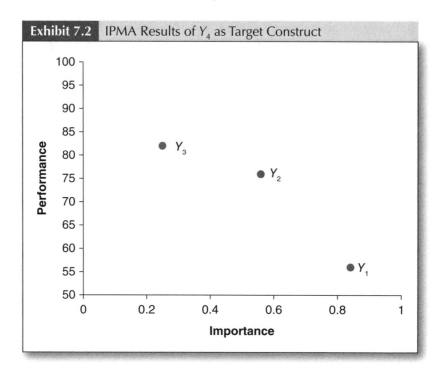

Exhibit 7.2   IPMA Results of Y_4 as Target Construct

The IPMA—as shown in the example in Exhibit 7.2—requires obtaining the **total effects** of the relationships of all the other constructs in the example (i.e., Y_1, Y_2, and Y_3) on the selected target construct Y_4 to indicate their importance. The total effect of a relationship between two constructs is the sum of all the **direct** and **indirect effects** in the structural model: total effect = direct effect + indirect effect. For instance, the direct effect of Y_1 on Y_4 has a value of 0.5. In addition, there are three indirect path relationships that range from Y_1 to Y_4: (i) $Y_1 \rightarrow Y_2 \rightarrow Y_4$, (ii) $Y_1 \rightarrow Y_2 \rightarrow Y_3 \rightarrow Y_4$, and (iii) $Y_1 \rightarrow Y_3 \rightarrow Y_4$. The estimated values of each relevant indirect relationship must be multiplied and added. Thus, in the case of the indirect effect of Y_1 on Y_4, the following applies:

$$
\begin{array}{llll}
= & Y_1 \rightarrow Y_2 \rightarrow Y_4 & = 0.50 \cdot 0.50 & = 0.250 \\
+ & Y_1 \rightarrow Y_2 \rightarrow Y_3 \rightarrow Y_4 & = 0.50 \cdot 0.25 \cdot 0.25 & = 0.031 \\
+ & Y_1 \rightarrow Y_3 \rightarrow Y_4 & = 0.25 \cdot 0.25 & = 0.063 \\
& & & = 0.344
\end{array}
$$

Exhibit 7.3 shows the total effects of the constructs Y_1, Y_2, and Y_3 on the target construct Y_4.

Next, we need to obtain the performance values of the latent variables in the PLS path model. To make the results comparable across different scales, we use a performance scale of 0 to 100, whereby 0 represents the lowest and 100 the highest performance. As most people are used to interpreting percentage values, this kind of performance scale is easy to understand. **Rescaling** the latent variables to obtain **index values** requires the following computations to be performed: Subtract the minimum possible value of the latent variable's scale (i.e., 1 for a scale of 1 to 7) from an estimated data point and divide this data point by the difference between the minimum and maximum data points of the latent variable's scale (i.e., $7 - 1 = 6$ for a scale of 1 to 7):

$$Y_i^{rescaled} = \frac{(Y_i - \text{Minscale}[Y])}{(\text{Maxscale}[Y] - \text{Minscale}[Y])} \cdot 100$$

whereby Y_{ij} represents the ith data point (e.g., $i = 5$ with respect to the latent variable score of the fifth observation in the data set) of a specific latent variable in the PLS path model (Anderson & Fornell, 2000; Höck et al., 2010; Tenenhaus et al., 2005). This procedure results in rescaled latent variable scores on a scale of 0 to 100. The mean value of these rescaled scores of each latent variable produces the index value of their performance, indicated on a scale of 0 to 100, with the higher values usually indicating a latent variable's better performance. In our example, Y_1 has a performance of 56, Y_2 of 76, and Y_3 of 82. Exhibit 7.4 shows the data used for the IPMA of the latent variable Y_4 as illustrated in Exhibit 7.2.

Exhibit 7.3	IPMA Path Model Example and Total Effects		
	Direct Effect on Y_4	*Indirect Effect on* Y_4	*Total Effect on* Y_4
Y_1	0.50	0.34	0.84
Y_2	0.50	0.06	0.56
Y_3	0.25	0.00	0.25

Exhibit 7.4	Data of the IPMA Path Model Example	
	Importance	*Performance*
Y_1	0.84	56
Y_2	0.56	76
Y_3	0.25	82

Application of the IPMA needs to meet the following requirements: First, all the indicators must have the same direction; a low value represents a bad outcome and a high value a good outcome. Otherwise, the scale cannot be interpreted in a way that allows the latent variables' higher mean values (i.e., toward 100) to represent a better performance. If this is not the case, the direction needs to be changed by reversing the scale (e.g., on a 1- to 5-point scale, 5 becomes 1 and 1 becomes 5, 2 becomes 4 and 4 becomes 2, and 3 remains unchanged). Second, the outer weights (formative measurement model) or outer loadings (reflective measurement model) that are used must have positive expected and estimated values. If this condition cannot be met in terms of a measurement model of a certain latent variable, the extracted performance value will not be on a scale of 0 to 100 but, for example, on a scale of –5 to 95.

Case Study Illustration

To illustrate the case study, we continue using the PLS path model example of corporate reputation presented in the previous chapters. To view the examples in this chapter, download the **Corporate_Reputation_Advanced.zip** file from http://www.pls-sem.com. This file contains the SmartPLS project file for this chapter, all data files used, and an MS Excel example of how to conduct an IPMA. After extracting the zip file, import the **Corporate Reputation Extended–Advanced Analyses.splsp** project file into SmartPLS (see explanations in the previous chapters) and estimate the PLS-SEM results of the **Base Model.** Exhibit 7.5 again shows the model and the estimated path coefficients as well as the R^2 values.

The goal is to conduct an IPMA of the key target construct customer loyalty (*CUSL*). Before running the analysis, the data need to be rescaled. The rescaling of the latent variables and the index value computation are carried out automatically by the

Exhibit 7.5 SmartPLS Results of the Corporate Reputation Model

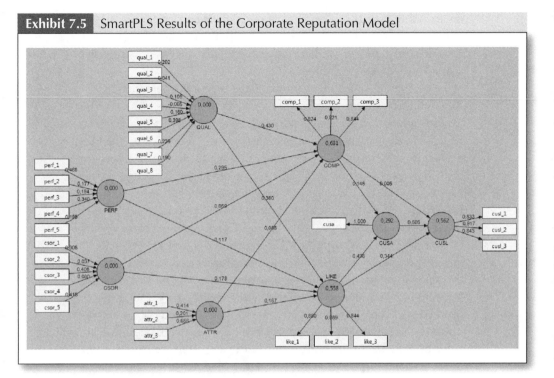

SmartPLS software when rescaled indicator data are used. Rescaling the indicators uses the following equation but on all indicators used as input for the PLS-SEM algorithm:

$$x_i^{rescaled} = \frac{(x_i - \text{Minscale}[x])}{(\text{Maxscale}[x] - \text{Minscale}[x])} \cdot 100$$

whereby x_i represents the ith observation of a specific indicator variable in the PLS path model (e.g., *attr_2*). For example, the response of observation number 199 of the *attr_2* indicator has a value of 6 on a given scale of 1 to 7. Then, with a Minscale[*attr_2*] = 1 and Maxscale[*attr_2*] = 7, the value of 6 as a response in data point 199 of indicator *attr_2* becomes

$$\frac{(6-1)}{(7-1)} \cdot 100 = 71.43$$

on a scale of 0 to 100. This kind of rescaling is carried out for all the indicator data. Using these data as an input for SmartPLS gives the same PLS path model estimation results but also delivers the rescaled scores of the latent variables.

The original data set for estimating the corporate reputation model (i.e., **Full Data.csv**) has missing values and data on a scale of 1 to 7. The easiest way to use the automatic capabilities of SmartPLS to generate the rescaled latent variable scores on a scale of 0 to 100 is to run the **PLS algorithm** as described, for example, in Chapter 6 and to open the **Default Report** (Exhibit 7.6). This report offers the **Processed** (Data) **Matrix** in which the selected missing value treatment option in SmartPLS has treated the missing values (i.e., mean value replacement).

The data can be copied (by clicking **CTRL+A** to select the results table and **CTRL+C** to copy the table) and pasted (by clicking **CTRL+V**) into a spreadsheet program such as Microsoft Excel for further processing. More specifically, in a spreadsheet, the row header with the variable names needs to be copied, after which every data entry is rescaled by subtracting the minimum value of the interval scale and dividing this difference by the difference between the maximum scale value and the minimum scale value. For example, in the new sheet of the spreadsheet application, the first data point *attr_1*, which is 5 on a 1 to 7 scale, is transformed as follows: $(5 - 1)/(7 - 1) \cdot 100 = 66.67$. This kind of computation is applied to all data and the file is saved as **Full Data(100).csv**. This rescaled data set is available in the **Corporate_ Reputation_Advanced.zip** file (http://www.pls-sem.com). Next, the **Full Data(100).csv** file must be imported into the **Corporate Reputation Extended–Advanced Analyses** project by using the SmartPLS **Import Indicator Data** option. In the SmartPLS **Projects** window, click on the **Corporate Reputation Extended–Advanced Analyses** project. This project has now been selected. Clicking the right mouse button opens the dialog box with several options as shown in Exhibit 7.7. Choosing the **Import Indicator Data** option allows you to add an additional set of indicator data to this selected SmartPLS project (i.e., Corporate Reputation Extended–Advanced Analyses).

Now, the SmartPLS data **Import Wizard** opens as shown in Exhibit 7.8. In the first step, you need to specify the location where you saved the **Full Data(100).csv** file. If you know the location, you can directly type in the path and the file name (e.g., C:\SmartPLS\Full Data(100).cvs). Otherwise, click on the ▣ button (Exhibit 7.8) that opens your file browser to search and double-click on the **Full**

Exhibit 7.6 Missing Value Treated Data

- Data Preprocessing
  - Results (chronologically)
    - Step 0 (Original Matrix)
    - Step 1 (Processed Matrix)
- Index Values
- Model
- PLS

attr_1	attr_2	attr_3	comp_1	comp_2	comp_3	csor_1	csor_2	csor_3	csor_4	csor_5
5.0000	1.0000	3.0000	4.0000	5.0000	5.0000	3.0000	3.0000	3.0000	3.0000	3.0000
6.0000	6.0000	6.0000	6.0000	7.0000	6.0000	2.0000	5.0000	6.0000	4.0000	6.0000
5.0000	6.0000	5.0000	4.0000	5.0000	2.0000	3.0000	1.0000	5.0000	2.0000	4.0000
3.0000	7.0000	6.0000	6.0000	4.0000	6.0000	3.0000	3.0000	5.0000	3.0000	5.0000
6.0000	6.0000	5.0000	3.0000	4.0000	4.0000	4.0000	3.0000	4.0000	3.0000	4.0000
4.0000	1.0000	3.0000	7.0000	5.0000	7.0000	7.0000	5.0000	7.0000	3.0000	3.0000
5.0000	7.0000	5.0000	6.0000	6.0000	6.0000	4.0000	1.0000	3.0000	3.0000	3.0000
4.0000	1.0000	5.0000	5.0000	7.0000	6.0000	7.0000	5.0000	6.0000	4.0000	2.0000
6.0000	3.0000	7.0000								6.0000

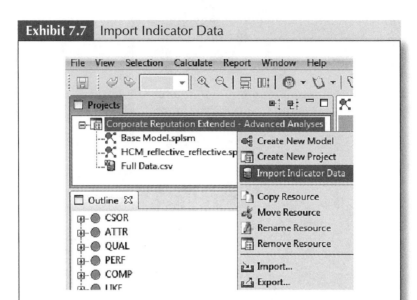

| Exhibit 7.7 | Import Indicator Data |

Data(100).csv file. Then, the file name and path appear in the text field (e.g., C:\SmartPLS\Full Data(100).cvs) as displayed in Exhibit 7.8.

Click on the **Next** button and the second dialog window of the SmartPLS **Import Wizard** (i.e., **Missing Values Settings**) opens (Exhibit 7.9). If your data set has missing values, check the box as shown in Exhibit 7.9. The text field allows you to indicate which number represents missing values. The **Full Data(100).csv** file contains missing values, so you must check the box. This file does not contain any missing values because these have treated with mean value replacement in the first step of the analysis. Therefore, simply click on the **Finish** button. Your data file has now been imported into the selected SmartPLS project. After importing the **Full Data(100).csv** file, this data set appears in the **Corporate Reputation Extended–Advanced Analyses** project, which is displayed in the SmartPLS **Projects** window. This project now has two data sets available. Note that you can switch between the data files for the PLS path model estimation. Click on a certain data file to select it. Then, press the right mouse button on this selected data file, which opens a menu with several options. Choose the option **Use Data for Calculation.** Then, a green tag (i.e., a green box with a white check-mark) appears next to the data file symbol to indicate that the PLS path model estimation uses this specific set of data.

Exhibit 7.8   SmartPLS Data Import (I)

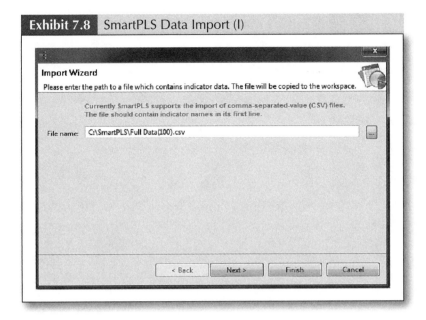

If the **Full Data(100).csv** file has a red tag after running the import procedure, it cannot be used for the estimation of the PLS path model. In that case, double-click on the data set in the SmartPLS **Projects** window. The **Data View** opens as shown in Exhibit 7.10. In most cases, SmartPLS was not able to identify the correct data separator when importing the data file. Try out the different options in the **Choose Delimiter** window of the **Data View** (i.e., comma, semicolon, space, tabulator) and select the one that gives you a proper preview in the data **Preview** window (Exhibit 7.10). Note that the data **Preview** window does not show the full set of data but only the header and the first couple of rows of the imported data set. When closing the **Data View**, SmartPLS asks you if you would like to save the changes, which you confirm by clicking on the **Yes** button. If the red tag still appears, you need to enter the **Data View** again. Now, press the **Validate** button. A window opens that contains the information in which column and which row you can find the invalid data points (see Chapter 2 for a description of data requirements in SmartPLS). Open the data file with a spreadsheet program such as Microsoft Office Excel or OpenOffice CALC and correct the invalid data. Then, save the data file in the comma separated value (i.e., .csv) or text (i.e., .txt) file format and import this set of data again into SmartPLS so that

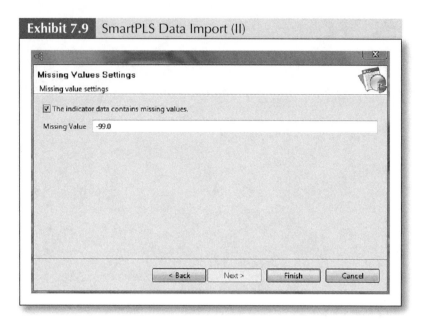

Exhibit 7.9 SmartPLS Data Import (II)

it appears within the chosen project in the SmartPLS **Projects** window. Before you import the corrected data set, you may want to delete the invalid data set with the red tag from your project. Just click on the data set in the SmartPLS **Projects** window to select it, and then press on the right mouse button. The dialog box as shown in Exhibit 7.7 appears and gives you the **Remove Resource** option, which deletes the selected file.

If the **Full Data(100).csv** file has a green tag, the data set is valid and can now be used to estimate the PLS path model. The PLS-SEM estimations for the path coefficients and the R^2 values do not change and are the same as described in the previous chapters. However, in the results, which are based on the rescaled input data, the **Default Report** of SmartPLS now offers **Index Values for Latent Variables** on a scale of 0 to 100, as displayed in Exhibit 7.11. Together with the total effects (Exhibit 7.11), this is the key information required to conduct an IPMA.

The information from the **Default Report** (i.e., index values and total effects) is needed for the IPMA of the key target construct *CUSL* in the PLS path model. Exhibit 7.12 presents the results of the total effects (importance) and index values (performance) used for the IPMA.

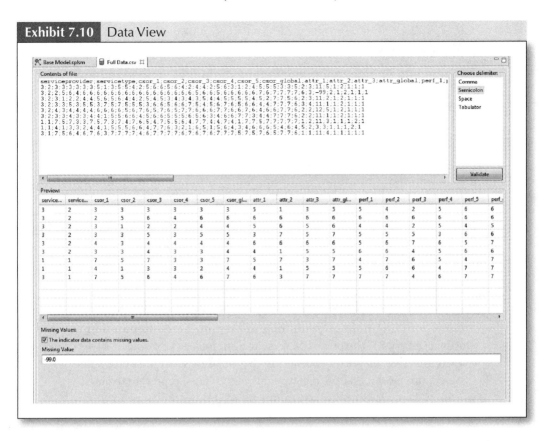

Exhibit 7.10	Data View

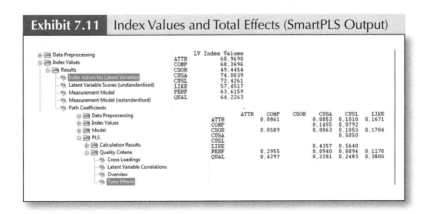

Exhibit 7.11	Index Values and Total Effects (SmartPLS Output)

Exhibit 7.12	Index Values and Total Effects for the IPMA of *CUSL*	
	Importance (Total Effects)	*Performance (Index Values)*
ATTR	0.101	60.969
COMP	0.079	68.370
CSOR	0.105	49.445
CUSA	0.505	74.004
LIKE	0.564	57.452
PERF	0.089	63.616
QUAL	0.248	64.226

These data allow for creating an IPMA representation, as shown in Exhibit 7.13, by using spreadsheet applications, such as Microsoft Excel or CALC in OpenOffice. The **Corporate_Reputation_ Advanced.zip** file (http://www.pls-sem.com) includes the **CR_IPMA_ Example.xlsx** file, which contains the full IPMA of this example based on the SmartPLS results and a graphical representation of results. This file can serve as a template for other studies as well.

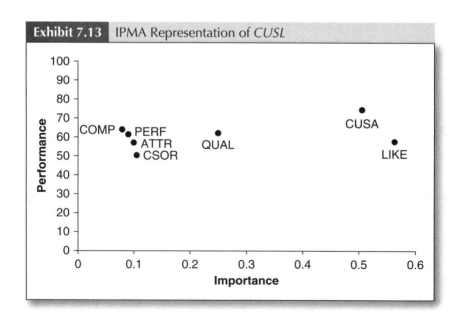

Exhibit 7.13 IPMA Representation of *CUSL*

As shown in Exhibit 7.13, the IPMA of *CUSL* reveals that *LIKE* is of primary importance for eastablishing customer loyalty. However, its performance is slightly below the average when compared with the other constructs. *CUSA* is of similar importance but has a considerably higher performance. *COMP,* on the other hand, has little relevance because it is of low importance even though it has relatively high performance. Consequently, managerial activities to improve *CUSL* should focus on the *LIKE* construct. Another IPMA of the indicators of *LIKE* (i.e., the outer weights represent the importance and the mean value of each indicator's performance) could provide additional information on how to best improve the performance of the *LIKE* construct. With respect to the indirect predecessors of *CUSL* (i.e., *ATTR, CSOR, PERF,* and *QUAL*), the *QUAL* construct has the highest impact on *CUSL* while simultaneously exhibiting an intermediate performance compared with the other constructs. Managerial action may also focus on improving the performance of the *QUAL* construct on the basis of an IPMA of this construct's indicators. This kind of analysis has become increasingly popular to extend the findings of PLS-SEM analyses. Höck et al. (2010) and Rigdon et al. (2011) present examples of IPMAs in PLS-SEM.

MEDIATOR ANALYSIS

Method

Mediation and **moderation** are two important topics in the context of PLS-SEM, but the concepts are also often confused. In this section, we deal with mediation. In Chapter 8, we address moderation, using both categorical and continuous variables.

Mediation focuses on a theoretically established direct path relationship (i.e., path p_{13} in Exhibit 7.14) between Y_1 and Y_3, as well as on an additional theoretically relevant component Y_2, which indirectly provides information on the direct effect via its indirect effect (i.e., $p_{12} \cdot p_{23}$) from Y_1 to Y_3 via Y_2 (Exhibit 7.14). Thereby, the indirect relationship via the Y_2 mediator affects the direct relationshipy from Y_1 to Y_3 in the mediator model.

We could, for example, develop the following hypothesis H_1: The higher the seawater temperature (Y_1), the lower the number of incidents (e.g., swimmers needing to be rescued) (Y_3). The logic of this simple cause-effect relationship is shown in Exhibit 7.15: Cold

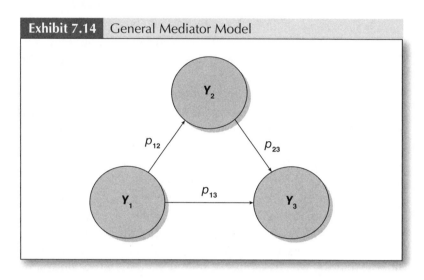

Exhibit 7.14 General Mediator Model

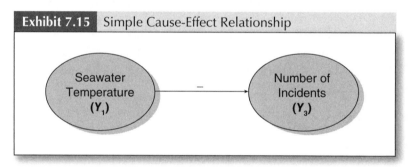

Exhibit 7.15 Simple Cause-Effect Relationship

water exhausts swimmers more quickly; therefore, they are more likely to misjudge their chances of swimming out to sea and returning safely.

Many coastal cities have daily empirical data on the seawater temperature and the number of swimming incidents over many years readily available. However, when estimating the relationship (i.e., the correlation between the seawater temperature and the number of incidents), we obtain either a nonsignificant or a significantly positive result for the hypothesized relationship. Since we had good reason to expect a negative relationship, there must be something missing in the model. In this example, the number of swimmers at the selected shoreline (Y_2) would make sense. Hence, hypothesis H_2 would posit that the higher the seawater temperature, the more swimmers there will be at the specific beach. Moreover, hypothesis H_3 would posit that the more swimmers there are in the water, the higher the likelihood of incidents occurring (e.g., swimmers needing to be rescued), both of which would make sense. Exhibit 7.16 illustrates this more complex cause-effect relationship.

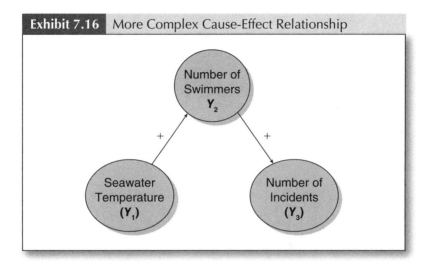

Exhibit 7.16	More Complex Cause-Effect Relationship

Empirical data could substantiate the positive effects illustrated in Exhibit 7.16. When the more complex cause-effect relationship is examined, however, it is possible that we could conclude that swimming in warmer water is more dangerous than swimming in colder water. This conclusion could also be examined empirically with regard to the simple cause-effect model (i.e., positive estimations of the relationship between the seawater temperature and the number of incidents instead of a negative relationship), although this would contradict our theoretical underpinnings.

We therefore combine the simple and the more complex cause-effect relationships models in a **mediator model** (Exhibit 7.17). In addition to H_1, H_2, and H_3, we would need to establish hypothesis H_4: The direct relationship between the seawater temperature and number of incidents is mediated by the number of swimmers.

If we use the available data to empirically estimate the model in Exhibit 7.17, we would obtain the estimated relationships with the expected signs. When extending the model by the number of swimmers, we obtain the "true" relationship between the seawater temperature and the number of incidents. This relationship is systematically affected by the number of swimmers, which in turn can be explained by the seawater temperature.

This example points out that mediation is a challenging field. The estimated cause-effect relationship results may not be the "true" effect because a systematic influence—a certain phenomenon (i.e., a mediator)—must first be accounted for theoretically. Mediating effects have been suggested, but these are often not explicitly tested. Only when the possible mediation is theoretically taken into account and also empirically tested can the nature of the cause-effect relationship be fully and accurately understood, as this type of analysis identifies its "true" result. Again, theory always precedes the findings of empirical analyses.

Exhibit 7.17	Mediator Model

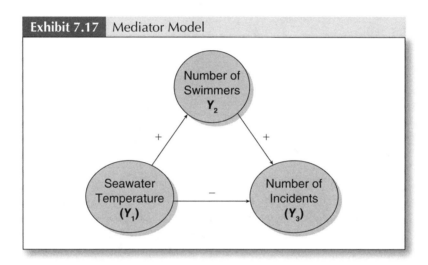

Technically, a variable functions as a mediator when it meets the following conditions (Baron & Kenny, 1986):

- Variations in the levels of the independent variable account significantly for the variations in the presumed mediator (i.e., path p_{12} in Exhibit 7.14).

- Variations in the mediator account significantly for the variations in the dependent variable (i.e., path p_{23} in Exhibit 7.14).

- When paths p_{12} and p_{23} are controlled, a previously significant relation between the independent and dependent variables (i.e., path p_{13} in Exhibit 7.14) changes its value significantly.

Consequently, empirical tests must answer the following questions:

- Is the direct effect p_{13} significant when the mediator variable is excluded from the PLS path model?

- Is the indirect $p_{12} \cdot p_{23}$ effect via the mediator variable significant after this variable has been included in the PLS path model? A necessary (but not sufficient) condition for the significance of the product of path p_{12} and path p_{23} is that the two paths themselves are both significant.

- How much of the direct effect p_{13} does the indirect effect (i.e., $p_{12} \cdot p_{23}$) absorb? Do we have a situation of full or partial mediation?

A commonly used approach for testing mediating effects is the Sobel (1982) test, which examines the relationship between the independent variable and the dependent variable compared with the relationship between the independent variable and dependent variable, including the mediation construct (Helm, Eggert, & Garnefeld, 2010). However, this test relies on distributional assumptions, which usually do not hold for the indirect effect $p_{12} \cdot p_{23}$ (specifically, the multiplication of two normally distributed coefficients results in a nonnormal distribution of their product). Furthermore, the Sobel test requires unstandardized path coefficients as input for the test statistic and lacks statistical power, especially when applied to small sample sizes.

When testing mediating effects, researchers should rather follow Preacher and Hayes (2004, 2008) and bootstrap the sampling distribution of the indirect effect, which works for simple and multiple mediator models (please note that we do not cover the latter case in this book; see Preacher & Hayes, 2008). Bootstrapping makes no assumptions about the shape of the variables' distribution or the sampling distribution of the statistics and can be applied to small sample sizes with more confidence. The approach is therefore perfectly suited for the PLS-SEM method. In addition, the approach exhibits higher levels of statistical power compared with the Sobel test. To apply this approach, we have to follow the procedure shown in Exhibit 7.18.

To begin with, the direct effect (i.e., path p_{13}) should be significant if the mediator is not included in the model. Even though this is not a necessary condition (Zhao, Lynch, & Chen, 2010), this kind of situation makes the mediator analysis much easier to understand and interpret. The significance test is conducted by carrying out the bootstrapping

Exhibit 7.18   Mediator Analysis Procedure in PLS-SEM

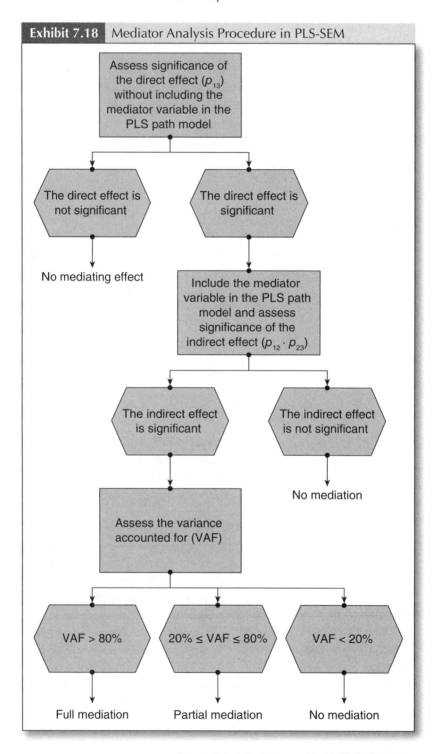

procedure as explained in the previous chapters. If this relationship is significant, the mediator may absorb some of this effect or the entire effect. Hence, we continue the mediator analysis if there is a significant direct path relationship between the exogenous and endogenous latent variables and include the mediator construct in the PLS path model.

When including the mediator, the indirect effect (i.e., $p_{12} \cdot p_{23}$) must be significant. The significance of each individual path p_{12} and p_{23} is a requirement for this condition. Only if the paths turn out to be significant after the bootstrapping procedure has been run can we assess if their product, which represents the indirect effect, is significant. If the indirect effect is significant, the mediator absorbs some of the direct effect. For example, in a PLS path model without the mediator variable, a positive direct effect (i.e., path p_{13}) would become smaller after the inclusion of the mediator variable. The question is how much the mediator variable absorbs. The **variance accounted for** (**VAF**) determines the size of the indirect effect in relation to the total effect (i.e., direct effect + indirect effect): VAF $= (p_{12} \cdot p_{23})/(p_{12} \cdot p_{23} + p_{13})$. Thereby, we can determine the extent to which the variance of the dependent variable is directly explained by the independent variable and how much of the target construct's variance is explained by the indirect relationship via the mediator variable.

If the indirect effect is significant but does not absorb any of the exogenous latent variable's effect on the endogenous variable, the VAF is rather low. This occurs when the direct effect is high and declines only very slightly after a mediator variable with a significant but very small indirect effect is included. In this situation, the VAF would be less than 20%, and one can conclude that (almost) no mediation takes place. In contrast, when the VAF has very large outcomes of above 80%, one can assume a **full mediation**. A situation in which the VAF is larger than 20% and less than 80% can be characterized as **partial mediation**.

A **suppressor effect,** which characterizes the sign change of the direct relationship after the mediator variables have been included, is an exception to the VAF-based assessment of mediating effects. For example, when a significant positive path relationship without the mediator variable becomes significantly negative after the inclusion of the mediator variable, a suppressor effect occurs. The swimmer example at the beginning of this section represents a situation with a suppressor effect. The VAF becomes larger than one or, in some instances, even negative with suppressor effects and can no longer be interpreted. This kind of situation always represents full mediation.

Case Study Illustration

The case study illustration uses the PLS path model of the previous chapters and as shown in Exhibit 7.5. We focus on the constructs *COMP* and *LIKE* and their relationship with *CUSL*. Subsequently, the following question arises: Are the two relationships mediated by *CUSA?*

To begin the analysis, the PLS path model must be estimated without the potential mediator variable *CUSA*. Exhibit 7.19 shows these path coefficients' significance, which results from conducting the bootstrapping procedure (i.e., with 344 observations per subsample, 5,000 subsamples, and no sign changes). The relationship between *LIKE* and *CUSL* is significant, while the *COMP* to *CUSL* relationship is not significant. Hence, we do not assume that the latter relationship is mediated by *CUSA* and focus the mediator analysis on the relationship between *LIKE* and *CUSL*.

In the next step, the mediator variable must be included. The assessment focuses on analyzing whether the indirect effect of *LIKE,* via the *CUSA* mediator variable, on *CUSL* is significant. A necessary (but not sufficient) condition is the significance of the relationship between *LIKE* and *CUSA* (i.e., 0.436), as well as between *CUSA* and *CUSL* (i.e., 0.505). This was confirmed by the evaluation of the structural model results in Chapter 6. The indirect effect's size is $0.436 \cdot 0.505 = 0.220$, and its significance is again tested using the bootstrapping results (i.e., with 344 observations per subsample, 5,000 subsamples, and no sign changes). To obtain the bootstrapping result for the product of two path coefficients, the results table of the bootstrap subsamples (Exhibit 7.20) needs to be copied and pasted into a spreadsheet application, such as Microsoft Excel or CALC in OpenOffice.

In the spreadsheet application, a new column is created for the indirect effect via the mediator (Exhibit 7.21). The indirect effect is

Exhibit 7.19	Significance Analysis of Path Coefficients Without the Mediator (Ringle et al., 2012)	
	Path Coefficient	p *Value*
COMP → *CUSL*	0.078	0.248
LIKE → *CUSL*	0.568	0.000

Exhibit 7.20 Bootstrapping Results of the Direct Effects

	ATTR -> COMP	ATTR -> LIKE	COMP -> CUSA	COMP -> CUSL	CSOR -> COMP	CSOR -> LIKE	CUSA -> CUSL
Sample 0	0.180	0.138	0.151	0.016	0.017	0.264	0.487
Sample 1	0.083	0.158	0.197	-0.030	0.024	0.278	0.477
Sample 2	0.021	0.162	0.150	-0.091	0.018	0.269	0.537
Sample 3	0.102	0.208	0.161	-0.018	-0.091	0.163	0.504
Sample 4	0.061	0.166	0.110	0.022	-0.006	0.190	0.500
Sample 5	0.135	0.301	0.153	0.050	0.167	0.119	0.456
Sample 6	-0.038	0.156	0.229	-0.076	0.151	0.181	0.532
Sample 7	0.018	0.125	0.082	-0.085	0.106	0.235	0.457
Sample 8	0.022	0.161	0.102	-0.030	0.072	0.120	0.473
Sample 9	0.099	0.122	0.232	-0.046	-0.019	0.164	0.558
Sample 10	0.167	0.219	0.063	0.016	-0.002	0.276	0.568
Sample 11	0.055	0.161	0.140	-0.074	0.033	0.225	0.469
Sample 12	0.109	0.112	-0.030	-0.047	0.129	0.221	0.537
Sample 13	0.060	0.167	0.049	0.023	0.001	0.242	0.417
Sample 14	0.100	0.174	0.132	-0.006	0.057	0.278	0.534
Sample 15	0.163	0.152	0.213	-0.007	0.092	0.243	0.529
Sample 16	0.100	0.236	-0.010	-0.029	-0.086	0.149	0.499
Sample 17	-0.104	0.150	0.121	0.022	-0.053	0.126	0.391
Sample 18	-0.004	0.265	0.122	-0.004	-0.025	0.144	0.538
Sample 19	0.108	0.174	0.073	-0.036	0.032	0.305	0.456
Sample 20	0.095	0.097	0.155	0.057	0.103	0.250	0.479
Sample 21	0.110	0.145	0.096	0.016	0.083	0.250	0.553
Sample 22	-0.021	0.137	0.269	0.033	0.064	0.135	0.505
Sample 23	0.035	0.143	0.185	0.012	-0.013	0.096	0.458

Bootstrapping
- Bootstrapping
  - Outer Loadings
  - Outer Loadings (Mean, STDEV, T-Val...
  - Outer Weights
  - Outer Weights (Mean, STDEV, T-Valu...
  - Path Coefficients
  - Path Coefficients (Mean, STDEV, T-V...
  - Total Effects
  - Total Effects (Mean, STDEV, T-Values...
- Data Preprocessing
- Results (chronologically)
  - Step 0 (Original Matrix)
- Model
- Specification
  - Manifest Variable Scores (Original)
  - Measurement Model Specification
  - Structural Model Specification

Note: The full table displayed in this exhibit contains results of 5,000 subsamples and all path relationships in the structural model.

the product of the direct effects between *LIKE* and *CUSA* as well as between *CUSA* and *CUSL*. The product of these direct effects needs to be computed for each of the 5,000 subsamples. The standard deviation can be computed for the new column of bootstrapping results for the indirect effect (e.g., with the function STDEV in MS Excel). In this example, the bootstrapping standard deviation (which equals the standard error in bootstrapping) has a value of 0.035. (note that your result is likely going to be slightly different because the bootstrapping procedure is a random process) The empirical *t* value of the indirect effect is the original value divided by the bootstrapping standard error. Hence, the empirical *t* value of the indirect effect of *LIKE* on *CUSL* is 0.220/0.035 = 6.2857, and we can conclude that this relationship via the *CUSA* mediator is significant ($p > 0.01$). Chapters 5 and 6 provide additional details for significance testing in PLS-SEM when using the bootstrap routine.

Exhibit 7.21	Bootstrapping Results of the Indirect Effect		
	LIKE → CUSA	CUSA → CUSL	*Indirect Effect*
Sample 0	0.425	0.487	0.207
Sample 1	0.457	0.477	0.218
Sample 2	0.413	0.537	0.222
Sample 3	0.454	0.504	0.229
Sample 4	0.397	0.500	0.199
Sample 5	0.481	0.456	0.219
. . .	. . .	. . .	. . .
Sample 4,999	0.382	0.533	0.204

The significant indirect effect is required to conclude that *CUSA* mediates the relationship between *LIKE* and *CUSL*. In the final step, we need to determine the strength of this mediation. This kind of assessment can be done by using the VAF. The direct effect of *LIKE* on *CUSL* has a value of 0.344, while the indirect effect via *CUSA* has a value of 0.220. Thus, the total effect has a value of 0.344 + 0.220 = 0.564. The VAF equals the direct effect divided by the total effect and has a value of 0.220/0.564 = 0.390. Consequently, 39% of *LIKE's* effect on *CUSL* is explained via the *CUSA* mediator. Since the VAF is larger than 20% but smaller than 80%, this situation can be characterized as partial mediation.

HIGHER-ORDER MODELS/HIERARCHICAL COMPONENT MODELS

Method

Thus far, we have dealt with first-order models in which we consider a single layer of constructs. In some instances, however, the constructs researchers wish to examine are quite complex and can also be operationalized at higher levels of abstraction. Establishing such **higher-order models** or **hierarchical component models** (**HCMs**), as they are usually called in the context of PLS-SEM (Lohmöller, 1989), most often involve testing second-order structures that contain two layers of constructs. As described in Chapter 2, satisfaction can be defined at different levels of abstraction. Specifically, satisfaction can be represented by numerous first-order constructs that capture separate attributes of satisfaction. In the context of services, these might include satisfaction with the quality of the service, the service personnel, the price, or the service scape. These first-order constructs might form the more abstract **second-order construct** satisfaction. (see Exhibit 2.5 in Chapter 2)

Conceptually, HCMs can be established following a bottom-up or top-down approach. In the bottom-up approach, several latent variables' information is combined into a single, more general construct. Alternatively, an HCM can be established top-down in which a general construct is defined that consists of several subdimensions. While the more general construct becomes part of the structural model, additional information can be found on the subdimensions by using a second-order model. Modeling customer satisfaction as described above and in Chapter 2 is an example of such a top-down approach.

There are three main reasons for the inclusion of an HCM in PLS-SEM. First, by establishing HCMs, researchers can reduce the number of relationships in the structural model, making the PLS path model more parsimonious and easier to grasp (Exhibit 7.24 later in this chapter illustrates this point). Second, HCMs prove valuable if the constructs are highly correlated; the estimations of the structural model relationships may be biased as a result of collinearity issues, and discriminant validity may not be established. In situations characterized by collinearity among constructs, a second-order construct can reduce such collinearity issues and may solve discriminant validity problems. Third, establishing HCMs can also prove valuable if formative indicators exhibit high levels of collinearity. Provided that theory supports this step, researchers can split up the set of indicators and establish separate constructs in a higher-order structure.

Exhibit 7.22 illustrates the four main types of HCMs discussed in the extant literature (Jarvis et al., 2003; Wetzels et al., 2009) and used in applications (Ringle et al., 2012). These types of models have two elements: the **higher-order component (HOC)**, which captures the more abstract entity, and the **lower-order components (LOCs)**, which capture the subdimensions of the abstract entity. Each of the HCM types is characterized by different relationships between (1) the HOC and the LOCs and (2) the constructs and their indicators. For example, the reflective-reflective type of HCM indicates a (reflective) relationship between the HOC and the LOCs, whereby each of the constructs is measured by reflective indicators. Conversely, the reflective-formative type indicates (formative) relationships between the LOCs and the HOC, whereby each construct is measured by reflective indicators.

As can be seen in Exhibit 7.22, the HOC has a measurement model with the same orientation (i.e., reflective or formative) as in the LOCs. To establish the HOC's measurement model, researchers usually assign all the indicators from the LOCs to the HOC in the form of a **repeated indicators approach.** In the HCM examples shown in Exhibit 7.22, the HOC uses the indicators x_1 to x_9 of its underlying components LOC_1, LOC_2, and LOC_2 in the measurement model.

While the repeated indicators approach is easy to implement, it warrants attention in two respects. First, the number of indicators should be similar across the LOCs; otherwise, the relationships between the HOC and LOCs may be significantly biased by the inequality of the number of indicators per LOC (Becker, Klein, & Wetzels, 2012). For example, an HCM has two LOCs, one with two indicators (LOC_1) and another one with eight indicators (LOC_2). When using the repeated indicator approach, all 10 indicators are assigned to the HOC. A stronger relationship between the HOC and LOC_1 emerges from this kind of setup since they share a large number of indicators in the HCM.

Exhibit 7.22	Types of Hierarchical Component Models (Ringle et al., 2012)

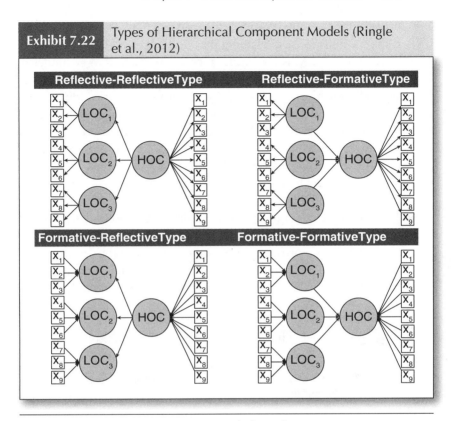

Note: LOC$_2$ = lower-order component; HOC = higher-order component.

Source: Copyright 2012 by the Regents of the University of Minnesota. Reprinted by permission.

Second, when using the repeated indicators approach, the same measurement model evaluation criteria apply to the HOC as for any other construct in the PLS path model. For instance, when the HOC has a reflective measurement model, all relevant reliability and validity criteria must be met (Chapter 4). The only exception is the discriminant validity between the HOC and the LOCs, as well as between the LOCs in **reflective-reflective HCMs** (see Exhibit 7.22).

As indicated above, the relationships between the LOCs and the HCM can be either reflective or formative. This decision depends on the theoretical/conceptual reasoning behind and the goal of the analysis. The reflective relationship between the LOCs and the HCM may be selected if there is a general or more global factor that explains all the correlations between the first-order factors as shown in Exhibit 7.23. Hence, there should be substantial correlation levels between the LOCs that can be explained by HOC. Thereby, the HOC is the spurious cause explaining the correlations between the LOCs. This kind of HCM is also useful if correlations need to be modeled. PLS-SEM does not allow path models to be estimated with nonrecursive relationships (i.e., causal loops). This includes bidirectional relationships, such as correlations in the structural model. Reflective relationships between the LOCs and the HOC can be used to model and estimate such correlations in PLS-SEM. For example, the estimate for the path between HOC and LOC_1 multiplied by the estimate for the path between HOC and LOC_2 approximately represents the correlation between LOC_1 and LOC_2 (Exhibit 7.23).

Formative relationships between the LOCs and the HOC reveal the relative contribution of each LOC in explaining the HOC. If the HOC itself explains one or more other latent variables in the structural model, the interpretation of this kind of HCM changes even more. As shown in Exhibit 7.24, the HOC is expected to fully mediate

Exhibit 7.23 Reflective Relationships Between HOC and LOCs

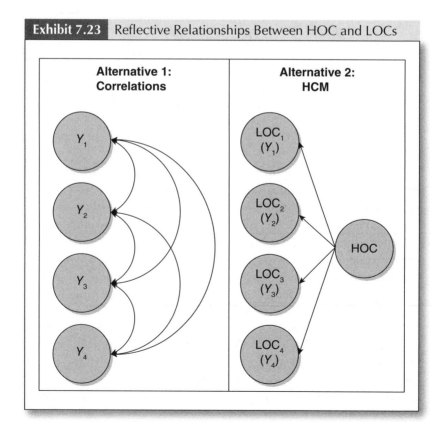

Exhibit 7.24	Formative Relationships Between HOC and LOCs

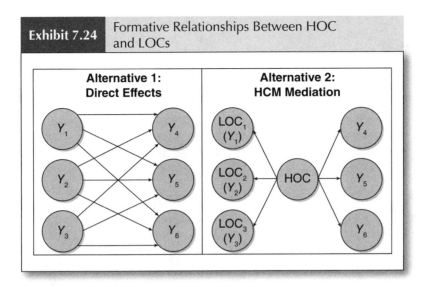

the relationship between the LOCs and the dependent variables in the PLS path model. Hence, there is a general construct (i.e., the HOC) that represents all the LOCs, thereby fully mediating their relationships with their target variables.

In many **formative-formative** and **reflective-formative HCM** applications, the HOC has (insignificant) predecessors other than the LOCs in the structural model (Ringle et al., 2012). These model setups require particular attention when the repeated indicator approach is used in the HOC's measurement model, since almost all of the HOC variance is explained by its LOCs ($R^2 \approx 1.0$). Consequently, the path relationship between any additional latent variable as a predecessor and the endogenous HOC is always approximately zero and nonsignificant.

In this kind of situation, a mixture of the repeated indicator approach and the use of latent variable scores in a **two-stage approach**—which is similar to the two-stage approach in moderator analyses (Chapter 8) in PLS-SEM (Henseler & Chin, 2010)—is appropriate. In the first stage, the repeated indicator approach is used to obtain the latent variable scores for the LOCs, which, in the second stage, serve as manifest variables in the HOC measurement model (Exhibit 7.25). Thereby, the HOC is embedded in the nomological net in such a way that it allows other latent variables as predecessors to explain some of its variance, which may result in significant path relationships.

Exhibit 7.25	Two-Stage Approach for HCM Analysis (Ringle et al., 2012)

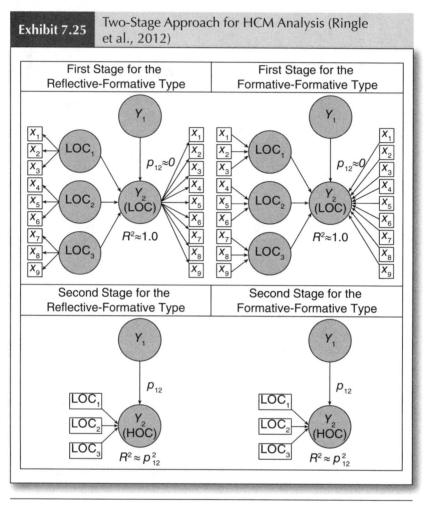

Note: LOC = lower-order component; HOC = higher-order component; Y_1 = exogenous latent variable in the structural model (its measurement model is not further specified in this illustration); Y_2 = endogenous latent variable in the structural model; p_{12} = standardized path coefficient for the structural model relationship between the latent variables Y_1 and Y_2.

Source: Copyright 2012 by the Regents of the University of Minnesota. Reprinted by permission.

A final note of caution is connected with the estimation of HCM using the PLS-SEM algorithm. Not all weighting schemes for the inner PLS path model (i.e., centroid, factor, and path; Chapter 3) work equally well for HCM. While the factor and path weighting schemes provide reasonable outcomes for HCM in PLS-SEM, one should not use the centroid weighting scheme (Hair et al., 2012b).

Case Study Illustration

In this case study application, we want to create an HCM for corporate reputation. Up to this point, we have focused on the *COMP* and *LIKE* constructs, which are two dimensions of corporate reputation. However, they could be handled as subdimensions of a more general *corporate reputation* construct in the PLS path model. From a theoretical/conceptual point of view, the reasons for this may be to simplify the model setup by using a single dimension (i.e., an HOC) that represents all the LOCs (i.e., the reflective relationships between the HOC and the LOCs) or to mediate all the relationships between the LOCs and their target constructs in the PLS path model (i.e., the formative relationships between the LOCs and the HOC). From an empirical point of view, LOCs' lack of discriminant validity and the potential collinearity issues in the structural model may be reasons for using HCMs. In this example, however, we have established the discriminant validity of the *COMP* and *LIKE* constructs, and collinearity is not a critical issue. Nevertheless, we select the HCM to represent *COMP* and *LIKE* as the LOCs of the HOC *corporate reputation,* which results in a reflective-reflective HCM (Exhibit 7.26). The PLS path model is thus becoming more parsimonious, and we can directly model the correlation between the LOCs, which is the product of the reflective relationships via the HOC. Note that, with PLS-SEM, an HOC can be formed with two LOCs, whereas with CB-SEM, there must be a minimum of three LOCs.

In the reflective-reflective HCM of *corporate reputation,* the constructs *COMP* and *LIKE* represent the LOCs. The HOC (i.e., *corporate reputation*) is created by reusing the indicators of the LOCs. Hence, all indicators of the reflective LOCs are assigned to the reflective measurement model of the HOC (Exhibit 7.26). Thereafter, the HOC representing corporate reputation is related to its actionable drivers (i.e., *ATTR, CSOR, QUAL,* and *PERF*) and its consequences (i.e., *CUSA* and *CUSL*) in the PLS path model. The **HCM_reflective_reflective** model in the **Corporate Reputation Extended–Advanced Analyses** project contains this PLS path model.

Subsequent to estimating the PLS path model, we need to evaluate the measurement models. The evaluation results of the formative and reflective measurement models differ only slightly from the analyses presented in Chapters 4 and 5. Hence, we need to focus only on the new HOC. All the outer loadings are well above the critical value of 0.70. The only exception is the

Exhibit 7.26   Reflective-Reflective HCM Example

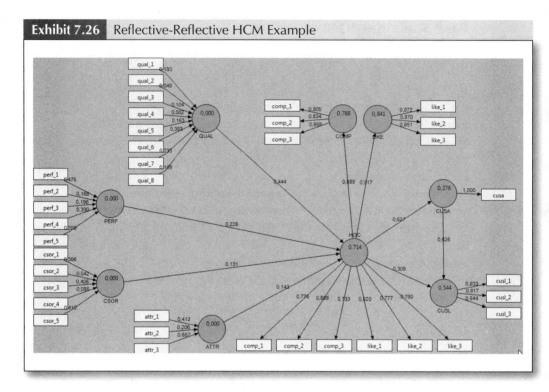

Exhibit 7.27   Discriminant Validity Assessment

	ATTR	CSOR	CUSA	CUSL	HOC	PERF	QUAL
ATTR	Formative						
CSOR	0.593	Formative					
CUSA	0.417	0.422	Single item				
CUSL	0.439	0.416	0.689	0.865			
HOC	0.676	0.668	0.527	0.586	0.765		
PERF	0.666	0.626	0.426	0.480	0.752	Formative	
QUAL	0.689	0.702	0.491	0.534	0.812	0.788	Formative

indicator *comp_2*. However, with an outer loading of 0.698, this indicator is only slightly below the critical value. Since the criteria for reliability and convergent validity were met, the *comp_2* indicator is retained in the measurement model. Specifically, the HOC's composite reliability (0.894) is well above its critical value of 0.70, thus supporting internal consistency reliability. The HOC's average variance extracted (AVE) has a value of 0.585, thereby providing evidence of convergent validity. However, as shown in exhibit 727 we cannot establish discriminant validity between the HOC *corporate reputation* and *QUAL*. Consequently, as discussed in previous chapters, it is reasonable to directly include the *COMP* and *LIKE* dimensions (i.e., the LOCs) in the PLS path model.

If discriminant validity had been established for this HCM application, the structural model results could—as explained in Chapter 6—have been further evaluated and interpreted. All the structural model relationships are significant ($p < 0.01$). The HOC has strong relationships with its LOCs *COMP* (0.888) and *LIKE* (0.917). Hence, *COMP* and *LIKE* are sufficiently highly correlated for the HOC to explain more than 50% of each LOC's variance.

The driver construct *QUAL* (0.444) and *PERF* (0.226) have the strongest effects on the HOC *corporate reputation,* while *CSOR* (0.131) and *ATTR* (0.143) are less relevant. The HOC itself has a strong effect on *CSUA* (0.527), which is in turn strongly related to *CUSL* (0.526). The direct relationship between *corporate reputation* (i.e., the HOC) and *CUSL* is somewhat weaker (0.309). The R^2 value of all the endogenous latent variables is relatively high if the number of indicators that explain each construct is taken into account (Chapter 6).

SUMMARY

• **Understand how to conduct a PLS-SEM importance-performance matrix analysis (IPMA).** PLS-SEM focuses on estimating the relationships of a PLS path model. This provides researchers and practitioners with information about the significance and relevance (i.e., relative importance) of constructs that explain other endogenous constructs in the PLS path model. This kind of analysis can be expanded to also take the performance of the latent variables into consideration by including the mean value obtained from an IPMA rescaling of the latent variable scores. This will enable practitioners and researchers to better characterize and prioritize activities to improve a selected target construct's performance.

- **Explain mediator analysis and how to execute it using PLS-SEM.** Mediator variables absorb part of the relationship between an exogenous and an endogenous construct in the PLS path model via the indirect effect, which is the relationship between the exogenous latent construct and the mediator variable and between the mediator variable and the endogenous latent construct. Thereby, mediators reveal the "true" relationship between an exogenous and an endogenous construct. Mediating effects must be theoretically/conceptually postulated a priori. The analysis then focuses on testing such hypothesized relationships empirically. If there is a significant mediation effect, it fully or partially absorbs a direct relationship or can even change its direction (i.e., suppressor effect).

- **Understand higher-order constructs and how to apply this concept in PLS-SEM.** HCMs are used to establish a more general HOC that represents or summarizes the information of several LOCs. Four major types of HCM represent different relationships between the HOC and the LOCs as well as the measurement models used to operationalize the constructs: reflective-reflective, reflective-formative, formative-reflective, and formative-formative. Generally, the HOC of reflective-reflective and formative-reflective HCMs represents a more general construct that simultaneously explains all the underlying LOCs (i.e., similar to reflective measurement models; Chapters 2 and 4). Conversely, the HOC is formed by the LOCs in reflective-formative and formative-formative HCMs (i.e., similar to formative measurement models; Chapters 2 and 5). Besides this issue, each of the four different HCM types must be assessed very carefully. We usually expect to have the same (or a comparable) number of indicators per LOC, while the relationship between reflective-formative or formative-formative HOCs and other constructs in the PLS path model that explain it requires a two-stage approach. HCMs are becoming increasingly popular in research since they offer means to establishing more parsimonious path models.

REVIEW QUESTIONS

1. What is the purpose of the IPMA?

2. How do you interpret the results of an IPMA?

3. What does mediation in PLS-SEM mean? Provide an example.

4. What are the necessary conditions for substantiating a partial or full mediation?

5. What is a suppressor effect?

6. What is an HCM? Visualize each of the four different types of HCMs introduced in this chapter.

7. Why do you need a two-stage approach in a reflective-formative or formative-formative HCM if the HOC has an additional construct (other than the LOCs) in the structural model that explains it?

8. What are the consequences when LOCs have substantially unequal numbers of indicators?

CRITICAL THINKING QUESTIONS

1. Name an additional (third) interesting dimension of an IPMA.

2. How would you characterize a situation when a nonsignificant direct effect (without the meditator) becomes significant (positive or negative) after including a significant mediator for this relationship in the PLS path model?

3. Provide examples of the four different major types of HCMs.

4. Can HCMs be used to solve discriminant validity problems in PLS-SEM?

KEY TERMS

Direct effect: is the direct relationship between an exogenous and an endogenous latent variable in a PLS path model.

Formative-formative HCM: has formative measurement models of all constructs in the HCM and path relationships between the LOCs and the HOC (i.e., the LOCs form the HOC).

Formative-reflective HCM: has formative measurement models of all constructs in the HCM and path relationships from the HOC to the LOCs.

Full mediation: occurs if inclusion of the mediator variable drops the relationship between the independent variable and dependent variable to almost zero.

HCM: see *Hierarchical component model.*

Hierarchical component model (HCM): is a higher-order structure (usually second-order) that contains several layers of constructs and involves a higher level of abstraction. HCMs involve a more abstract *higher-order component (HOC),* related to two or more *lower-order components (LOCs)* in a reflective or formative way.

Higher-order component (HOC): is a general construct that represents all underlying LOCs in an HCM.

Higher-order model: see *Hierarchical component model (HCM).*

HOC: see *Higher-order component.*

Importance: see *Total effect.*

Importance-performance matrix analysis (IPMA): combines the importance results and the performance results of PLS-SEM in a two-dimensional results representation.

Index value: see *Performance.*

Indirect effect: represents a relationship between an exogenous and an endogenous latent variable via a third (e.g., mediator) construct in the PLS path model. If *a* is the relationship between the exogenous latent variable and the mediator variable, and *b* is the relationship between the mediator variable and the endogenous latent variable, the indirect effect is the product of path *a* and path *b*.

IPMA: see *Importance-performance matrix analysis.*

LOC: see *Lower-order component.*

Lower-order component (LOC): is a subdimension of the HOC in an HCM.

Mediation: represents a situation in which a mediator variable to some extent absorbs the effect of an exogenous on an endogenous latent variable in the PLS path model.

Mediator model: see *Mediation.*

Moderation: occurs when the effect of an exogenous latent variable on an endogenous latent variable depends on the values of another variable, which moderates the relationship (see Chapter 8).

Partial mediation: maintains that the mediating variable accounts for some but not all of the relationships between the independent variable and a dependent variable.

Performance: is a term used in the context of *IPMA*. It is the mean value of the unstandardized (and rescaled) scores of a latent variable or an indicator.

Reflective-formative HCM: has reflective measurement models of all constructs in the HCM and path relationships from the LOCs to the HOC.

Reflective-reflective HCM: has reflective measurement models of all constructs in the HCM and path relationships from the HOC to the LOCs.

Repeated indicators approach for HCM: is a type of measurement model setup in HCM that uses the indicators of the LOCs as indicators of the HOC to create an HCM in PLS-SEM.

Rescaling: changes the direction and the values of a variable's scale.

Second-order construct: see *Hierarchical component model.*

Suppressor effect: occurs when the integration of a mediator variable changes the sign of a path relationship between the independent and dependent variable.

Total effect: is the sum of the direct effect and the indirect effect between an exogenous and an endogenous latent variable in the PLS path model.

Two-stage approach for HCM: is needed to estimate path relationships between an exogenous latent variable and a *reflective-formative HCM* or a *formative-formative HCM* in PLS-SEM.

VAF: see *Variance accounted for.*

Variance accounted for: is the size of the indirect effect relative to the total effect. This value is normed between 0 and 1 (or 0% to 100%). Higher results indicate a stronger mediation.

SUGGESTED READINGS

Baron, R. M., & Kenny, D. A. (1986). The moderator-mediator variable distinction in social psychological research: Conceptual, strategic and statistical considerations. *Journal of Personality and Social Psychology, 51,* 1173–1182.

Becker, J. M., Klein, K., & Wetzels, M. (2012). Hierarchical latent variable models in PLS-SEM: Guidelines for using reflective-formative type models. *Long Range Planning, 45*(5/6), 359–394.

Höck, C., Ringle, C. M., & Sarstedt, M. (2010). Management of multipurpose stadiums: Importance and performance measurement of service interfaces. *International Journal of Services Technology and Management, 14,* 188–207.

Preacher, K. J., & Hayes, A. F. (2008). Asymptotic and resampling strategies for assessing and comparing indirect effects in simple and multiple mediator models. *Behavior Research Methods, 40,* 879–891.

Ringle, C. M., Sarstedt, M., & Straub, D. W. (2012). A critical look at the use of PLS-SEM in *MIS Quarterly. MIS Quarterly, 36,* iii–xiv.

Wetzels, M., Odekerken-Schroder, G., & van Oppen, C. (2009). Using PLS path modeling for assessing hierarchical construct models: Guidelines and empirical illustration. *MIS Quarterly, 33,* 177–195.

Wilson, B. (2010). Using PLS to investigate interaction effects between higher order branding constructs. In V. Esposito Vinzi, W. W. Chin, J. Henseler & H. Wang (Eds.), *Handbook of partial least squares: Concepts, methods and applications* (Springer handbooks of computational statistics series, vol. II) (pp. 621–652). New York: Springer.

Zhao, X., Lynch, J. G., & Chen, Q. (2010). Reconsidering Baron and Kenny: Myths and truths about mediation analysis. *Journal of Consumer Research, 37,* 197–206.

C H A P T E R   8

Modeling Heterogeneous Data

LEARNING OUTCOMES

1. Understand the importance of modeling heterogeneity in PLS-SEM.

2. Know the concepts that enable you to identify heterogeneity.

3. Execute a PLS-SEM multigroup analysis (PLS-MGA).

4. Comprehend the concept of unobserved heterogeneity.

5. Use the SmartPLS software to model continuous moderator variables in a PLS path model.

CHAPTER PREVIEW

Cause-effect relationships in PLS path models imply that exogenous latent variables directly affect endogenous latent variables without any systematic influences of other variables. In many instances, however, this assumption does not hold. For example, respondents are likely to be heterogeneous in their perceptions and evaluations of latent variables, yielding significant differences in, for example, path coefficients across two or more groups of respondents. Recognizing that heterogeneous data structures are often present, researchers are increasingly interested in identifying and understanding such differences. In fact, failure to consider heterogeneity can be a threat to the validity of PLS-SEM results.

In this chapter, we learn about different concepts that enable researchers to model heterogeneous data. The chapter begins with **multigroup analysis** that is used to compare parameters (usually path coefficients) between two or more groups of data. It is typically applied when researchers want to explore differences that can be traced back to observable characteristics such as gender or country of origin. In this situation, it is assumed that there is a categorical moderator variable (e.g., gender) that influences the relationships in the PLS path model. The aim of multigroup analysis is therefore to disclose the effect of this categorical moderator variable. When the true sources of heterogeneity in data sets are unknown, however, heterogeneity is considered unobserved. To identify and treat unobserved heterogeneity, researchers can apply latent class approaches such as finite mixture PLS (FIMIX-PLS) that we briefly introduce. The chapter then explains how to include continuous (rather than categorical) moderator variables in the model that might affect the strength or even direction of specific path relationships.

MODELING CATEGORICAL MODERATOR EFFECTS

Introduction

Researchers are often interested in comparing PLS path models across two or more groups of data to see whether different parameter estimates occur for each group. For example, a researcher may aim at finding out whether the path coefficients in a PLS path model differ significantly across countries or industries. **Heterogeneity** exists when two or more groups of respondents exhibit significant differences in their model relationships (the focus is usually on the relationships between the latent constructs in the PLS path model). Comparing several groups of respondents is beneficial from a practical and theoretical perspective. But the most important reason for understanding group-specific effects is that it facilitates obtaining further differentiated findings. Indeed, failure to consider heterogeneity can be a threat to the validity of PLS-SEM results since it can lead to incorrect conclusions (Becker, Rai, Ringle, & Völckner, in press; Hair et al., 2012b).

To illustrate the problems stemming from failure to treat heterogeneity in the context of structural equation models, consider the model shown in Exhibit 8.1, in which customer satisfaction with a product (Y_3) depends on the two perceptual dimensions: satisfaction with the quality (Y_1) and satisfaction with the price (Y_2). Suppose there are two segments of equal size. Group 1 is quality conscious, whereas Group 2 is price conscious, as indicated by the different segment-specific path coefficients. More specifically, the effect of quality (Y_1) on satisfaction (Y_3) is much higher in Group 1 $(p_{13}^{(1)} = 0.50$; the superscript in parentheses indicates the group) than in Group 2 $(p_{13}^{(2)} = 0.10)$. Similarly, with an absolute difference of 0.40, the path from price (Y_2) to satisfaction (Y_3) is much higher in Group 2 compared with Group 1. If we fail to recognize the heterogeneity between the groups and analyze the model using the full set of data, the path coefficients would be substantially biased. That is, both estimates equal 0.30 when using the full set of data, thus leading the researcher to conclude that price and quality are equally important for establishing customer satisfaction when in fact they are not.

In this example, heterogeneity is the result of one group of customers exhibiting preference for price, while a second group prefers quality over price. From a technical perspective, there is a categorical moderator variable that splits the data set into two customer groups (price conscious and quality conscious) and thus requires estimating two separate models. Usually, such a (categorical) **moderator variable** captures some observable trait of the respondents such as their gender (male vs. female) or income (low vs. high) and is known a priori. However, a moderator can also capture some unobservable trait, as is the case in our example (preference for quality vs. price). Note that a categorical moderator does not necessarily have to represent only two groups. It is also possible to have more than two groups (e.g., low income, intermediate income, high income). Likewise, the moderator variable can also be continuous. We discuss continuous moderator variables later in this chapter.

Path coefficients based on different samples are almost always different (in a mathematical sense), but the question is whether these differences are statistically significant. Specifically, when conducting a multigroup analysis, we want to test the null hypotheses H_0 that the path coefficients are not significantly different (e.g., $p_{13}^{(1)} = p_{13}^{(2)}$), which amounts to the same as saying that the absolute difference between the path coefficients is zero (i.e., H_0: $\left| p_{13}^{(1)} - p_{13}^{(2)} \right| = 0$). The

Exhibit 8.1 Heterogeneity in a Structural Model

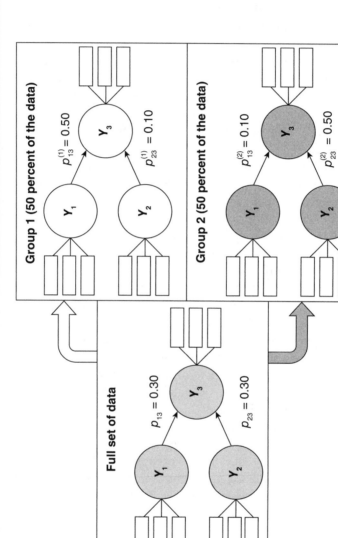

corresponding alternative hypothesis H_1 is that the path coefficients are different in the population (i.e., H_1: $p_{13}^{(1)} \neq p_{13}^{(2)}$ or, put differently, H_1: $\left| p_{13}^{(1)} - p_{13}^{(2)} \right| > 0$).

To find out whether there is a significant difference between coefficients, researchers need to run a PLS-SEM multigroup analysis (PLS-MGA). **PLS-MGA** refers to a set of different techniques that have been developed for comparing PLS model estimates across groups of data. Usually, PLS-MGA is used to explore differences between path coefficients in the structural model, but one can also compare, for example, loadings or weights. PLS-MGA is a rather new research field, and several approaches have recently been proposed (see Sarstedt, Henseler, et al., 2011, for an overview). For this introductory text, we limit our coverage to the **parametric approach to PLS-MGA** proposed by Keil et al. (2000), which can be used to compare two groups of data.

The Parametric Approach to PLS-MGA

Keil et al. (2000) proposed a modified version of a two-independent-samples t test (Mooi & Sarstedt, 2011) to compare path coefficients across two groups of data. None of the PLS-SEM software packages executes PLS-MGA, so researchers must calculate this test by hand, which requires them to specify several parameters.

1. The number of observations in Group 1 and Group 2 (i.e., $n^{(1)}$ and $n^{(2)}$) must be known.

2. The path coefficients of Group 1 and Group 2 (referred to as $p^{(1)}$ and $p^{(2)}$), which will be compared, must be estimated. To obtain these, separate PLS path models for each group of data must be estimated.

3. Last, the standard errors of the parameter estimates of Group 1 and Group 2 (i.e., $se(p^{(1)})$ and $se(p^{(2)})$) must be determined. As described in Chapter 5, the standard errors of the PLS parameter estimates can be obtained via bootstrapping. As a result, the bootstrapping procedure must be run for each group.

These six elements (i.e., two group-specific numbers of observations, path coefficients and standard errors) are then used as input to calculate a test statistic whose form depends on whether the variances of the parameter estimates (as obtained from bootstrapping) differ significantly across the groups. To check whether this is the case, Levene's test is used (Mooi & Sarstedt [2011] provide a more detailed discussion of Levene's test).

If the standard errors are equal, the test statistic (i.e., the empirical t value) is computed as follows:

$$t = \frac{\left| p^{(1)} - p^{(2)} \right|}{\sqrt{\frac{\left(n^{(1)} - 1 \right)^2}{\left(n^{(1)} + n^{(2)} - 2 \right)} \cdot se\left(p^{(1)} \right)^2 + \frac{\left(n^{(2)} - 1 \right)^2}{\left(n^{(1)} + n^{(2)} - 2 \right)} \cdot se\left(p^{(2)} \right)^2} \cdot \sqrt{\frac{1}{n^{(1)}} + \frac{1}{n^{(2)}}}}.$$

To reject the null hypothesis of equal path coefficients, the empirical t value must be larger than the critical value from a t distribution with $n^{(1)} + n^{(2)} - 2$ degrees of freedom.

If the standard errors are unequal, the test statistic takes the following form:

$$t = \frac{\left| p^{(1)} - p^{(2)} \right|}{\sqrt{\frac{\left(n^{(1)} - 1 \right)}{n^{(1)}} \cdot se\left(p^{(1)} \right)^2 + \frac{\left(n^{(2)} - 1 \right)}{n^{(2)}} \cdot se\left(p^{(2)} \right)^2}}.$$

This test statistic is also asymptotically t distributed but with the following degrees of freedom (df):

$$df = \left\| \frac{\left(\frac{\left(n^{(1)} - 1 \right)}{n^{(1)}} \cdot se\left(p^{(1)} \right)^2 + \frac{\left(n^{(2)} - 1 \right)}{n^{(2)}} \cdot se\left(p^{(2)} \right)^2 \right)^2}{\frac{\left(n^{(1)} - 1 \right)}{n^{(1)^2}} \cdot se\left(p^{(1)} \right)^4 + \frac{\left(n^{(2)} - 1 \right)}{n^{(2)^2}} \cdot se\left(p^{(2)} \right)^4} - 2 \right\|.$$

As implied by its name, the parametric approach assumes that the data follow a normal distribution. This is inconsistent, however, with the distribution-free character of the PLS-SEM approach. Hence, more comprehensive approaches for PLS-MGA have been introduced by Chin and Dibbern (2010), Henseler (2007), Henseler et al. (2009), and Sarstedt, Henseler, et al. (2011), who propose nonparametric procedures to execute PLS-MGA. Parallel to the concept of an F test in regression, Sarstedt, Henseler, et al. (2011)

outlined a technique to compare more than two groups. Since these methods are not available in software packages, we focus on the parametric approach and refer the reader to Sarstedt, Henseler, et al. (2011) for additional information on nonparametric alternatives and recent developments.

Measurement Invariance

A primary concern when comparing path coefficients across groups is ensuring that the construct measures are invariant across the groups. Among other criteria, as described by Steenkamp and Baumgartner (1998), **measurement invariance** (also referred to as **measurement equivalence**) implies that the categorical moderator variable's effect is restricted to the path coefficients and does not entail group-related differences in the measurement models.

However, in many cases, especially in cross-cultural research, the measurement invariance assumption is questionable or even implausible. Thus, researchers should consider group membership effects on both measurement and structural model estimates, for instance, by reverting to the approaches proposed by Haenlein and Kaplan (2011) or Ringle, Sarstedt, and Zimmermann (2011). In contrast, Rigdon et al. (2010) provide a different perspective on invariance in PLS-SEM, saying that "on the other hand, PLS-SEM is avowedly a method based on approximation, and designed for situations involving a less firmly established theoretical base. . . . Therefore, it may be best for researchers to express appropriate caution in interpreting results from PLS path analysis involving multiple groups" (p. 269). For this introductory text, we recommend this view and refer the interested reader to further literature on this issue (Haenlein & Kaplan, 2011; Ringle et al., 2011).

Case Study Illustration

To illustrate the use of the parametric approach to PLS-MGA, we will examine the simple PLS path model from Chapter 2 in which we analyzed the effect of the two corporate reputation dimensions (likeability and competence) on customer satisfaction and customer loyalty. Rather than analyzing the aggregate data set with 344 observations, we are interested in analyzing whether the effects of competence and likeability on satisfaction and loyalty differ significantly for customers with prepaid cell phone plans from those with contract plans. The research study obtained data on customers with a contract plan ($plan = 1$; $n^{(1)} = 219$) versus those with a prepaid plan ($plan = 2$; $n^{(2)} = 125$), and we will compare those two groups. When engaging in PLS-MGA, researchers need to ensure that the number of observations in each group meets the rules of thumb for minimum sample size requirements (Chapter 1). As the maximum number of arrows pointing at a latent variable is three, we would need $3 \cdot 10 = 30$ observations per group, according to the 10 times rule. Following the more rigorous recommendations from a power analysis (Chapter 1), 59 observations per group are needed to detect R^2 values of around 0.25 at a significance level of 5% and a power level of 80%. Therefore, the group-specific sample sizes can be considered sufficiently large.

To download the corresponding SmartPLS project file, go to the http://www.pls-sem.com website, right-click on **Corporate_ Reputation_Moderation.zip,** save the file on your hard drive and extract it (e.g., in the C:\SmartPLS\ folder). Then, run the SmartPLS software and press on **File → Import** in the menu to import the ready-to-use SmartPLS project file **Corporate Reputation Moderation.splsp** as described in detail in Chapter 2. Thereafter, a new project appears with the name **Corporate Reputation Moderation** in the SmartPLS **Projects** window on the left-hand side. This project contains four models (**Simple Model.splsm, Simple Model–Moderation–Product Indicator.splsm, Simple Model–Moderation–Two Stage 1.splsm,** and **Simple Model–Moderation–Two Stage 2.splsm**) and four data sets (**Full Data.csv, Full Data_LVS.csv, Full Data_contract.csv,** and **Full Data_prepaid.csv**). After double-clicking on **Simple Model.splsm,** the PLS path model opens as displayed in Exhibit 8.2.

Alternatively, you can draw the model yourself following the instructions from the earlier chapters. Rather than drawing separate models for each group, you can simply use one model and estimate it with the different group-specific data sets. Therefore, you need to import the group-specific data (the **Corporate_Reputation_ Moderation.zip** file, which you can download from http://www .pls-sem.com, also contains the single data sets for this case study) by using the SmartPLS data **Import Wizard** as explained in Chapter 7 (i.e., for the IPMA case study). In the SmartPLS **Projects** window, right-click on the specific project (or any .splsm, .csv, or .txt file of

Exhibit 8.2	Simple Model for PLS-MGA

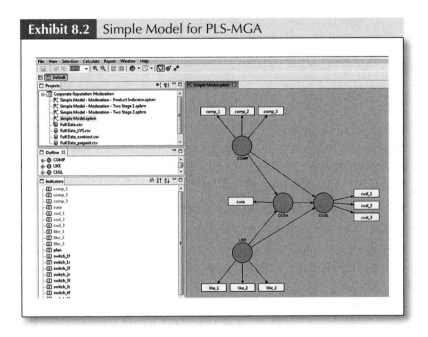

the specific project) in which you would like to import the data set. A menu opens where you need to select the **Import Indicator Data** option. Then, the SmartPLS data **Import Wizard** opens and allows you to choose the data set that you wish to import (**Full Data_contract.csv** or **Full Data_prepaid.csv**) from your hard drive. The newly imported data set will then appear with a green tag (i.e., a green box with the white checkmark) below the .splsm file in your SmartPLS project (if the data set has a red tag, check the procedures explained in Chapter 7 for the IPMA case study).

In the next step, we need to select and activate the data set that we want to use for the model estimation. To activate the data set with customers who use a contract plan, right-click on **Full Data_contract .csv** and choose **Use Data for Calculation** (Exhibit 8.3). The green tag will now appear next to **Full Data_contract.csv** and indicates that this data set has been selected for estimating the PLS path model. This data set has missing values, so you must check to see if the missing values are correctly specified. Double-click on the data set, and a screen for the data set will appear. Look at the lower left corner of the screen and make sure the box is checked indicating the data contain missing values and that missing values are coded −99.0. If not, you must check the box **The indicator data contains missing values** and insert **–99.0** in the field below. Close the data set tab and confirm that these changes should be saved.

We can now proceed with the regular model estimation for the **Full Data_contract.csv** group of data by (i.e., the group of customers with a contract plan) going to **Calculate → PLS Algorithm.** This provides us with the path coefficients that we are going to use as input for the PLS-MGA. Of course, when estimating the model, we need to make sure that all criteria discussed in the previous chapters (e.g., convergence of the algorithm, reliability and validity of construct measures) are fulfilled. Since this is the case, we can simply proceed with the analysis. The results of running the model are displayed in Exhibit 8.4.

As described above, the parametric PLS-MGA approach also requires us to specify the standard errors of the path coefficient estimates. Consequently, we need to run the bootstrapping procedure for each of the groups. To do so, go to **Calculate → Bootstrapping** and follow the instructions presented in Chapter 5. Note that you need to adjust the number of bootstrap cases according to the number of observations in the data sets (i.e., $n^{(1)} = 125$ for **Full Data_contract.csv**). This

Exhibit 8.3	Activate a Data Set

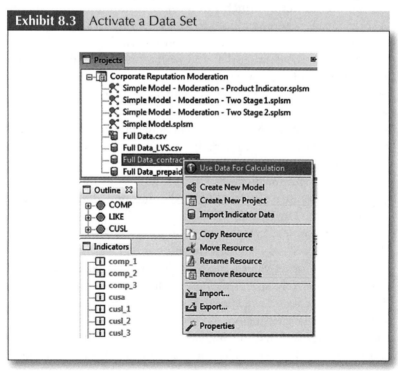

sample size change is completed by inserting the number of observations in the space beside **Cases** in the lower portion of the **Run the Bootstrapping Algorithm** screen. You also need to specify the number of bootstrapping **Samples** (i.e., 5,000). Next, open the default report (**Report → Default Report**). Under **Bootstrapping → Path Coefficients (Mean, STDEV, T-Values)** in the default report, you will find the standard errors.

Once you have finished the analyses and recorded the path coefficients and bootstrap standard errors, switch to the other data set by right-clicking on **Full Data_prepaid.csv** and choose **Use Data for Calculation** (Exhibit 8.3). The green box with the white checkmark will appear next to the **Full Data_prepaid.csv** file and indicates that this data set has been selected for the analysis. Again, you need to ensure the missing values box is checked and that missing values are coded −99.0. Now run the standard PLS-SEM algorithm and the bootstrapping procedure (using $n^{(2)} = 219$ bootstrap cases, 5,000 bootstrap samples, and the no sign changes option) and record the path coefficients and bootstrap standard errors. Exhibit 8.4 shows the results of these analyses. Note that because the bootstrapping procedure is a random process, your bootstrap standard errors will likely diverge (although only slightly) from those shown here.

In the next step, you need to enter the values into the formula presented above. On http://www.pls-sem.com, in the **Corporate_Reputation_Moderation.zip** file, you will find the Microsoft Excel file **PLS-MGA_Parametric.xlsx** that does the calculations of t values and p values automatically for you. When you open the Excel file, you will see six cells marked in yellow on the top left in which you have to enter the group-specific path coefficients and standard errors for one specific relationship. You also need to specify the number of observations per group. Start with the relationship $COMP \rightarrow CUSL$ and enter the corresponding values into the cells, as shown in Exhibit 8.5.

The selection of the appropriate parametric test statistic depends on whether the standard errors can be assumed to be equal or unequal in the population. Therefore, we first need to examine the results of Levene's test, indicated under **Test for equality of standard errors** in the Excel sheet (Exhibit 8.5). In the present example, the resulting p value (0.832) is higher than 0.05 and lower than 0.95, which implies that we cannot reject the null hypothesis of equal standard errors. Thus, we have to consider the results under **Equal standard errors assumed** in the

Exhibit 8.4 PLS-MGA Results

| | Group 1: Contract | | Group 2: Prepaid | | | Group 1 vs. Group 2 | | |
	$p^{(1)}$	$se(p^{(1)})$	$p^{(2)}$	$se(p^{(2)})$	$|p^{(1)} - p^{(2)}|$	t Value	Significance Level	p Value
COMP → CUSL	0.133	0.087	−0.050	0.071	0.183	1.595		0.112
COMP → CUSA	0.224	0.111	0.130	0.083	0.094	0.682		0.500
CUSA → CUSL	0.598	0.058	0.440	0.055	0.158	1.983	**	0.048
LIKE → CUSL	0.206	0.082	0.418	0.073	0.212	1.852	*	0.065
LIKE → CUSA	0.358	0.096	0.480	0.079	0.122	0.962		0.337
n	125		219					

Note: $p^{(1)}$ and $p^{(2)}$ are path coefficients of Group 1 and Group 2, respectively; $se(p^{(1)})$ and $se(p^{(2)})$ are the standard error of $p^{(1)}$ and $p^{(2)}$, respectively.

*$p < .10.$ **$p < .05.$

Excel sheet. As shown in Exhibit 8.5, the resulting t value is 1.595, which yields a p value of approximately .112, thus indicating that there is no significant difference in the effect of competence on loyalty between customers with a contract and customers with a prepaid plan.

While Exhibit 8.5 provides an example only for the $COMP \rightarrow CUSL$ relationship, Exhibit 8.4 summarizes the results for all the relationships in the model. As can be seen, only two relationships (path coefficients) differ significantly across the two groups. The effect of customer satisfaction on customer loyalty is significantly ($p < .05$) higher for customers with a contract plan. This finding makes intuitive sense considering the nature of their business relationship compared with customers with a prepaid plan. Conversely, the effect of likeability on loyalty is significantly higher ($p < .10$) for customers with a prepaid plan, implying that the affective dimension of reputation plays a greater role when the business relationship is more short term in nature.

MODELING UNOBSERVED HETEROGENEITY

Because heterogeneity is often present in empirical research, researchers should always consider potential sources of heterogeneity, for example, by forming groups of data based on observable characteristics such as demographics (e.g., age or gender). When heterogeneous data structures can be traced back to observable characteristics, we refer to this situation as **observed heterogeneity.** Unfortunately, the sources of heterogeneity in data can never be fully known a priori. Consequently, situations arise in which differences related to **unobserved heterogeneity** prevent the PLS path model from being accurately estimated. Since researchers never know if unobserved heterogeneity is causing estimation problems, they need to apply complementary techniques for response-based segmentation (so-called **latent class techniques**) that allow for identifying and treating unobserved heterogeneity.

Several latent class techniques have recently been proposed that generalize statistical concepts such as finite mixture modeling, typological regression, or genetic algorithms to PLS-SEM (see Sarstedt, 2008, for a review). One of the most prominent latent class approaches is **finite mixture partial least squares** (FIMIX-PLS; Hahn, Johnson, Herrmann, & Huber, 2002; Sarstedt, Becker, et al., 2011). Based on a mixture regression concept, **FIMIX-PLS** simultaneously estimates the

Exhibit 8.5 Excel Template for Parametric Test

		Group 1	Group 2								
Please enter values here					**Output: Two-tailed test**						
	Path coefficient	0,133	-0,050			Equal standard errors assumed	Unequal standard errors assumed		**Test for equality of standard errors**		
	Std. error	0,087	0,071		t-value	1,595	1,630			0,832	
	Sample size	125	219		df	342	273				
					p-value	0,112	0,104				

Reject test if value < 0.05 or > 0.95 (for Aplha = 0.10)

path coefficients and ascertains the data's heterogeneity by calculating the probability of the observations' segment membership so that they fit into a predetermined number of groups. In light of the approach's performance in prior studies (e.g., Ringle, Wende, et al., 2010; Sarstedt & Ringle, 2010) and its availability through the software application SmartPLS, Hair, Ringle, and Sarstedt (2011) suggest that researchers should routinely use the technique to evaluate whether PLS-SEM results are distorted by unobserved heterogeneity. For a more detailed discussion and step-by-step illustration of the approach on empirical data, see Ringle, Sarstedt, et al. (2010) and Rigdon et al. (2010). For applications of FIMIX-PLS, see, for example, Sarstedt et al. (2009), Money, Hillenbrand, Henseler, & Da Camara (2012), Navarro, Acedo, Losada, & Ruzo (2011), or Rigdon et al. (2011).

Research on ways to account for unobserved heterogeneity is ongoing, and recent research has highlighted genetic algorithm segmentation in PLS-SEM (PLS-GAS; Ringle et al., 2012) and prediction-oriented segmentation in PLS-SEM (PLS-POS; Becker, Rai, et al., 2012) as two approaches that perform favorably compared with FIMIX-PLS. Since PLS-GAS and PLS-POS have not yet been readily implemented in any PLS-SEM software package, we advise researchers to use FIMIX-PLS, which is a suitable means to uncover unobserved heterogeneity.

CONTINUOUS MODERATOR EFFECTS

Method

Cause-effect relationships in a PLS path model imply that exogenous latent variables directly affect endogenous latent variables without any systematic influences of other variables. In the previous section, we learned about a situation where this is not necessarily the case. For instance, in the case study, we evaluated whether the customers' type of cell phone plan has a significant bearing on the effects of competence and likeability on customer satisfaction and loyalty. In other words, we used the categorical moderator variable type of plan (contract vs. prepaid) to divide the data set into two groups and evaluated whether this moderator variable has a significant effect on our model estimates.

In many situations, however, researchers have a continuous (rather than a categorical) **moderator variable** that they believe can affect the strength of one specific relationship between two latent variables. Moderators may also change the direction of relationships.

For example, a path coefficient may be positive for those observations that have high value in the moderator variable, whereas the structural relationship is negative for observations where this is not the case.

In both cases, this kind of heterogeneity explained by a continuous moderator variable occurs when the relationship between the latent variables is not constant but rather depends on the values of a moderating variable. Returning to our previously discussed introductory example in the context of PLS-MGA, we could, for example, hypothesize that the relationship between satisfaction with the price (Y_1) and overall satisfaction (Y_2) is influenced by the customers' income. This would mean that the expected change in customer loyalty based on customer satisfaction (as expressed by the path coefficient linking the two constructs) might be lower for customers with low incomes and higher for customers with higher incomes. The **moderator effect** tells us that this relationship changes, depending on the customer income level. If this moderator effect were not present, we would assume that satisfaction has a constant effect on loyalty without significant changes across different income levels.

The concept of moderator effects parallels that of a mediator variable (Chapter 7) with the crucial difference that the moderator variable does not depend on the predictor variable (Y_1 in our example). In addition, the concept of a continuous moderator can also be considered a general form of a multigroup analysis. Specifically, a situation researchers often encounter is where they have a continuous moderator variable, but instead of modeling its original effect on the relationship as continuous, they transform the continuous variable into a categorical variable and then conduct a multigroup analysis. When the researcher wants to execute this type of analysis, the most often followed approach is to dichotomize the moderator variable. That is, divide the variable into two categories, such as "high" and "low," based on the values of the moderator. In the past, a common approach to dichotomize the variable was by using either a median or a mean split. Thus, for example, observations whose moderator score is above the median are said to have a high moderator value, while observations whose moderator construct score is (equal to or) below the median are said to have a low moderator value. In our example from above, this would involve splitting the data set into low and high income groups, based on either the mean or the median income level.

Dividing the data into groups based on the mean or median is arbitrary and difficult to achieve when more than one continuous moderator variable is included. Instead, researchers have been applying cluster analysis to the continuous moderator variables to identify natural groupings that exhibit meaningful differences (Hair, Wolfinbarger Celsi, et al., 2011). Using such an approach, researchers can identify subgroups objectively and scientifically. Moreover, researchers may wish to compare three or more groups, and this is easy to do using cluster analysis.

Finally, researchers can use cluster analysis to execute a polar extremes approach (Hair et al., 2010). An example of a **polar extremes approach** is when the researcher first uses cluster analysis to identify three groups. Then the middle group is removed from the analysis and only the extreme groups are compared to determine if there is a moderator effect. Of course, the sample size requirements of PLS-SEM of the individual groups must be considered when applying this or other approaches to dividing a total sample into subgroups.

Exhibit 8.6 illustrates the situation where the effect from satisfaction with price (Y_1) on overall satisfaction (Y_2) is influenced by a moderator variable (M), the income. In this situation, the moderator effect (p_3) is symbolized by an arrow pointing at the effect p_1 linking Y_1 and Y_2, which is hypothesized as being moderated by M.

Exhibit 8.6	Example of a Moderating Effect

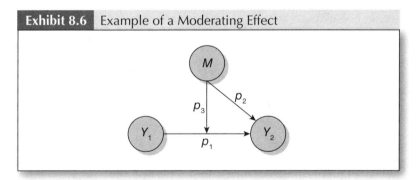

In a main effect model without moderation where there is only an arrow linking Y_1 and Y_2, the effect p_1 is referred to as a **main effect** (e.g., the relationship between customer satisfaction and customer loyalty of the corporate reputation example used in the previous chapter). Such main effects are different compared with the model shown in Exhibit 8.6, which includes the moderator variable. Here, in contrast, p_1 is referred to as a **simple effect,** expressing the effect of Y_1 on Y_2 that is moderated by M. More specifically, the estimated value of p_1 represents the strength of the relationship between Y_1 and

Y_2 when the moderator variable M has a value of zero. If the level of the moderator variable is increased (or decreased) by one standard deviation unit, the simple effect p_1 is expected to change by the size of p_3. For example, if the simple effect p_1 equals 0.30 and the moderating effect p_3 has a value of –0.10, one would expect the relationship between Y_1 and Y_2 to decease to a value of $0.30 + (-0.10) = 0.20$, if (*ceteris paribus*) the mean value of the moderator variable M increases by one standard deviation unit (Henseler and Fassott, 2010).

However, in many model setups, zero is not an existing value on the scale of M or, as in the case in our example, is not a sensible value for the moderator. This situation (i.e., the moderator has a value of zero) makes the interpretation of the simple effect problematic. For this reason, one needs to mean-center the moderator variable. This is done by subtracting the latent variable's mean from each observation. Mean-centering shifts the reference point from an income of zero to the average income and thus facilitates interpretation of the effects. Finally, one needs to include the moderator variable's simple effect (p_2) on the endogenous latent variable Y_2. This additional path is important (and a frequent source of mistake) to account for mean value changes in the endogenous latent variable. If the path p_2 is omitted, the effect of M on the relationship between Y_1 and Y_2 (i.e., p_3) would be inflated.

As the nature of the effect between Y_1 and Y_2 (i.e., p_1) differs for models with and without the moderator, we need to include an important note of caution. If one is interested in testing the significance of the main p_1 effect between Y_1 and Y_2, the PLS-SEM analysis should be initially executed without the moderator. The evaluation and interpretation of results should follow the procedures explained in Chapter 6. Then, moderator models represent complementary analyses for this relationship that may follow the initial PLS-SEM analysis. This issue is important because main effects become a simple effect in the moderator model that differ in their estimated values and their meaning. They represent the relationship between an exogenous and an endogenous latent variable in the structural model when the moderator variable's value is equal to its mean value (provided mean-centering has been applied). Hence, interpreting the simple effect results of a moderator model as if it were a main effect (e.g., for testing the hypothesis of a significant relationship p_1 between Y_1 and Y_2) may involve false and misleading conclusions (Henseler and Fassott, 2010).

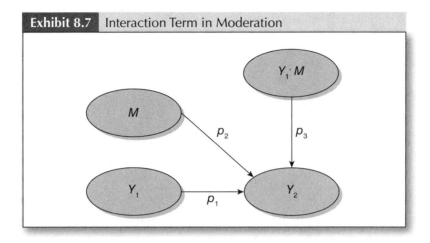

Exhibit 8.7 Interaction Term in Moderation

Modeling Continuous Moderating Effects

To gain an understanding of how moderating effects are modeled, let's consider the following formula expressing the structural model with the moderator effect as depicted in Exhibit 8.6:

$$Y_2 = (p_1 + p_3 \cdot M) \cdot Y_1 + p_2 \cdot M.$$

As can be seen, the influence of Y_1 on Y_2 depends not only on the strength of the simple effect p_1 but also on the product of p_3 and M. To understand how a moderator variable can be integrated in the model, we need to rewrite the equation as follows:

$$Y_2 = p_1 \cdot Y_1 + p_2 \cdot M + p_3 \cdot (Y_1 \cdot M).$$

This equation shows that including a moderator effect requires the specification of the simple effect of the exogenous latent variable (i.e., $p_1 \times Y_1$), the simple effect of the moderator variable (i.e., $p_2 \times M$), and the product term $p_3 \times (Y_1 \times M)$, which is also called the **interaction term**. As a result, the coefficient p_3 expresses how the simple effect p_1 (Exhibit 8.7) changes when the moderator variable M is increased or decreased by one standard deviation. Exhibit 8.7 illustrates the concept of an interaction term. As can be seen, the model includes the interaction term as an additional latent variable

Exhibit 8.8	Three-Way interaction

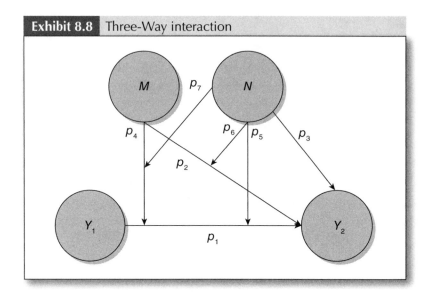

covering the product of the exogenous latent variable Y_1 and the moderator M. Because of this interaction term, researchers often refer to **interaction effects** when modeling moderator variables.

Three-Way Interactions

So far, we have looked at a **two-way interaction** because the moderator interacts with one other variable, the exogenous latent variable Y_1. However, it is also possible to model higher levels of interaction where the moderating effect is again moderated. Such a setup is also referred to as **cascaded moderator analysis** (Henseler & Fassott, 2010).

The most common form of a cascaded moderator analysis is **a three-way interaction.** Returning to our example above, we could imagine that the moderating effect of income is not constant but is itself influenced by other variables such as age. We would thus have to include a second moderator variable N into the model (Exhibit 8.8).

Including a second moderator variable N into our model changes the equation for the moderator model as follows:

$$Y_2 = p_1 \cdot Y_1 + p_2 \cdot M + p_3 \cdot N + p_4 \cdot (Y_1 \times M) + p_5 \cdot (Y_1 \cdot N) + p_6 \cdot (M \cdot N) + p_7 \cdot (Y_1 \cdot M \cdot N).$$

The corresponding PLS path model would then include three direct effects from Y_1, M, and N and four interaction terms (Exhibit 8.9).

Exhibit 8.9 Three-Way Interaction in PLS-SEM

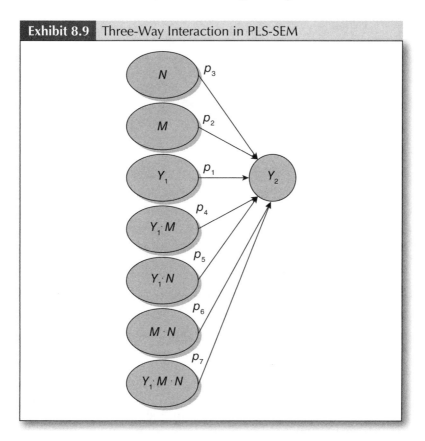

Creating the Interaction Term

In PLS-SEM, two approaches are usually employed to create the interaction term. The **product indicator approach** involves multiplying each (mean-centered) indicator of the exogenous latent variable with each indicator of the moderator variable. These so-called **product indicators** become the indicators of the interaction term. Therefore, if the exogenous latent variable has I indicators, and the moderator is measured by J indicators, the interaction term will have $I \cdot J$ product indicators. Exhibit 8.10 illustrates the interaction term when both Y_1 and M are measured by means of two (reflective) indicators. Thus, the interaction term has four product indicators.

When the exogenous latent variable or the moderator variable has a formative measurement model, the product indicator approach cannot be applied. Instead, researchers should use the **two-stage approach** that extends the product indicator approach to formative measures by making explicit use of PLS-SEM's advantage to estimate

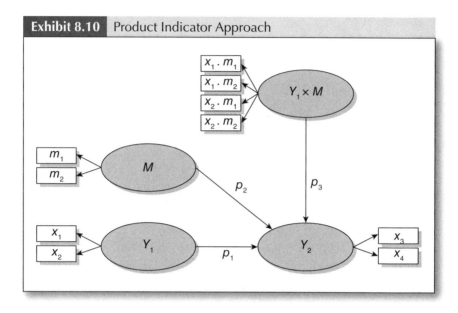

Exhibit 8.10 Product Indicator Approach

latent variable scores (Henseler and Chin, 2010; Rigdon et al. 2010). The two stages are as follows:

> Stage 1: The main effects model is estimated without the interaction term to obtain the scores of the latent variables. These are saved for further analysis in the second stage.

> Stage 2: The latent variable scores of the exogenous latent variable and moderator variable from Stage 1 are multiplied to create a single-item measure used to measure the interaction term. All other latent variables are represented by means of single items of their latent variable scores from Stage 1.

Exhibit 8.11 illustrates the two-stage approach for our previous model, but two formative indicators are used to measure the moderator variable. In Stage 1, the main effects model is run to obtain the latent variable scores for Y_1, Y_2, and M (i.e., $LVS(Y_1)$, $LVS(Y_2)$, and $LVS(M)$). The latent variable scores of Y_2 and M are then multiplied to form the single item used to measure the interaction term $Y_1 \cdot M$ in Stage 2. The latent variables Y_1, Y_2, and M are each measured with a single item of the latent variable scores from Stage 1. Note that all single items in Stage 2 could also have been specified as formative (rather than reflective). The reason is that in PLS-SEM, latent variables measured with only one indicator are set equal to this indicator, no matter which measurement model setup is chosen (single-item constructs).

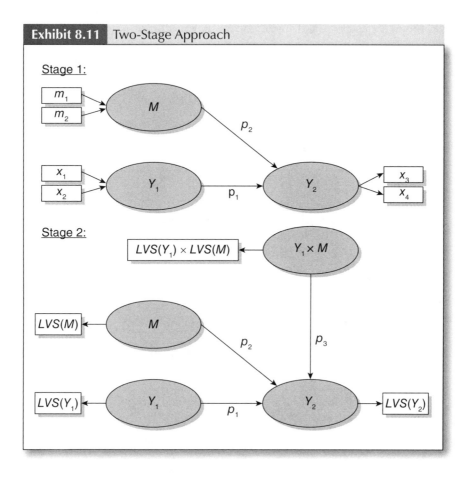

Exhibit 8.11   Two-Stage Approach

The two-stage approach is not restricted to models that include formative measurement approaches but can also be used when all constructs are measured by reflective indicators. Henseler and Chin's (2010) simulation study on the use of these alternative approaches in PLS-SEM shows that the product indicator approach performs favorably when parameter accuracy is a major issue of concern. Thus, it is the best choice for hypothesis testing. When prediction represents the major or only purpose of an analysis, however, researchers should use the two-stage approach.

Case Study Illustration

To illustrate the estimation of moderation effects, let's consider the simple model on the effects of competence and likeability on customer satisfaction and loyalty again. If you do not have the model readily available, please go back to the case study on PLS-MGA in the previous section and import the SmartPLS project file **Corporate Reputation Moderation.splsp.** Next, open the model by double-clicking on **Simple Model.splsm.** The model shown in Exhibit 8.2 will appear in the modeling window.

In the following discussion, we focus on the relationship between customer satisfaction and customer loyalty. Specifically, we introduce switching costs as a moderator variable that can be assumed to negatively influence the relationship between satisfaction and loyalty. The higher the perceived switching costs, the weaker the relationship between these two constructs. Following prior literature (Barroso & Picón, 2012; Jones, Mothersbaugh, & Beatty, 2000), switching costs can be measured both reflectively and formatively. First, switching costs are measured using reflective indicators to illustrate the use of the product indicator approach. Next, we use a formative measurement model operationalization of switching costs to illustrate the two-stage approach.

Exhibit 8.12	Indicators for Measuring Switching Costs
Switching Costs (SC): Reflective Indicators (Jones et al., 2000)	
switch_1r	It takes me a great deal of time and effort to get used to a new company.
switch_2r	It costs me too much to switch to another company.
switch_3r	In general it would be a hassle switching to another company.
Switching Costs (SC): Formative Indicators (Barroso & Picón, 2012)	
switch_1f	Benefit loss costs
switch_2f	Personal relationship loss costs
switch_3f	Economic risk costs
switch_4f	Evaluation costs
switch_5f	Setup costs
switch_6f	Monetary loss costs

The Product Indicator Approach

To implement the product indicator approach, we first need to extend the original model by including the moderator variable (note that the **Corporate Reputation Moderation** project file also includes a model, **Simple Model–Moderation–Product Indicator.splsm,** which contains the model setup described in this section). To do so, enter a new construct in the model, rename it as *SC* (i.e., switching costs), and draw a path relationship from the newly added moderator variable to the *CUSL* construct, as shown in Exhibit 8.12. Next, we need to assign indicators to the *SC* construct. Following Jones et al. (2000), we first measure switching costs reflectively using three indicators (*switch_1r* to *switch_3r;* Exhibit 8.12), measured on a 5-point Likert scale (1 = *fully disagree*, 5 = *fully agree*).

Exhibit 8.13 shows the main effects model (i.e., the simple model plus *SC* linked to *CUSL*). Next, we need to include the interaction

---

Exhibit 8.13 Single-Effects Model

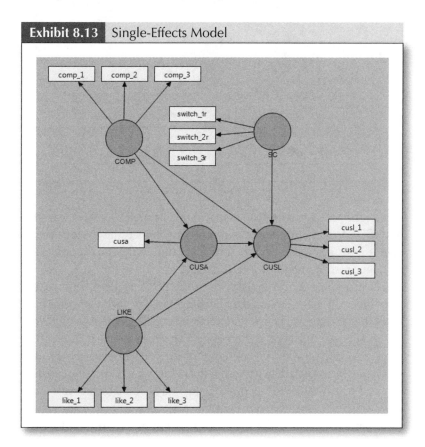

term. The SmartPLS software offers an option to automatically include an interaction term with product indicators. Right-click in the target construct *CUSL* and choose the option **Create Moderating Effect** (Exhibit 8.14).

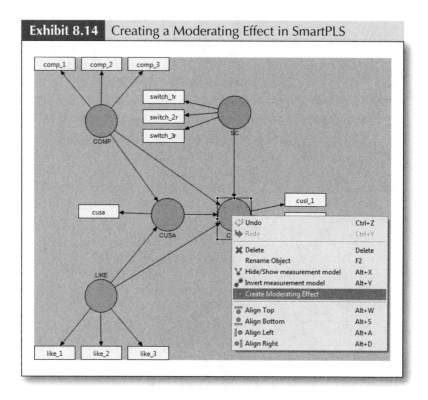

Exhibit 8.14 Creating a Moderating Effect in SmartPLS

In the screen that follows, specify *SC* as the moderator variable and *CUSA* as the predictor variable and choose the option **Mean-center indicator values before multiplication** in the **Interaction effect term generation** menu box (Exhibit 8.15).

When you click on **Finish**, SmartPLS will include the interaction term labeled *CUSA * SC* in the modeling window. Its violet color indicates that this construct is an interaction term. Right-click on *CUSA * SC* and choose the menu option **Hide/Show measurement model**. The three product indicators (i.e., *cusa*switch_1r, cusa*switch_2r,* and *cusa*switch_3r*) will then appear in the modeling window. We can now proceed with the analysis by running the PLS-SEM algorithm (using the path weighting scheme and mean value replacement for missing values) as described in the earlier chapters. It is important to note that the

| Exhibit 8.15 | Moderating Effect Dialog Box in SmartPLS |

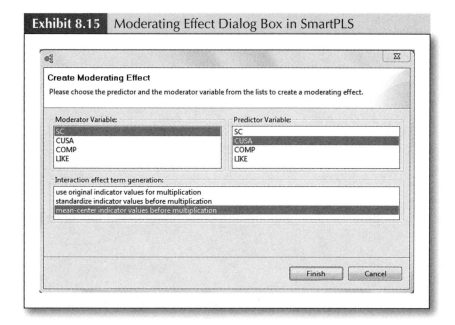

reflective evaluation criteria also apply for the interaction term. For instance, the assessment of the size and significance of the interaction term is useful only if the latent interaction variable is reliable. As a rule of thumb, the composite reliability of the interaction term equals the product of the composite reliabilities of the simple effect construct and the moderator construct. Hence, high levels of composite reliabilities are advantageous when conducting a moderator analysis via the product indicator approach.

A screenshot from SmartPLS showing the final model, including the model estimates, is shown in Exhibit 8.16. Examining the results, one may consider removing *switch_3r* from the measurement model of the latent moderator variable *SC*. This indicator has a relatively low loading (0.681), and deleting it would improve the composite reliability of *SC* and therefore of the interaction term. This kind of model adjustment has almost no effect on the final results displayed in Exhibit 8.16, however, and therefore does not lead to different conclusions. As can be seen, the interaction term *CUSA * SC* has a negative effect on *CUSL* (–0.045).

The interpretation of the negative interaction term would be as follows. A medium level of switching costs (i.e., the moderator variable *SC*) is the reference point. For this level of switching costs, the relationship between *CUSA* and *CUSL* (i.e., the simple effect in the moderator

Exhibit 8.16   Moderator Model in SmartPLS

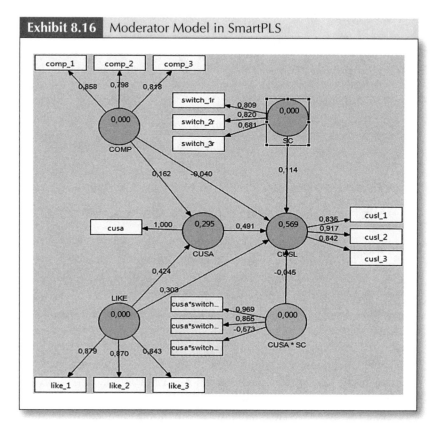

model) has a value of 0.491. If the switching costs become higher (i.e., SC is increased by one standard deviation point), this would imply that the relationship between CUSA and CUSL would decrease by the size of the interaction term and obtain the value of 0.491 − 0.045 = 0.446. Hence, when switching costs get higher, CUSA becomes less important for the explanation of CUSL. Exactly the opposite kind of interpretation holds for situations of lower switching costs (i.e., SC is decreased by one standard deviation point). Here, CUSA would increase in its importance for explaining CUSL.

Such conclusions only hold, however, when the interaction term is significant. Consequently, we run the bootstrapping procedure with 344 bootstrap cases, 500 bootstrap samples using the no sign changes option, and mean replacement for missing values to conduct the significance test for the relationship between the interaction term and CUSL. The analysis yields a t value of 1.065 for the path linking the interaction term and CUSL (again, note that your t value will likely differ due to the random nature of the bootstrapping process).

Therefore, we do not find support for a significant moderating effect of *SC* on the relationship between *CUSA* and *CUSL*.

The Two-Stage Approach

We want to explore again whether switching costs exert a significant effect on the relationship between customer satisfaction and customer loyalty. Different from above, however, is that we draw on Barroso and Picón (2012) and operationalize switching costs using six formative indicators (*switch_1f* to *switch_6f*), measured on a scale from 1 (*low*) to 5 (*high*). Because of *SC*'s formative measurement model, the product indicator approach is not applicable, and we therefore use the two-stage approach.

The starting point for our analysis is again the simple model (Exhibit 8.2) with only the constructs *COMP*, *LIKE*, *CUSA*, and *CUSL*. Similar to the product indicator approach, we first include the moderator variable switching costs as a new construct in our model (note that the **Corporate Reputation Moderation** project file also includes two models, **Simple Model–Moderation–Two Stage 1.splsm** and **Simple Model–Moderation–Two Stage 2.splsm**, which contain the model setups described in this section). Draw a path from the moderator variable (which again is renamed *SC* as done above) and assign the six indicators *switch_1f* to *switch_6f* to the construct. Make sure that you specify the measurement model for this new construct as formative by right-clicking on the *SC* construct and choosing the menu option **Invert measurement model** (see case study in Chapter 5). Next, run the standard PLS-SEM algorithm (using the path weighting scheme and mean value replacement). This will yield the results shown in Exhibit 8.17. Of course, we need to ensure that all criteria for the measurement model evaluation have been met (see Chapters 4 and 5). Since this is the case for all reflective and formative measures, we can proceed with the analysis.

While we need to ensure that all constructs have been validly measured, there is no need to interpret the path coefficients at this point. The only purpose of this initial analysis step (i.e., Stage 1) is to obtain the latent variable scores we are going to use as input for Stage 2.

To access the latent variable scores, go to **Report** → **Default Report** and left-click on the file tab that will appear in the modeling window. You will find the latent variable scores in the menu **PLS** → **Calculation Results** → **Latent Variable Scores** of the default report (Exhibit 8.18).

Exhibit 8.17 Two-Stage Approach (Stage 1)

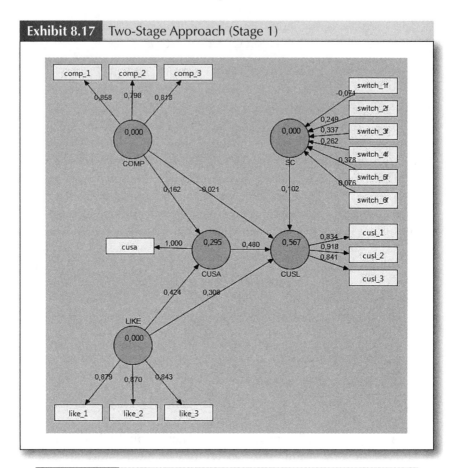

Exhibit 8.18 Latent Variable Scores in SmartPLS Default Report

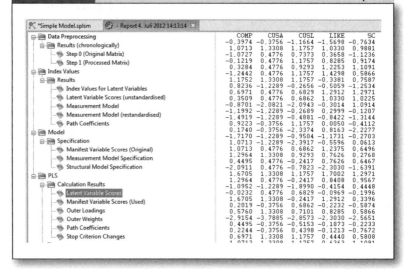

Since we use the latent variable scores as input for Stage 2, we need to copy/paste the scores into a new data set. Therefore, select all values in the table, click the right mouse button, and choose **Copy.** Next, open any spreadsheet software program such as Microsoft Excel and paste the entire set of latent variable scores (including the top row with the latent variable names *COMP, CUSA, CUSL, LIKE,* and *SC*) into the table. Now save the file as a .csv file to your hard drive (e.g., as **Full Data_LVS.csv**). Then, go back to our project in SmartPLS, right-click on **Simple model.splsm,** and select **Import Indicator Data** (Exhibit 8.3). After following the steps described in the SmartPLS data **Import Wizard** (see IPMA case study in Chapter 7), the newly generated data set **Full Data_LVS.csv** will appear below the **Simple model.splsm.** The green box with a white checkmark indicates that the data set has been successfully imported. If a red box appears, you need to double-click on the data set **Full Data_LVS.csv.** In the screen that follows, you need to choose the correct delimiter (i.e., semicolon) and click on **Validate.** SmartPLS will confirm that the data set is valid. Now close the window (i.e., the file tab **Full Data_LVS. csv**) and confirm that changes should be saved.

Next, go back to the modeling window. You will see that because we are using a new data set that only includes the latent variable scores, the original model is invalid, as indicated by the red color of constructs and paths in the model (Exhibit 8.19).

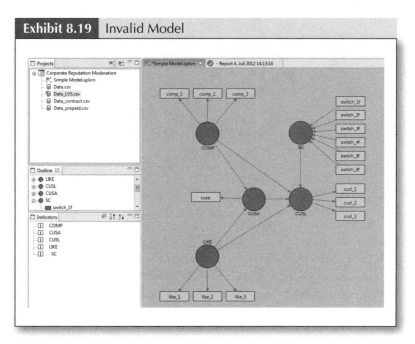

Exhibit 8.19 Invalid Model

Stage 2 of the two-stage approach only includes latent variable scores. Therefore, we need to remove all prior indicators (e.g., *comp_1* to *comp_3*) from the model and assign the indicators shown in the **Indicators** menu at the bottom left of the screen (Exhibit 8.19) as single-item measures to the corresponding constructs. The resulting (main effects) model is shown in Exhibit 8.20.

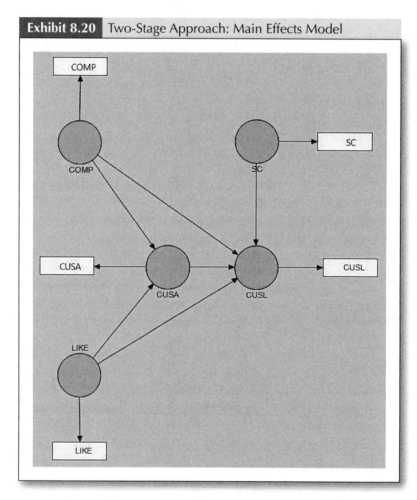

| **Exhibit 8.20** | Two-Stage Approach: Main Effects Model |

Similar to the product indicator approach, we now need to specify the interaction term. Right-click on the target construct *CUSL* and select the **Create Moderating Effect** option (Exhibit 8.14). In the screen that follows (Exhibit 8.15), choose *SC* as the moderator variable and *CUSA* as the predictor variable and select the **Mean-center**

indicator values before multiplication option. After clicking on **Finish,** the interaction term will again appear in the model (if you like, you can show the interaction term's measurement model by right-clicking on the interaction term and choosing the corresponding option). Running the standard PLS-SEM algorithm will yield the results shown in Exhibit 8.21.

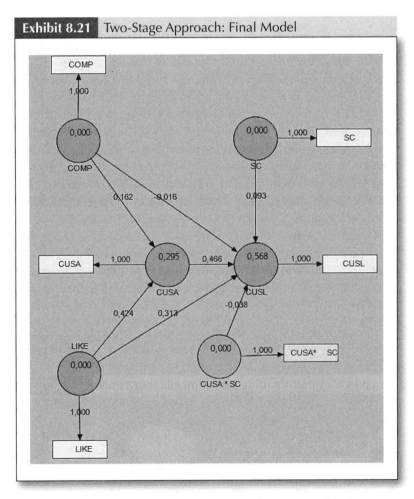

Exhibit 8.21 Two-Stage Approach: Final Model

Before drawing the conclusion that the relationship between *CUSA* and *CUSL* would decrease when switching costs become higher (and vice versa for situations of lower switching costs), we again need to determine if the relationship between the interaction term and *CUSL* is significant. Running the bootstrapping procedure with 344 cases and 500 samples results in a *t* value of 1.104, indicating that the moderator effect is not significant. Hence, we cannot conclude that *SC* affects the relationship between *CUSA* and *CUSL*.

SUMMARY

- **Understand the importance of modeling heterogeneity in PLS-SEM.** Applications of PLS-SEM are usually based on the assumption that the data stem from a single population. In such cases, the estimation of a unique global PLS path model represents all observations. In many real-world applications, however, the assumption of homogeneity is unrealistic because respondents are likely to be heterogeneous in their perceptions and evaluations of latent phenomena. While the consideration of heterogeneity is promising from a practical and theoretical perspective to learn about differences between groups of respondents, it is oftentimes also necessary to obtain valid results. For example, when there are significant differences between path coefficients across groups, an analysis on the aggregate data level could cancel out group-specific effects. The results of such an analysis would likely be seriously misleading and render erroneous recommendations to managers and researchers. Researchers are well advised, therefore, to consider the issue of heterogeneous data structures in their modeling efforts.

- **Know the concepts that enable you to identify heterogeneity.** Traditionally, heterogeneity implies the existence of distinct groups of respondents. These groups may be defined a priori on the basis of, for instance, geographic variables, gender, or stated preferences. Yet heterogeneity is frequently unobservable, and its true sources are unknown to the researcher. Including moderating effects in a model is another way to identify heterogeneity across respondents. Moderator variables imply that the relationship between two latent variables varies by respondent groups, depending on the respondent's score on the moderating variable.

- **Execute a PLS-SEM multigroup analysis (PLS-MGA).** PLS-MGA refers to a set of different techniques that have been developed for comparing PLS-SEM model estimates across two or more groups of data. Usually, PLS-MGA is used to explore differences between path coefficients in the structural model, but one can also compare, for example, loadings or weights. PLS-MGA is a rather new research field, and several approaches have recently been proposed. The most prominent one is the parametric approach, a modified version of an independent samples t test that is used to compare differences between two groups of respondents. The parametric test is easy to apply and only requires the specification of group-specific path coefficients, standard errors (as obtained from the bootstrapping procedure), and sample sizes. As the name already implies, however, the parametric approach to PLS-MGA requires that the data follow a normal distribution, which runs contrary to PLS-SEM's distribution-free nature.

- **Comprehend the concept of unobserved heterogeneity.** Traditionally, heterogeneity is taken into account by partitioning the data into groups, based on a priori information (usually observable characteristics). Oftentimes, the true sources of heterogeneous data structures are unknown a priori, however, and heterogeneity must therefore be considered unobserved. Methodological research on PLS-SEM has proposed a set of techniques that enable researchers to identify and understand unobserved heterogeneity. Among these methods, FIMIX-PLS is the most prominent approach to date, and several researchers call for its routine use to ascertain whether estimates are affected by unobserved heterogeneity.

- **Use the SmartPLS software to model continuous moderator variables in a PLS path model.** Besides examining the direct (or single) effects of PLS path models, the additional analysis of moderator effects is an issue of increasing interest to researchers. Moderator effects are evoked by variables whose variation has an effect on the strength or even direction of a relationship between an exogenous and an endogenous latent variable (i.e., simple effect). Modeling moderator variables in PLS-SEM requires researchers to include an interaction term that accounts for the interrelation between the exogenous latent variable and the moderator variable. The product indicator approach and the two-stage approach are two prominent concepts to model the interaction term. The product indicator approach is restricted to setups where the exogenous latent variable and moderator variable are both measured reflectively. The two-stage approach can be used when formative measures are involved.

REVIEW QUESTIONS

1. What is the difference between observed and unobserved heterogeneity?

2. How do you run a multigroup analysis in PLS-SEM?

3. What is FIMIX-PLS?

4. What are the two approaches to moderator analysis in PLS-SEM? When should each approach be used?

5. Why should the indicators be mean-centered when generating an interaction term in a moderator analysis?

6. What is the interaction term and what does its value mean?

CRITICAL THINKING QUESTIONS

1. Why is the consideration of heterogeneity so important when analyzing PLS path models?

2. Critically comment on the following statement: "Measurement invariance is not an issue in PLS-SEM because of the method's focus on prediction and exploration."

3. Discuss why the product indicator approach to moderation should not be used when formative measures are involved.

KEY TERMS

Cascaded moderator analysis: is a type of moderator analysis in which the strength of a moderating effect is influenced by another variable (i.e., the moderating effect is again moderated).

Direct effect: see *Single effect.*

FIMIX-PLS: see *Finite mixture partial least squares.*

Finite mixture partial least squares (FIMIX-PLS): is a latent class approach that allows for identifying and treating unobserved heterogeneity in PLS path models.

Heterogeneity: occurs when the data underlie groups of data characterized by significant differences in terms of model parameters.

Heterogeneity can be either observed or unobserved, depending on whether its source can be traced back to observable characteristics (e.g., demographic variables) or whether the sources of heterogeneity are not fully known.

Interaction effect: see *Moderator effect.*

Interaction term: is an auxiliary variable entered into the PLS path model to account for the interaction of the moderator variable and the exogenous latent variable.

Latent class techniques: form a class of procedures that allow for identifying and treating unobserved heterogeneity in PLS models. Several approaches are available that generalize, for example, typological regression, finite mixture, or genetic algorithm concepts to PLS-SEM. Among those, *finite mixture partial least squares* is the most prominent approach in the field.

Main effect: is a relationship between an exogenous and an endogenous latent variable in the PLS path model without the presence of a moderating effect. After inclusion of the moderator variable, the main effect usually changes its size and becomes the single effect of the moderator model.

Measurement equivalence: see *Measurement invariance.*

Measurement invariance: deals with the comparability of responses to particular (sets of) items. Among other things, measurement invariance implies that the categorical moderator variable's effect is restricted to the path coefficients and does not entail group-related differences in the measurement models.

Moderator effect: occurs when the effect of an exogenous latent variable on an endogenous latent variable depends on the values of another variable that moderates the relationship.

Moderator variable (categorical): see *Multigroup analysis.*

Moderator variable (continuous): is a variable that affects the direction and/or strength of the relation between an exogenous latent variable and an endogenous latent variable.

Multigroup analysis: also referred to as PLS-MGA, is a type of moderator analysis where the moderator variable is categorical (usually with two categories) and is assumed to potentially affect all relationships in the structural model.

Observed heterogeneity: occurs when the sources of heterogeneity are known and can be traced back to observable characteristics such as demographics (e.g., gender, age, income).

Parametric approach to PLS-MGA: is a modified version of a two-independent-samples t test that can be used to compare parameters across two groups of data.

PLS-MGA: see *Multigroup analysis.*

Polar extremes approach: is a type of multigroup analysis that involves partitioning the sample into three or more groups and only comparing the two most extreme ones.

Product indicator approach: is an approach to model the interaction term when including a continuous moderator variable in the model. It involves multiplying the indicators of the moderator with the indicators of the exogenous latent variable to establish a measurement model of the interaction term. The approach is only applicable when both moderator and exogenous latent variables are operationalized reflectively. When formative measures are involved, the *two-stage approach* should be used.

Product indicators: are indicators of an interaction term, generated by multiplication of each indicator of the predictor variable with each indicator of the moderator variable.

Simple effect: is a cause-effect relationship in a moderator model. The estimated value represents the size of the relationship between the exogenous and endogenous latent variable when the moderator variable has a value of zero. For this reason, main effects and effects (simple) usually have different sizes.

Three-way interaction: is an extension of *two-way interaction* where the moderator effect is again moderated by one other moderator variable.

Two-stage approach: is an approach to model the interaction term when including a continuous moderator variable in the model. Unlike the product indicator approach, it can be used in situations where the exogenous latent variable and/or the moderator variable are measured formatively.

Two-way interaction: is the standard approach to moderator analysis where the moderator variable interacts with one other exogenous latent variable.

Unobserved heterogeneity: occurs when the sources of heterogeneous data structures are not (fully) known.

SUGGESTED READINGS

Carte, T. A., & Russell, C. J. (2003). In pursuit of moderation: Nine common errors and their solutions. *MIS Quarterly, 27,* 479–501.

Henseler, J., & Chin, W. W. (2010). A comparison of approaches for the analysis of interaction effects between latent variables using partial least squares path modeling. *Structural Equation Modeling, 17,* 82–109.

Henseler, J., & Fassott, G. (2010). Testing moderating effects in PLS path models: An illustration of available procedures. In V. Esposito Vinzi, W. W. Chin, J. Henseler, & H. Wang (Eds.), *Handbook of partial least squares: Concepts, methods and applications in marketing and related fields* (pp. 713–735). Berlin: Springer.

Money, K. G., Hillenbrand, C., Henseler, J., & Da Camara, N. (2012). Exploring Unanticipated Consequences of Strategy Amongst Stakeholder Segments: The Case of a European Revenue Service. Long Range Planning, 45(5/6), 395-423.

Navarro, A., Acedo, F. J., Losada, F., & Ruzo, E. (2011). Integrated model of export activity: Analysis of heterogeneity in managers' orientations and perceptions on strategic marketing management in foreign markets. *Journal of Marketing Theory and Practice, 19*(2), 187–204.

Rigdon, E. E., Ringle, C. M., & Sarstedt, M. (2010). Structural modeling of heterogeneous data with partial least squares. In N. K. Malhotra (Ed.), *Review of marketing research* (pp. 255–296). Armonk, NY: Sharpe.

Ringle, C. M., Sarstedt, M., & Mooi, E. A. (2010). Response-based segmentation using finite mixture partial least squares: Theoretical foundations and an application to American customer satisfaction index data. *Annals of Information Systems, 8,* 19–49.

Sarstedt, M. (2008). A review of recent approaches for capturing heterogeneity in partial least squares path modelling. *Journal of Modelling in Management, 3,* 140–161.

References

Albers, S. (2010). PLS and success factor studies in marketing. In V. Esposito Vinzi, W. W. Chin, J. Henseler, & H. Wang (Eds.), *Handbook of partial least squares: Concepts, methods and applications in marketing and related fields* (pp. 409–425). Berlin: Springer.

Anderson, E. W., & Fornell, C. G. (2000). Foundations of the American Customer Satisfaction Index. *Total Quality Management, 11,* 869–882.

Bagozzi, R. P. (2007). On the meaning of formative measurement and how it differs from reflective measurement: Comment on Howell, Breivik, and Wilcox (2007). *Psychological Methods, 12,* 229–237.

Barclay, D. W., Higgins, C. A., & Thompson, R. (1995). The partial least squares approach to causal modeling: Personal computer adoption and use as illustration. *Technology Studies, 2,* 285–309.

Baron, R. M., & Kenny, D. A. (1986). The moderator-mediator variable distinction in social psychological research: Conceptual, strategic and statistical considerations. *Journal of Personality and Social Psychology, 51,* 1173–1182.

Barroso, C., & Picón, A. (2012). Multi-dimensional analysis of perceived switching costs. *Industrial Marketing Management, 41,* 531–543.

Bearden, W. O., Netemeyer, R. G., & Haws, K. L. (2011). *Handbook of marketing scales: Multi-item measures of marketing and consumer behavior research.* Thousand Oaks, CA: Sage.

Becker, J.-M., Klein, K., & Wetzels, M. (2012). Formative hierarchical latent variable models in PLS-SEM: Recommendations and guidelines. *Long Range Planning, 45,* 359–394.

Becker, J.-M., Rai, A., Ringle, C. M., & Völckner, F. (in press). Discovering unobserved heterogeneity in structural equation models to avert validity threats. *MIS Quarterly.*

Bollen, K. A., & Lennox, R. (1991). Conventional wisdom on measurement: A structural equation perspective. *Psychological Bulletin, 110,* 305–314.

Bruner, G. C., James, K. E., & Hensel, P. J. (2001). *Marketing scales handbook: A compilation of multi-item measures.* Oxford, UK: Butterworth-Heinemann.

Cassel, C., Hackl, P., and Westlund, A. H. (1999). Robustness of partial least squares method for estimating latent variable quality structures. *Journal of Applied Statistics, 26*(4), 435–446.

Cenfetelli, R. T., & Bassellier, G. (2009). Interpretation of formative measurement in information systems research. *MIS Quarterly, 33,* 689–708.

Chin, W. W. (1998). The partial least squares approach to structural equation modeling. In G. A. Marcoulides (Ed.), *Modern methods for business research* (pp. 295–358). Mahwah, NJ: Lawrence Erlbaum.

Chin, W. W. (2003). *PLS Graph 3.0.* Houston, TX: Soft Modeling, Inc.

Chin, W. W. (2010). How to write up and report PLS analyses. In V. Esposito Vinzi, W. W. Chin, J. Henseler, & H. Wang (Eds.), *Handbook of partial least squares: Concepts, methods and applications in marketing and related fields* (pp. 655–690). Berlin: Springer.

Chin, W. W., & Dibbern, J. (2010). A permutation based procedure for multi-group PLS analysis: Results of tests of differences on simulated data and a cross cultural analysis of the sourcing of information system services between Germany and the USA. In V. Esposito Vinzi, W. W. Chin, J. Henseler, & H. Wang (Eds.), *Handbook of partial least squares: Concepts, methods and applications in marketing and related fields* (pp. 171–193). Berlin: Springer.

Chin, W. W., & Newsted, P. R. (1999). Structural equation modeling analysis with small samples using partial least squares. In R. H. Hoyle (Ed.)., *Statistical strategies for small sample research* (pp. 307–341). Thousand Oaks, CA: Sage.

Cohen, J. (1988). *Statistical power analysis for the behavioral sciences.* Mahwah, NJ: Lawrence Erlbaum.

Cohen, J. (1992). A power primer. *Psychological Bulletin, 112,* 155–159.

Davison, A. C., & Hinkley, D. V. (1997). *Bootstrap methods and their application.* Cambridge, UK: Cambridge University Press.

DeVellis, R. F. (2011). *Scale development.* Thousand Oaks, CA: Sage.

Diamantopoulos, A. (2006). The error term in formative measurement models: Interpretation and modeling implications. *Journal of Modelling in Management, 1,* 7–17.

Diamantopoulos, A. (2011). Incorporating formative measures into covariance-based structural equation models. *MIS Quarterly, 35,* 335–358.

Diamantopoulos, A., & Riefler, P. (2011). Using formative measures in international marketing models: A cautionary tale using consumer animosity as an example. *Advances in International Marketing, 10,* 11–30.

Diamantopoulos, A., Riefler, P., & Roth, K. P. (2008). Advancing formative measurement models. *Journal of Business Research, 61,* 1203–1218.

Diamantopoulos, A., Sarstedt, M., Fuchs, C., Kaiser, S., & Wilczynski, P. (2012). Guidelines for choosing between multi-item and single-item scales for construct measurement: A predictive validity perspective. *Journal of the Academy of Marketing Science, 40,* 434–449.

Diamantopoulos, A., & Siguaw, J. A. (2006). Formative vs. reflective indicators in measure development: Does the choice of indicators matter? *British Journal of Management, 13,* 263–282.

Diamantopoulos, A., & Winklhofer, H. M. (2001). Index construction with formative indicators: An alternative to scale development. *Journal of Marketing Research, 38,* 269–277.

Drolet, A. L., & Morrison, D. G. (2001). Do we really need multiple-item measures in service research? *Journal of Service Research, 3,* 196–204.

Eberl, M. (2010). An application of PLS in multi-group analysis: The need for differentiated corporate-level marketing in the mobile communications industry. In V. Esposito Vinzi, W. W. Chin, J. Henseler, & H. Wang (Eds.), *Handbook of partial least squares: Concepts, methods and applications in marketing and related fields* (pp. 487–514). Berlin: Springer.

Eberl, M., & Schwaiger, M. (2005). Corporate reputation: Disentangling the effects on financial performance. *European Journal of Marketing, 39,* 838–854.

Edwards, J. R., & Bagozzi, R. P. (2000). On the nature and direction of relationships between constructs and measures. *Psychological Methods, 5,* 155–174.

Efron, B., & Tibshirani, R. (1986). Bootstrap methods for standard errors, confidence intervals, and other measures of statistical accuracy. *Statistical Science, 1,* 54–75.

Falk, R. F., & Miller, N. B. (1992). *A primer for soft modeling.* Akron, OH: University of Akron Press.

Fornell, C. G. (1982). A second generation of multivariate analysis: An overview. In C. Fornell (Ed.), *A second generation of multivariate analysis* (pp. 1–21). New York: Praeger.

Fornell, C. G. (1987). A second generation of multivariate analysis: Classification of methods and implications for marketing research. In M. J. Houston (Ed.), *Review of marketing* (pp. 407–450). Chicago: American Marketing Association.

Fornell, C. G., & Bookstein, F. L. (1982). Two structural equation models: LISREL and PLS applied to consumer exit-voice theory. *Journal of Marketing Research, 19,* 440–452.

Fornell, C. G., Johnson, M. D., Anderson, E. W., Cha, J., & Bryant, B. E. (1996). The American Customer Satisfaction Index: Nature, purpose, and findings. *Journal of Marketing, 60,* 7–18.

Fuchs, C., & Diamantopoulos, A. (2009). Using single-item measures for construct measurement in management research: Conceptual issues and application guidelines. *Die Betriebswirtschaft, 69,* 197–212.

Geisser, S. (1974). A predictive approach to the random effects model. *Biometrika, 61,* 101–107.

Goodhue, D. L., Lewis, W., & Thompson, R. (2012). Does PLS have advantages for small sample size or non-normal data? *MIS Quarterly, 36,* 891–1001.

Götz, O., Liehr-Gobbers, K., & Krafft, M. (2010). Evaluation of structural equation models using the partial least squares (PLS) approach. In V. Esposito Vinzi, W. W. Chin, J. Henseler, & H. Wang (Eds.), *Handbook of partial least squares: Concepts, methods and applications in marketing and related fields* (pp. 691–711). Berlin: Springer.

Gudergan, S. P., Ringle, C. M., Wende, S., & Will, A. (2008). Confirmatory tetrad analysis in PLS path modeling. *Journal of Business Research, 61,* 1238–1249.

Haenlein, M., & Kaplan, A. M. (2004). A beginner's guide to partial least squares analysis. *Understanding Statistics, 3,* 283–297.

Haenlein, M., & Kaplan, A. M. (2011). The influence of observed heterogeneity on path coefficient significance: Technology acceptance within the marketing discipline. *Journal of Marketing Theory and Practice, 19,* 153–168.

Hahn, C., Johnson, M. D., Herrmann, A., & Huber, F. (2002). Capturing customer heterogeneity using a finite mixture PLS approach. *Schmalenbach Business Review, 54,* 243–269.

Hair, J. F., Black, W. C., Babin, B. J., & Anderson, R. E. (2010). *Multivariate data analysis*. Englewood Cliffs, NJ: Prentice Hall.

Hair, J. F., Ringle, C. M., & Sarstedt, M. (2011). PLS-SEM: Indeed a silver bullet. *Journal of Marketing Theory and Practice, 19*, 139–151.

Hair, J. F., Sarstedt, M., Pieper, T., & Ringle, C. M. (2012a). The use of partial least squares structural equation modeling in strategic management research: A review of past practices and recommendations for future applications. *Long Range Planning 45*, 320–340.

Hair, J. F., Sarstedt, M., Ringle, C. M., & Mena, J. A. (2012). An assessment of the use of partial least squares structural equation modeling in marketing research. *Journal of the Academy of Marketing Science, 40*, 414–433.

Hair, J. F., Wolfinbarger Celsi, M., Money, A. H., Samouel, P., & Page, M. J. (2011). *Essentials of business research methods*. Armonk, NY: Sharpe.

Hayduk, L.A. & Littvay, L. (2012). Should researchers use single indicators, best indicators, or multiple indicators in structural equation models? *BMC Medical Research Methodology, 12*(159), 12–159.

Helm, S., Eggert, A., & Garnefeld, I. (2010). Modelling the impact of corporate reputation on customer satisfaction and loyalty using PLS. In V. Esposito Vinzi, W. W. Chin, J. Henseler, & H. Wang (Eds.), *Handbook of partial least squares: Concepts, methods and applications in marketing and related fields* (pp. 515–534). Berlin: Springer.

Henseler, J. (2007, September 5–7). *A new and simple approach to multigroup analysis in partial least squares path modeling*. Paper presented at the 5th International Symposium on PLS and Related Methods (PLS'07), Oslo, Norway.

Henseler, J. (2010). On the convergence of the partial least squares path modeling algorithm. *Computational Statistics, 25*, 107–120.

Henseler, J., & Chin, W. W. (2010). A comparison of approaches for the analysis of interaction effects between latent variables using partial least squares path modeling. *Structural Equation Modeling, 17*, 82–109.

Henseler, J., & Fassott, G. (2010). Testing moderating effects in PLS path models: An illustration of available procedures. In V. Esposito Vinzi, W. W. Chin, J. Henseler, & H. Wang (Eds.), *Handbook of partial least squares: Concepts, methods and applications in marketing and related fields* (pp. 713–735). Berlin: Springer.

Henseler, J., Ringle, C. M., & Sarstedt, M. (2012). Using partial least squares path modeling in international advertising research: Basic concepts and recent issues. In S. Okazaki (Ed.), *Handbook of research in international advertising* (pp. 252–276). Cheltenham, UK: Edward Elgar.

Henseler, J., Ringle, C. M., & Sinkovics, R. R. (2009). The use of partial least squares path modeling in international marketing. *Advances in International Marketing, 20*, 277–320.

Henseler, J., & Sarstedt, M. (in press). Goodness-of-fit indices for partial least squares path modeling *Computational Statistics*.

Höck, C., Ringle, C. M., & Sarstedt, M. (2010). Management of multipurpose stadiums: Importance and performance measurement of service interfaces. *International Journal of Services Technology and Management, 14*, 188–207.

Homburg, C., & Giering, A. (2001). Personal characteristics as moderators of the relationship between customer satisfaction and loyalty—an empirical analysis. *Psychology and Marketing, 18,* 43–66.

Hui, B. S., & Wold, H. (1982). Consistency and consistency at large of partial least squares estimates. In K. G. Jöreskog & H. Wold (Eds.), *Systems under indirect observation, Part II* (pp. 119–130). Amsterdam: North-Holland.

Hulland, J. (1999). Use of partial least squares (PLS) in strategic management research: A review of four recent studies. *Strategic Management Journal, 20,* 195–204.

Jarvis, C. B., MacKenzie, S. B., & Podsakoff, P. M. (2003). A critical review of construct indicators and measurement model misspecification in marketing and consumer research. *Journal of Consumer Research, 30,* 199–218.

Jones, M. A., Mothersbaugh, D. L., & Beatty, S. E. (2000). Switching barriers and repurchase intentions in services. *Journal of Retailing, 76,* 259–274.

Keil, M., Saarinen, T., Tan, B. C. Y., Tuunainen, V., Wassenaar, A., & Wei, K.-K. (2000). A cross-cultural study on escalation of commitment behavior in software projects. *MIS Quarterly, 24,* 299–325.

Kim, G., Shin, B., & Grover, V. (2010). Investigating two contradictory views of formative measurement in information systems research. *MIS Quarterly, 34,* 345–365.

Kristensen, K., Martensen, A., & Grønholdt, L. (2000). Customer satisfaction measurement at Post Denmark: Results of application of the European Customer Satisfaction Index Methodology. *Total Quality Management, 11,* 1007–1015.

Little, R. J. A., & Rubin, D. B. (2002). *Statistical analysis with missing data.* New York: John Wiley.

Lohmöller, J.-B. (1987). *LVPLS 1.8.* Cologne, Germany: Zentralarchiv für Empirische Sozialforschung.

Lohmöller, J.-B. (1989). *Latent variable path modeling with partial least squares.* Heidelberg, Germany: Physica.

Loo, R. (2002). A caveat on using single-item versus multiple-item scales. *Journal of Managerial Psychology, 17,* 68–75.

MacKenzie, S. B., Podsakoff, P. M., & Podsakoff, N. P. (2011). Construct measurement and validation procedures in MIS and behavioral research: Integrating new and existing techniques. *MIS Quarterly, 35,* 293–295.

Marcoulides, G. A., & Saunders, C. (2006). PLS: A silver bullet? *MIS Quarterly, 30,* iii–ix.

Mateos-Aparicio, G. (2011). Partial least squares (PLS) methods: Origins, evolution, and application to social sciences. *Communications in Statistics–Theory and Methods, 40*(13), 2305–2317.

Money, K. G., Hillenbrand, C., Henseler, J., & Da Camara, N. (2012). Exploring unanticipated consequences of strategy amongst stakeholder segments: The case of a European revenue service. *Long Range Planning, 45*(5/6), 395–423.

Mooi, E. A., & Sarstedt, M. (2011). *A concise guide to market research: The process, data, and methods using IBM SPSS Statistics.* Berlin: Springer.

Navarro, A., Acedo, F. J., Losada, F., & Ruzo, E. (2011). Integrated model of export activity: Analysis of heterogeneity in managers' orientations and perceptions on strategic marketing management in foreign markets. *Journal of Marketing Theory and Practice, 19*(2), 187–204.

Nunally, J. C., & Bernstein, I. (1994). *Psychometric theory.* New York: McGraw-Hill.

Preacher, K. J., & Hayes, A. F. (2004). SPSS and SAS procedures for estimating indirect effects in simple mediation models. *Behavior Research Methods, Instruments, and Computers, 36,* 717–731.

Preacher, K. J., & Hayes, A. F. (2008). Asymptotic and resampling strategies for assessing and comparing indirect effects in simple and multiple mediator models. *Behavior Research Methods, 40,* 879–891.

Raithel, S., Wilczynski, P., Schloderer, M. P., & Schwaiger, M. (2010). The value-relevance of corporate reputation during the financial crisis. *Journal of Product and Brand Management, 19,* 389–400.

Ramirez, E., David, M. E., & Brusco, M. J. (in press). Marketing's SEM based nomological network: Constructs and research streams in 1987–1997 and in 1998–2008. *Journal of Business Research.*

Reinartz, W., Haenlein, M., & Henseler, J. (2009). An empirical comparison of the efficacy of covariance-based and variance-based SEM. *International Journal of Research in Marketing, 26,* 332–344.

Rigdon, E. E. (2012). Rethinking partial least squares path modeling: In praise of simple methods. *Long Range Planning, 45,* 341–358.

Rigdon, E. E., Ringle, C. M., & Sarstedt, M. (2010). Structural modeling of heterogeneous data with partial least squares. In N. K. Malhotra (Ed.), *Review of marketing research* (pp. 255–296). Armonk, NY: Sharpe.

Rigdon, E. E., Ringle, C. M., Sarstedt, M., & Gudergan, S. P. (2011). Assessing heterogeneity in customer satisfaction studies: Across industry similarities and within industry differences. *Advances in International Marketing, 22,* 169–194.

Ringle, C. M., Götz, O., Wetzels, M., & Wilson, B. (2009). *On the use of formative measurement specifications in structural equation modeling: A Monte Carlo simulation study to compare covariance-based and partial least squares model estimation methodologies* (METEOR Research Memoranda RM/09/014). Maastricht, the Netherlands: Maastricht University.

Ringle, C. M., Sarstedt, M., & Mooi, E. A. (2010). Response-based segmentation using finite mixture partial least squares: Theoretical foundations and an application to American customer satisfaction index data. *Annals of Information Systems, 8,* 19–49.

Ringle, C. M., Sarstedt, M., Schlittgen, R., & Taylor, C. R. (in press). PLS path modeling and evolutionary segmentation. *Journal of Business Research.*

Ringle, C. M., Sarstedt, M., & Straub, D. W. (2012). A critical look at the use of PLS-SEM in *MIS Quarterly. MIS Quarterly, 36,* iii–xiv.

Ringle, C., Sarstedt, M., & Zimmermann, L. (2011). Customer satisfaction with commercial airlines: The role of perceived safety and purpose of travel. *Journal of Marketing Theory and Practice, 19,* 459–472.

Ringle, C. M., Wende, S., & Will, A. (2005). SmartPLS 2.0 [Computer software]. Retrieved from www.smartpls.de

Ringle, C. M., Wende, S., & Will, A. (2010). Finite mixture partial least squares analysis: Methodology and numerical examples. In V. Esposito

Vinzi, W. W. Chin, J. Henseler, & H. Wang (Eds.), *Handbook of partial least squares: Concepts, methods and applications in marketing and related fields* (pp. 195–218). Berlin: Springer.

Roldán, J. L. & Sánchez-Franco, M. J. (2012). Variance-based structural equation modeling: Guidelines for using partial least squares in information systems research. In *Research methodologies, innovations and philosophies in software systems engineering and information systems* (pp. 192–221). Hershey, PA: IGI Global.

Rossiter, J. R. (2002). The C-OAR-SE procedure for scale development in marketing. *International Journal of Research in Marketing, 19,* 305–335.

Sarstedt, M. (2008). A review of recent approaches for capturing heterogeneity in partial least squares path modelling. *Journal of Modelling in Management, 3,* 140–161.

Sarstedt, M., Becker, J.-M., Ringle, C. M., & Schwaiger, M. (2011). Uncovering and treating unobserved heterogeneity with FIMIX-PLS: Which model selection criterion provides an appropriate number of segments? *Schmalenbach Business Review, 63,* 34–62.

Sarstedt, M., Henseler, J., & Ringle, C. M. (2011). Multi-group analysis in partial least squares (PLS) path modeling: Alternative methods and empirical results. *Advances in International Marketing, 22,* 195–218.

Sarstedt, M., & Ringle, C. M. (2010). Treating unobserved heterogeneity in PLS path modelling: A comparison of FIMIX-PLS with different data analysis strategies. *Journal of Applied Statistics, 37,* 1299–1318.

Sarstedt, M., & Schloderer, M. P. (2010). Developing a measurement approach for reputation of non-profit organizations. *International Journal of Nonprofit & Voluntary Sector Marketing, 15,* 276–299.

Sarstedt, M., Schwaiger, M., & Ringle, C. M. (2009). Do we fully understand the critical success factors of customer satisfaction with industrial goods? Extending Festge and Schwaiger's model to account for unobserved heterogeneity. *Journal of Business Market Management, 3,* 185–206.

Sarstedt, M., & Wilczynski, P. (2009). More for less? A comparison of single-item and multi-item measures. *Die Betriebswirtschaft, 69,* 211–227.

Sarstedt, M., Wilczynski, P., & Melewar, T. (in press). Measuring reputation in global markets: A comparison of reputation measures' convergent and criterion validities. *Journal of World Business.*

Sattler, H., Völckner, F., Riediger, C., & Ringle, C. (2010). The impact of brand extension success factors on brand extension price premium. *International Journal of Research in Marketing, 27,* 319–328.

Schafer, J. L., & Graham, J. L. (2002). Missing data: Our view of the state of the art. *Psychological Methods, 7,* 147–177.

Schwaiger, M. (2004). Components and parameters of corporate reputation: An empirical study. *Schmalenbach Business Review, 56,* 46–71.

Schwaiger, M., Raithel, S., & Schloderer, M. P. (2009). Recognition or rejection: How a company's reputation influences stakeholder behavior. In J. Klewes & R. Wreschniok (Eds.), *Reputation capital: Building and maintaining trust in the 21st century* (pp. 39–55). Berlin: Springer.

Schwaiger, M., Sarstedt, M., & Taylor, C. R. (2010). Art for the sake of the corporation: Audi, BMW Group, DaimlerChrysler, Montblanc, Siemens, and Volkswagen help explore the effect of sponsorship on corporate reputations. *Journal of Advertising Research, 50,* 77–90.

Slack, N. (1994). The importance-performance matrix as a determinant of improvement priority. *International Journal of Operations and Production Management, 44,* 59–75.

Sobel, M. E. (1982). Asymptotic confident intervals for indirect effects in structural equation models. *Sociological Methodology, 13,* 290–312.

Steenkamp, J. B. E. M., & Baumgartner, H. (1998). Assessing measurement invariance in cross national consumer research. *Journal of Consumer Research, 25,* 78–107.

Stone, M. (1974). Cross-validatory choice and assessment of statistical predictions. *Journal of the Royal Statistical Society, 36,* 111–147.

Tenenhaus, M., Amato, S., & Esposito Vinzi, V. (2004). A global goodness-of-fit index for PLS structural equation modeling. In *Proceedings of the XLII SIS Scientific Meeting* (pp. 739–742). Padova, Italy: CLEUP.

Tenenhaus, M., Esposito Vinzi, V., Chatelin, Y.-M., & Lauro, C. (2005). PLS path modeling. *Computational Statistics & Data Analysis, 48,* 159–205.

Völckner, F., Sattler, H., Hennig-Thurau, T., & Ringle, C. M. (2010). The role of parent brand quality for service brand extension success. *Journal of Service Research, 13,* 359–361.

Walsh, G., Mitchell, V.-W., Jackson, P. R., & Beatty, E. (2009). Examining the antecedents and consequences of corporate reputation: A customer perspective. *British Journal of Management, 20,* 187–203.

Wanous, J. P., Reichers, A., & Hudy, M. J. (1997). Overall job satisfaction: How good are single-item measures? *Journal of Applied Psychology, 82,* 247–252.

Wetzels, M., Odekerken-Schroder, G., & van Oppen, C. (2009). Using PLS path modeling for assessing hierarchical construct models: Guidelines and empirical illustration. *MIS Quarterly, 33,* 177–195.

Wilson, B., Callaghan, W., Ringle, C. M., & Henseler, J. (2007). Exploring causal path directionality for a marketing model using Cohen's path method. In H. Martens, T. Næs, & M. Martens (Eds.), *Causalities explored by indirect observation: Proceedings of the 5th International Symposium on PLS and Related Methods (PLS'07)* (pp. 57–61). Åas, Norway: MATFORSK.

Wold, H. (1975). Path models with latent variables: The NIPALS approach. In H. M. Blalock, A. Aganbegian, F. M. Borodkin, R. Boudon, & V. Capecchi (Eds.), *Quantitative sociology: International perspectives on mathematical and statistical modeling* (pp. 307–357). New York: Academic Press.

Wold, H. (1982). Soft modeling: The basic design and some extensions. In K. G. Jöreskog & H. Wold (Eds.), *Systems under indirect observations: Part II* (pp. 1–54). Amsterdam: North-Holland.

Wold, H. (1985). Partial least squares. In S. Kotz & N. L. Johnson (Eds.), *Encyclopedia of statistical sciences* (pp. 581–591). New York: John Wiley.

Zhang, Y., & Schwaiger, M. (2009). An empirical research of corporate reputation in China. *Communicative Business, 1,* 80–104.

Zhao, X., Lynch, J. G., & Chen, Q. (2010). Reconsidering Baron and Kenny: Myths and truths about mediation analysis. *Journal of Consumer Research, 37,* 197–206.

Author Index

Subject Index

italicized pages refer to exhibits